The King's Fellowship
A Layman's Guide to Christian Teaching
By Jonathan Flores

This book is dedicated to those people who have influenced me to seek and follow after our Lord Jesus Christ, who is the King of Kings. It starts with my mother, Dona Flores, who always has shown grace, mercy, faith, and most of all Godly love in all circumstances. Next is Pastor Dennis Keating of Emmanuel Faith Community Church. He taught me God's word as my college group pastor and later when I was married with young children as the lead pastor of the church, a position he stills occupies today.

Another great influence in my life has been Pastor Bill Trok and his wife Sharon Trok of Ridgeview Community Church. Bill and Sharon encouraged me to use my teaching gifts by trusting me to pastor the high school ministry of their church for more than three years. Some of the content of this book comes from those experiences we shared together. Bill and Sharon also stood by me and supported me during very difficult circumstances in my personal life, and for that I will always be grateful.

My children Leah and Christian have also served to motivate me to put Jesus Christ first in my life. I realized from the beginning that they needed and deserved a father who would "raise them in the training and instruction of the Lord." (Ephesians 6:4) This challenged me to get serious about growing my faith and leading them in the truth of the gospel.

Last, but certainly not least, is my wife Ciria Montano Flores. I prayed for God to bring me a partner who loves Him more than anything else, and she is that answer. She is my best friend, my loyal companion, my personal theologian, and an unashamed evangelist. Without her love and support I could not have written this book.

FOREWORD

This book had its beginnings with the idea of creating an online Facebook page for young Christian adults, particularly those away from their home churches attending college. Many college-age Christians struggle with their faith when they are confronted with the secular, atheistic teachings they receive in universities and institutions of higher learning. The thought was by having an online forum in which they could stay connected with their Christian peers and receive biblical instruction, that their faith would not diminish or be lost altogether.

Thus, in June of 2014 I launched the Facebook page named "The King's Fellowship" and began to post essays on Christian teachings and perspectives on life. In a short time it became apparent that Christians of all ages could benefit from reading the essays. Therefore, I decided to invest my resources into advertising, or boosting, the posts to people on Facebook of all ages in the United States. Since that time over 660,000 people have been officially reached on Facebook. Unofficially, including shares and organic reach, well over a million Americans have seen or read these posts. Praise God for this! Knowing that God's word does not come back void gives me encouragement that these posts are making a difference in the lives of so many!

Recently, the Lord laid it on my heart to compile these essays into a book that could be placed into the hands of people. The format of the book is that of a study guide, with focus questions and space to write notes. I encourage the readers to highlight, mark, and write questions and insights directly onto the pages. My hope is that this book will serve to help people grow in their faith and also be used as an evangelistic tool to reach the lost.

This book is for sale on Amazon and hopefully will soon be available on Kindle. This is a non-profit ministry project of my own and I will not use any proceeds as personal income. In fact, if you wish to have a free copy for yourself or someone you know then please visit "The King's Fellowship" facebook page and send me a message. May God richly bless you and prepare you for His imminent return!

Sincerely,

Jonathan Flores

Contents

Chapter 1

The Bible: A True Story of Epic Proportion!

Chapter 2

American Culture

Chapter 3

Skeptics and Hard Questions

Chapter 4

Sharing the Gospel

Chapter 5

Men's Leadership

Chapter 6

Christian Living

Chapter 7

Christian Doctrine

Chapter 8

Do Miracles Exist?

Chapter 1

The Bible: A True Story of Epic Proportion!

"Aim at heaven and you will get earth thrown in. Aim at earth and you get neither." **–C.S. Lewis**

The Bible: A True Story of Epic Proportion! Part 1

The Bible explains the Origin of the Universe

People are drawn toward epic stories. Consider the successes of Star Wars, the stories of Harry Potter, the Lord of the Rings Trilogy and the Hunger games. They are stories full of awesome wonder, miraculous feats, daring adventure, and of course, love. The heroes and heroines in these tales are faced with monumental struggles against evil forces. We identify emotionally with our favorite characters and we imagine what we would do if we were them. I think this is natural for us because all people, especially young people, have an innate desire to live an extraordinary life. A life full of adventure and purpose that makes a lasting impact, in other words, living a life that "makes a difference".

But these stories are fantasy. Fictional accounts created by great writers. But I present to you that there exists an epic struggle that is real, that has been happening since the creation of space and time, and is happening now. It is essentially a love story between the Creator of the universe and the pinnacle of His creation, namely mankind, this means you and me. And whether or not you believe it to be true, you and I are a part of this story.

This story is found in the sacred writings written by men under the direction of the One who made all things. It is the Holy Bible. The bible contains 66 books written by 40 authors over a period of about 1500 hundred years. It is a communication from the living God describing who He is, His character, and His purpose for mankind. It explains the origin of all things, including physical life and death, and it answers all of the essential questions we have about ourselves: where we came from, where we have been, and where we are headed in the future. It contains the stories of those who have preceded us in this epic tale. Ordinary people like you and me who have accomplished extraordinary things for the glory of God.

It teaches us the true meaning of love and leads us to the source that gives us the power to love others despite our selfish nature. Its words have the supernatural ability to change us and to give us hope, joy, and peace, despite living in a world full of evil. It is the guidebook that shows us how to live a life that has an everlasting impact!

Today we begin the first of several posts which will explore 10 points to help us grasp the eternal significance of these sacred writings. I pray you will find these posts both informative and inspirational and that you will be encouraged to read this magnificent book on your own. So let's begin. **Point 1: The Bible explains the Origin of the Universe**

The very first verse of the very first book, Genesis, written by the prophet Moses approximately 3500 years ago says: "In the beginning God created the heavens and the earth." (Genesis 1:1)

The book of Genesis tells how all things came to exist starting with the universe. Atheists and skeptics will point to the claims of Evolution theory that say the universe has always existed and therefore did not need a creator. However, are you aware that during the past 100 years there have been a series of remarkable discoveries in science which has uncovered convincing evidence that the universe indeed had a beginning?

In 1915 a German-born physicist by the name of Albert Einstein unveiled his famous General Theory of Relativity, which allowed scientists for the first time to talk meaningfully about the past history of the universe. Soon after, physicists Alexander Friedmann and George Lemaitre, each working with Einstein's equations, predicted that the universe is expanding. Then in 1929 Edwin Hubble, using the powerful 100-inch reflecting telescope at the Mount Wilson Observatory near Los Angeles, measured the red shift in light from distant galaxies. This empirical evidence confirmed not only that the universe is expanding but that it sprang into being from a single point in the finite past! It was a monumental discovery, almost beyond comprehension!

Not surprisingly, many scientists were not pleased with the implications of these findings and jokingly labeled them as "The Big Bang Theory". Alternative theories intent on proving an eternal universe have been continually presented, but one by one these models have failed to stand the test of time, solidifying The Big Bang Theory as the widely accepted scientific model today. It is important to note the Big Bang is a theory that explains an effect, namely the explosion of the universe into existence from nothing! It is not an attempt to explain the cause of that effect.

We can use deductive reasoning to logically come to the conclusion that the universe must have a cause. This is known as "The Kalam Cosmological Argument". It goes like this:

First premise: Whatever begins to exist has a cause.

Second premise: The universe began to exist.

Conclusion: Therefore, the universe has a cause.

We have just learned about the scientific evidence which supports the validity of the second premise "the universe began to exist." In addition, all of the scientific evidence we have about how the universe operates clearly shows us that all things which begin to exist have a cause. This is known as "The Law of Causality". This supports the first premise. Thus, our conclusion is supported by the reasonableness of both premises. In order for the universe to come into existence from nothing, it also must have a cause. That cause must be spaceless, timeless, immaterial, and incredibly powerful! That cause was written down for us 3500 years ago! That cause is the God of the bible.

FOCUS QUESTIONS

What remarkable discoveries in cosmology led to the formation of the Big Bang Theory?

How does the Big Bang Theory support Genesis 1:1?

Describe the Kalam Cosmological Argument.

A True Story of Epic Proportion! Part 2

The Bible tells us God has revealed Himself in Creation.

Psalm 19:1-4 says, "The heavens declare the glory of God; the skies proclaim the work of His hands. Day after day they pour forth speech; night after night they display knowledge. There is no speech or language where their voice is not heard. Their voice goes out into all the earth, their words to the ends of the world." And Romans 1:20 says, "For since the creation of the world God's invisible qualities—his eternal power and divine nature—have been clearly seen, being understood from what has been made, so that people are without excuse."

In part one we learned how recent discoveries in cosmology confirm what the bible tells us, that the universe had a beginning. And there are many other passages in scripture which have been proven scientifically true, even though they were written thousands of years ago. I will read just two of them but I encourage you to research the others for yourself.

Both passages are found in the book of Job. The first says, "He (God) stretches out the north over empty space; He hangs the earth on nothing." (Job 26:7) Job is one of the oldest books in the bible. It is estimated to be about 3,500 years old. During that time in human history, depending on the culture in which you lived, people thought the earth sat on the back of a turtle, or an elephant, or something else. Certainly, no culture we know of thought the earth was held up by nothing! Today, modern science has produced satellite images that prove beyond all doubt that the earth does indeed "hang on nothing" held in place by the invisible force of gravity. Also, it has recently been discovered that there exists a hole, or "empty space", in the ozone layer above the North Pole.

The second passage is Job 38:16, it says, "Have you entered into the springs of the sea or walked in the recesses of the deep?" The oceans are very deep, over 5 miles deep at some spots, and there is intense pressure with virtually no light beyond a depth of 656 feet. It wasn't until about 40 years ago that mankind was able to construct a vehicle that could withstand this extreme environment and explore the ocean floor. What scientists have discovered is the ocean floor has deep trenches (recesses) and "springs" of hot water welling up! So ask yourself, "Who would have known these scientific facts 3500 years ago?" Finally, before we conclude today's point, let's briefly discuss recent discoveries in biology.

Darwin's theory of evolution rests on the idea that the incredibly complex web of life today evolved from very simple ones. No creator was necessary, just random chance and the unguided powers of natural selection to preserve the fittest forms of life. Given enough time more complex forms of life would slowly evolve from the simpler ones. Never mind that

Darwinian evolution can't account for the origin of the first life form, which by the way is not simple at all! Biologists have discovered that individual cells are extremely complex and contain tiny machines similar to those engineered in our modern-day factories!

Along comes the discovery of the DNA molecule which science has shown contains the genetic code found in all living cells. <u>The keyword here is code</u>. DNA stores information using a 4 letter code of amino acids, A-G-C-T. The order of these letters determines the structure and function of proteins which make up all living organisms. These chains of DNA code are very long and only one misplaced letter renders the code useless! Bill Gates, founder of Microsoft, commented that "DNA is like a software program, only much more complex than anything we've ever devised."

The information stored in DNA is staggeringly large! So much so that one human DNA molecule contains enough information to fill a million-page encyclopedia, or about 1,000 books! If the information contained in the DNA of one human cell were to be written down on paper, that paper would stretch from the North Pole to Ecuador! Statistical analysis overwhelmingly rejects the probability that random chance and unguided natural selection could be the author of this code, despite having nearly 14 billion years of elapsed time (estimated age of the universe).

DNA is an information-based system and all of our human experience teaches us that information can only come from the activity of an intelligent mind. <u>If you have code, then you must have a code writer!</u> Therefore, it is perfectly reasonable to infer that the biochemical information in DNA should also come from an intelligent mind, a mind like the mind of God.

Just recently, one of the world's most famous atheists, Professor Antony Flew, admitted he couldn't explain how DNA was created and developed through evolution. He now accepts the need for an intelligent source to have been involved in the making of the DNA code. "What I think the DNA material has done is show that intelligence must have been involved in getting these extraordinary diverse elements together," he said (quoted by Richard Ostling, "Leading Atheist Now Believes in God," Associated Press report, Dec. 9, 2004).

Although written thousands of years ago, King David's words about our marvelous human bodies still ring true. Referring to God he wrote: "For you created my inmost being; you knit me together in my mother's womb. I praise you because I am fearfully and wonderfully made; your works are wonderful, I know that full well." (Psalm 139:13-14)

Again, we see secular evidence supporting the truth revealed to us in the scriptures, which says to look at creation is to see that God exists. When a person says they do not see evidence for God's existence, it is not because they can't see it; it is because they choose not to see it.

FOCUS QUESTIONS

Name a scientific fact in the bible that was not discovered until recent history.

Why is the discovery of DNA such a compelling reason for a Creator?

A True Story of Epic Proportion! Part 3

The Bible Reveals the Uniqueness of Man.

Genesis 1:26-27 says, "Then God said, "Let us make mankind in our image, in our likeness, so that they may rule over the fish in the sea and the birds in the sky, over the livestock and all the wild animals, and over all the creatures that move along the ground. So God created mankind in his own image, male and female he created them."

Having the "image" or "likeness" of God means that we were made to resemble God. John 4:24 says, "God is spirit, and those who worship Him must worship in spirit and truth." Thus, the image of God refers to the immaterial part of a person. Adam did not resemble God in the physical sense. He was unique among all God's creations because he was endowed with an immaterial soul/spirit. The human soul sets us apart from the animal world and fits us for the dominion God intended man to have over the earth. It also enables us to commune with our Maker and to reflect His likeness mentally, morally, and socially.

Mentally, man was created as a rational being. As a result, man has the special abilities to reason, discover, and to create. This is a reflection of God who has revealed Himself to all people through His creation. Think about it; Animals don't build space shuttles and skyscrapers. They don't write computer software, discover vaccines or do cancer research. They don't compose music, make the instruments to play it, and then create the electronic devices to record and listen to it! People have unique abilities! Don't miss the obvious!

Morally, man was created in righteousness and perfect innocence, a reflection of God's holiness. God gave man the ability to make moral and ethical judgments in ways that are unique from all other forms of life. God saw all He had made (mankind included) and called it "very good" (Genesis 1:31). Because God values freedom, He gave Adam and all people, including you and me, the right to make free choices. God did this because He wanted us to have the option to freely love Him in return. Despite being given a righteous nature, Adam made the choice to rebel against his Creator by violating the one and only law given to him. This action brought sin and death into the world and is the source of human suffering.

Socially, man was created for fellowship with God. This reflects God's triune nature and His love. Man's primary relationship is to be with God, but he also has the need for companionship with other people. God made the first woman because "it is not good for the man to be alone" (Genesis 2:18). Every time someone marries, makes a friend, hugs a child, or attends church, he is demonstrating the fact that we are made in the likeness of God. Now let us consider another unique human quality.

King Solomon wrote in Ecclesiastes 3:11, "He (God) has made everything beautiful in its time. He has also set eternity in the human heart; yet no one can fathom what God has done from beginning to end." This passage tells us people have the built-in awareness of eternity. It is not an idea we would logically arrive at on our own. Everything we know about our universe and how it works and the laws of nature would not lead us to conclude the infinite to be possible. Yet, we have a longing for something more than what is temporal, but we cannot comprehend or understand it. We have a notion that there is more to our existence than what we can see, feel, and touch; yet, it is literally beyond our physical grasp.

As people, you and I can look to the God of the Bible to explain our existence and we can read His sacred writings to help us understand that although we live in a physical realm, a realm we can see, feel, and touch, a realm that can be observed and quantified; we also live in a spiritual realm, a realm that is unseen, that exists outside of the laws of nature, that cannot be observed and quantified.

God's creation is too big and wondrous for us to comprehend, but its satisfactions are too small. Why? Because you and I are more than just material matter and energy! We have an eternal soul created by God for an eternal purpose! That eternal purpose is to know and have fellowship with the One who made us. And when you experience physical death, your soul will continue to exist. The bible tells us that the day is coming when each one of us must stand before our Maker and give an account for our actions in this life. Revelation 20:12-13 says, "And I saw the dead, great and small, standing before the throne, and books were opened...and each person was judged according to what they had done."

Therefore, listen to the calling of your Creator. Nothing should be more precious to you than the fate of your eternal soul! I implore you to seek after God and fulfill your ultimate purpose, and in the process find eternal life!

FOCUS QUESTIONS

What are three ways people reflect the likeness of God?

What does Ecclesiastes 3:11 teach us about the uniqueness of people?

A True Story of Epic Proportion! Part 4

The Bible details an Epic Struggle of Good vs. Evil

Today we are introduced to the arch enemy of God and of all people. His name is Lucifer, a.k.a. Satan, or the devil. So where does he come from and how does the bible describe him? Ezekiel 28:11, 14 says, "…You were the seal of perfection, full of wisdom and perfect in beauty… You were anointed as a guardian cherub, for so I ordained you. You were on the holy mount of God".

Lucifer was a "covering" cherub, or angel, created by God along with the other angels. He was a highly exalted angelic leader, full of wisdom and breathtaking in beauty. His brightness was awe-inspiring. Ezekiel 28:13 seems to indicate that his throat was specially prepared to make him an outstanding musician. Some think he led the angelic choir. But something happened in Lucifer's life that led him down the path of evil.

Ezekiel 28:17 says, "Your heart became proud on account of your beauty, and you corrupted your wisdom because of your splendor. So I threw you to the earth." And Isaiah 14:13-14 says, "You said in your heart, 'I will ascend to the heavens; I will raise my throne above the stars of God; I will sit enthroned on the mount of assembly, on the utmost heights of Mount Zaphon. I will ascend above the tops of the clouds; I will make myself like the Most High." These passages reveal that pride, jealousy, discontent, and self-exaltation arose in Lucifer.

Jesus gives us further insight into Lucifer's character in John 8:44. Speaking to the hypocritical religious leaders of his time, Jesus says, "You belong to your father, the devil, and you want to carry out your father's desires. He was a murderer from the beginning, not holding to the truth, for there is no truth in him. When he lies, he speaks his native language, for he is a liar and the father of lies." Satan is a murderer and the father of lies.

Lucifer wanted to unseat God and demand that all worship him. So he won the support of one-third of the angels (Revelation 12:3, 4) and caused an insurrection in heaven. It was treason of the worst kind! Revelation 12:7-9 says, "Then war broke out in heaven. Michael and his angels fought against the dragon, and the dragon and his angels fought back. But he was not strong enough, and they lost their place in heaven. The great dragon was hurled down—that ancient serpent called the devil, or Satan, who leads the whole world astray. He was hurled to the earth, and his angels with him." This was the greatest battle, by far, ever fought! God had no choice but to oust Lucifer and his rebel army. After his expulsion from heaven, Lucifer was called Satan (this means adversary) and the devil (this means slanderer), and his angels were called demons.

So where is Satan now? Job 2:2 says, "And the Lord said to Satan, "Where have you come from?" Satan answered the Lord, "From roaming throughout the earth, going back and forth on it." Contrary to popular belief, Satan resides on the earth, not in hell. When Jesus was tested in the desert, Satan offered Him the kingdoms of the world if only Jesus would bow down and worship him. (Matthew 4:8-9) Jesus did not dispute Satan's authority over these kingdoms leading us to the conclusion that they were his to give. But God originally gave Adam and Eve dominion over the earth (Genesis 1:26). So how did Satan gain the authority over the kingdoms of the world?

In part 3 we learned that God created mankind in His own image to have fellowship. Fellowship is a love relationship and true love requires freedom of choice. Therefore God established just one law for Adam and Eve to obey, giving them the choice to remain in fellowship with Him, or to reject Him by their transgression. Genesis 2:16-17 says, "And the LORD God commanded the man, "You are free to eat from any tree in the garden; but you must not eat from the tree of the knowledge of good and evil, for when you eat from it you will certainly die."

Satan used a serpent--the wisest, most appealing animal God made--to deceive Eve. Remember that Satan invented lying (father of lies) and he mixed truth with the lies he told Eve. <u>Lies that include some truth are the most effective</u>. Satan told Eve, "You will certainly not die...for God knows that when you eat from it your eyes will be opened, and you will be like God, knowing good and evil." (Genesis 3:4-5) It was true Adam and Eve would "know evil" after sinning. Out of love God had withheld from them the knowledge of heartache, grief, suffering, pain, and death! Satan made the knowledge of evil appear attractive and he continues to do so today. His lies malign God's character because he fears that people will turn to God if they understand His love for them.

Adam and Eve believed Satan's lies and ate the fruit, thus breaking God's law and breaking fellowship with God. God expelled them from Eden and they lost their dominion over the earth to Satan (Romans 6:16). Thus, Satan became ruler, or prince, of the earth (John 12:31). God's good creation was now corrupted and sin and death had entered the world. But all was not lost. God had a plan!

FOCUS QUESTIONS

What does the bible tell us about Lucifer's origin?

What led Lucifer to rebel against God?

What strategies does Satan use to make his lies convincing?

A True Story of Epic Proportion! Part 5

The Bible explains God's Plan of Salvation

In part 4 we learned that Adam and Eve rebelled against God by choosing to violate the one and only law He gave them. This choice ushered sin and death into the world and brought a separation to the fellowship they had shared with the Holy God who created them in His own image. Their sin also caused them to forfeit their dominion over the earth and cede it Lucifer, or Satan, the one who deceived them. The book of Genesis continues on to describe the unchecked growth of evil and the rampant wickedness of mankind.

Genesis 6:11 says, "Now the earth was corrupt in God's sight and was full of violence." And Genesis 6:5-6 says, "The LORD saw how great the wickedness of the human race had become on the earth, and that every inclination of the thoughts of the human heart was only evil all the time. The LORD regretted that he had made human beings on the earth, and his heart was deeply troubled." <u>It was evident that left alone mankind would destroy itself</u>! But all hope was not lost. God had a plan. God would establish the nation of Israel, the people through whom He would raise up a Messiah, the Savior for all mankind.

So who is this Messiah and what do we know about him? God foretold various signs and conditions to His prophets from the nation of Israel. They wrote details about the Messiah that people should watch for so that he would be recognized and believed. These prophecies were written down for us in the Old Testament. These sacred writings, written hundreds of years before Jesus' birth, contain over 300 prophecies that Jesus fulfilled through His life, death and resurrection. The New Testament, written 30-60 years after Jesus left earth, chronicles the fulfillment of these prophecies for us. Here are eight of them with the references from the Old and New Testaments:

Messiah would be born of a virgin. (Isaiah 7:14)(Matthew 1:22-23)

Messiah would be born in Bethlehem. (Micah 5:2) (Matthew 2:1)

Messiah would come from the tribe of Judah. (Genesis 49:10)(Luke 3:33)

Messiah would be heir to King David's throne. (2 Samuel 7:12-13)(Romans 1:3)

Messiah would spend a season in Egypt. (Hosea 11:1)(Matthew 2:14-15)

Messiah's hands and feet would be pierced. (Psalm 22:16) (John 20:25-27)

Messiah would be buried with the rich. (Isaiah 53:9)(Matthew 27:57-60)

The Messiah will resurrect from the dead. (Psalms 49:15)(Matthew 28:2-7)

Mathematically speaking, the odds of 1 person fulfilling just 8 prophecies are 1 in 100,000,000,000,000,000. And the odds of 1 person fulfilling 48 prophecies are 1 chance in 10 to the 157th power! This number is greater than the number of atoms in the entire universe!! The odds of 1 person fulfilling all 300+ prophecies are only Jesus! It is the magnificent detail of these prophecies that mark the Bible as the inspired Word of God. Only God could foreknow and accomplish all that was written about the Christ!

Jesus came to earth to restore the fellowship that had been severed between God and mankind. To do this He first had to place himself in our shoes. He had to live as a man and face the same trials and temptations that plague us. He had to choose to obey His heavenly Father and submit Himself to His Father's will. Finally, he had to voluntarily die in our place to pay the penalty of sin for us, which is death.

The Bible tells us that long before the world began, God had planned that the crucifixion of Jesus would be the method and payment for sin – the only payment that would reconcile sinners to a holy and loving God. 1 Peter 1:19-20 says, "For you know that it was not with perishable things such as silver or gold that you were redeemed from the empty way of life handed down to you from your ancestors, but with the precious blood of Christ, a lamb without blemish or defect. He was chosen before the creation of the world, but was revealed in these last times for your sake."

Check this out this fact about Jesus! John 1:1-3 says, "In the beginning was the Word, and the Word was with God, and the Word was God. He was with God in the beginning. Through him all things were made; without him nothing was made that has been made." Jesus is the Creator! He made everything! He is God! He is the One who walked in the garden with Adam and Eve! He is the One who created them to have fellowship with Him! And He is the One who gave them the freedom to choose Him or not. He also gives each one of us that same choice.

Sadly, there are many who choose to reject God's offer of salvation. But for those who believe and accept Jesus as Lord and Savior, their fellowship with God is restored for all eternity! 1 John 1:3 says, "We proclaim to you what we have seen and heard, so that you also may have fellowship with us. And our fellowship is with the Father and with his Son, Jesus Christ." And John 1:10-12 says, "He was in the world, and though the world was made through Him, the world did not recognize Him. He came to that which was His own, but His own did not receive Him. Yet to all who did receive Him, to those who believed in His name, He gave the right to become children of God."

FOCUS QUESTIONS

How did God tell mankind about the Messiah, and how does that prove that the bible is truly a book of sacred writings?

Why did the Messiah come to earth?

What astonishing fact do we learn about Jesus in John 1?

A True Story of Epic Proportion! Part 6

We are in a Spiritual War!

After Lucifer was cast out of heaven to earth, he deceived Adam and Eve into rebelling against God. In doing so, Lucifer, or Satan, gained dominion over the earth from mankind. But God had a plan of salvation to restore the fellowship between Himself and mankind that was lost when Adam and Eve sinned. That plan was for God to become a man, the Messiah Jesus Christ, and offer His life on a cross as payment for sin. This is summed up for us in the familiar bible verse John 3:16, which says, "For God so loved the world that He gave his one and only Son, that whoever believes in Him shall not perish but have eternal life."

Today we will learn that there is a spiritual war raging right now, and whether or not we believe this is true, we are all a part of it. It is a war to win the hearts and minds of people over to the truth of the gospel of Jesus Christ. Thus, it is a war to determine the eternal destiny for the souls of all people, including our family and friends.

The prophetic writings in the book of Revelation reveal that the outcome of this war has already been decided! Revelation 20:1-10 says, "And I saw an angel coming down out of heaven, having the key to the Abyss and holding in his hand a great chain. He seized the dragon, that ancient serpent, who is the devil, or Satan, and bound him for a thousand years. He threw him into the Abyss, and locked and sealed it over him, to keep him from deceiving the nations...When the thousand years are over, Satan will be released from his prison and will go out to deceive the nations...and to gather them for battle. In number they are like the sand on the seashore. They marched across the breadth of the earth and surrounded the camp of God's people, the city he loves. But fire came down from heaven and devoured them. And the devil, who deceived them, was thrown into the lake of burning sulfur, where the beast and the false prophet had been thrown. They will be tormented day and night for ever and ever." Satan's fate is certain and he wants to take as many people with him as he can!

When Jesus died on the cross and rose again, He not only conquered sin and death, He also reclaimed dominion over the earth that Adam and Eve lost to Satan. Jesus said to His disciples, "All authority in heaven and on earth has been given to me. Therefore go and make disciples of all nations, baptizing them in the name of the Father and the Son and the Holy Spirit, teaching them to obey everything I have commanded you. And remember, I am with you always, to the end of the age." (Matthew 28:18-20) This is known as the Great Commission. Christians are charged to spread the gospel message to the ends of the earth in order to give people from all nations the opportunity to choose to follow Christ and to receive the blessings of heaven for all eternity.

Satan knows this and he does not like it! Remember, he bitterly hates God and he hates humans because we are created in God's image. He can't touch God, so, instead, his venom is directed against people, especially Christians! The bible warns us of this. Writing to fellow Christians, Peter wrote, "Be alert and of sober mind. Your enemy the devil prowls around like a roaring lion looking for someone to devour." (1Peter 5:8) And Paul wrote, "For our struggle is not against flesh and blood, but against the rulers, against the authorities, against the powers of this dark world and against the spiritual forces of evil in the heavenly realms."(Ephesians 6:12) Satan wants nothing more than to destroy a Christian's faith in God and to limit their ability to spread the gospel.

Remember, Jesus called Satan the father of lies and a murderer. He works bits of truth into his lies in order to make them more convincing and he attacks God's character to draw people away from God's love. That is what he did in the garden with Adam and Eve and he is still doing it today! Think about it, the lie of Darwinian evolution takes bits of scientific truth from microevolution (change within species) and extends it to the lie that all life evolved on its own without the need of a Creator.

Satan uses human suffering to impeach God's character of love and mercy in order to paint Him as an uncaring tyrant. How often have we heard "How can a loving God allow evil and suffering?" Of course, he must discredit the bible and Christian leaders so people won't realize that the primary source of suffering is sin and that God actually paid for that sin with His own life in order to save us from death!

Perhaps his most powerful tactic is to deceive people using religion. 2 Corinthians 11:14-15 says, "...Satan himself masquerades as an angel of light. It is not surprising, then, if his servants also masquerade as servants of righteousness." And Galatians 1:7-8 says, "...Evidently some people are throwing you into confusion and are trying to pervert the gospel of Christ. But even if we or an angel from heaven should preach a gospel other than the one we preached to you, let them be under God's curse!"

Satan's demons can appear and pose as righteous people; even clergymen. He is the architect of false religions, including some which claim to be teaching the gospel of Jesus Christ! Therefore, we Christians must be very careful to read and study the sacred writings of the bible so that we are not deceived. The authentic gospel message says:

Jesus is the only way of salvation (John 14:6)

Salvation is a gift from God and cannot be earned (Ephesians 2:8-9)

A person must come to God with humility and repentance (2 Corinthians 7:10, Acts 20:21)

Salvation must be received by faith (John 1:12)

A person must confess Jesus is God and believe He has risen from the dead (Romans 10:9)

In conclusion, there is a spiritual war raging now for the souls of people. Satan is active in deceiving people with secular lies and false religions and Christians must fight back using the truth of the gospel message.

FOCUS QUESTIONS

What kind of war are Christians engaged in and what is the outcome going to be?

What tactics does Satan use to deceive people?

What does the authentic gospel teach?

A True Story of Epic Proportion! Part 7

The Bible Challenges us to Act!

The previous six posts have provided us a broad overview of the Bible. In part 1 we learned the Bible explains the origin of the universe. We noted that the Big Bang Theory shows that space, time, and matter sprang into existence from nothing in the finite past. Thus, modern science supports the Genesis account of the creation of the universe written down for us 3500 years ago!

This led to our next point in part 2, which is God has revealed Himself to us in creation. We learned that modern scientific discoveries in biology show DNA to be a genetic code for life containing vast amounts of information. And it is an accepted scientific fact that information can only come from an intelligent source, or mind, not an unguided process like Darwin's natural selection. The bible clearly tells us that the mind of God is that intelligent source.

In part 3 we learned man is unique in nature, having been created in God's image. The scriptures tell us that in the beginning mankind had a special personal relationship with God and that all of creation was perfect. But then in part 4 we learned about Lucifer, the most beautiful angel God had created. The bible tells us of Lucifer's pride and his desire to be god himself. He led a rebellion in heaven in which he and one-third of the angels were defeated and cast out of heaven to earth. Lucifer, or Satan, deceived the first people, Adam and Eve, into rebelling against God, and he continues to deceive people today.

He is the "father of lies" and a murderer who hates God and the people who are made in God's image. We learned in part 6 that the fate of Satan and his demons is the lake of fire for all eternity. He knows this and he is determined to take as many people with him as he can. Thus, we learned that we are living in the midst of a spiritual war for the souls of people. Satan uses lies, deception, and the pride of life to draw people away from the truth of God's word and away from the path of salvation.

In part 5 we learned that God has provided the way of salvation for all people. The prophetic writings of the Old Testament, written hundreds of years before the birth of Christ the Messiah, tell us of the signs to watch for so that people would recognize him. The New Testament records the accounts of those who were eyewitnesses of Jesus' life, miracles, teachings, and death on a cross. Their testimonies affirm the fulfillment of the Old Testament prophecies, confirming Jesus to be the Messiah, the Savior of the world. Most importantly, the New Testament provides evidence of Jesus' resurrection from the dead and the hope of eternal life He offers to all people!

If you have yet to accept Jesus Christ as your Lord and Savior, then you are in danger of being separated from God from all eternity! The book of Revelation tells us of this coming judgment. It says, "Then I saw a great white throne and Him who was seated on it. The earth and the heavens fled from his presence, and there was no place for them. And I saw the dead, great and small, standing before the throne, and books were opened. Another book was opened, which is the book of life. The dead were judged according to what they had done as recorded in the books. The sea gave up the dead that were in it, and death and Hades gave up the dead that were in them, and each person was judged according to what they had done. Then death and Hades were thrown into the lake of fire. The lake of fire is the second death. Anyone whose name was not found written in the book of life was thrown into the lake of fire." (Revelation 20:11-15)

Many people will think they are saved because they believe in Jesus, but that is not enough! Even the demons believe in Jesus and shudder (James 2:19). A person must put on the Lord Jesus Christ as their Savior by believing and accepting His atonement on the cross for them.

The following scenario is a good illustration of this principle: Imagine you have to jump out of an airplane 25,000 feet in the air and there is a parachute available to you. You believe the parachute can save you, but if you jump without it you will certainly die! You must put it on in order for it to save you. It is the same with Jesus. Believing He can save you is not enough, you must put Him on by trusting in Him as your Savior. This is done by humbly admitting your sin and asking Him into your heart.

Some people will think God should just forgive them and let them into heaven just as they are. They think because they are sorry for their sin and try not to do it that God should just forgive them. But consider this: A murderer is standing before a judge and is found to be 100% guilty. The evidence is clear and he has confessed to the crime. The murderer says to the judge, "Your honor, I am truly sorry for what I've done and I've tried very hard not to do it again. It's been 10 years since I've killed anyone. Can't you just forgive me and let me go?" The judge will say "Of course you should be sorry!" and "Of course you shouldn't do it again!" "You must receive the consequences for what you have done!"

Only a corrupt judge would let the murderer go free. God is righteous and holy. He is a good judge and therefore He must punish sin. You may be thinking to yourself, "I am not a murderer! Why should God condemn me?" However, you must understand that all sin is an abomination to holy God! If you have ever hated someone, God considers that the same as murder. (Matthew 5:21-22) In addition, God equates lust to adultery (Matthew 5:28), and all liars will be consigned to the lake of fire (Revelation 21:8).

Once you admit your guilt for sinning against God and recognize the punishment is being sent to hell, the following scenario can help you to understand what Jesus has done for you: Imagine you are the murderer and are about to be led away to prison when suddenly a man comes into the court and walks up to the judge. He says, "I love (your name) and I am going to pay (your) fine." The judge can accept the payment on your behalf and let you go free without compromising justice because your fine has been paid.

Ephesians 1:7 says "In Him (Christ) we have redemption through His blood, the forgiveness of sins, in accordance with the riches of God's grace…" That is what Jesus did for you on the cross! Wow! That is amazing love! Again, you must accept what the Lord Jesus Christ has done for you and put Him on in order to be set free from sin's punishment.

How do you do this? First, come before God with humility and repentance. (2 Corinthians 7:10, Acts 20:21). Understand that you cannot earn your own salvation, Jesus did that for you. It is a gift to be received by God's grace and by faith. (Ephesians 2:8-9, John 1:12). By yourself, pray to God and express your desire to receive Christ's payment for your sin. (Romans 10:9)

Finally, for all who have accepted God's plan of salvation through Jesus Christ, understand that your salvation is sure! Ephesians 2:8-9 tells us it was acquired by faith and by grace, not by works. In other words, you didn't earn it. And since you didn't earn it, you can't lose it! Romans 8:38-39 says, "For I am convinced that neither death nor life, neither angels nor demons, neither the present nor the future, nor any powers, neither height nor depth, nor anything else in all creation, will be able to separate us from the love of God that is in Christ Jesus our Lord."

The challenge for you and for all of us who have accepted Christ is to live up to His calling. We must see beyond ourselves and beyond the worldviews which conflict with God's purposes for our lives. But you may be thinking, "I can't do it!" It's too hard! You know what, you're right! You can't do it! None of us can! But He can!! The almighty God, who created the universe and everything in it can! We must pray to Him each day for strength and protection; we must read His word to give us guidance, peace and hope. Jesus said, "…Whoever wants to be my disciple must deny themselves daily and follow me." (Luke 9:23) And the Apostle Paul wrote, "…let us run with perseverance the race marked out for us, fixing our eyes on Jesus, the pioneer and perfecter of our faith." (Hebrews 12:1-2)

In closing, we (Christians) must make the daily choice to surrender ourselves to God in the name of Jesus Christ and walk in obedience to His commands. We will make mistakes and sin, but when we do we simply confess them to God and He will forgive them (1 John 1:9). Over time He will change us and give us new desires that reflect His glory and goodness to a world dominated by darkness. Thank you reading this and may God bless you all!

FOCUS QUESTIONS

Can a person believe in Jesus and not be saved? Explain.

Why can't God let us into heaven just as we are?

What steps must a person take to receive salvation?

Can a person lose their salvation? Explain.

Chapter 2

American Culture

"America will never be destroyed from the outside. If we falter and lose our freedoms, it will be because we destroyed ourselves."

Abraham Lincoln

The Walking Dead

The Walking Dead television program is one of the most popular in American culture. The theme is about people who have died, but for some reason they are still able to walk and function at a primal level. And of course they want to destroy the living by eating them! There always seems to be more of them then the people who are trying to stay alive and not become a "walker" and the living are constantly in danger and on the edge of becoming one of the walking dead.

Are you aware the Bible describes people who seem to be living, but whose condition is actually that of a dead person? Even though these people are walking, talking, breathing, and going about their daily activities, they are in reality the "walking dead", and the world is full of them right now! These walking dead are those people who have yet to surrender their lives to Jesus Christ, the author of life, and receive salvation from death by God's grace through faith. Those who don't have Christ are the WALKING DEAD. (This is the meaning of "walking dead" for the remainder of this essay.)

Ephesians 2:1 says, "As for you, you were DEAD IN your transgressions and sins". Paul wrote to the Christians in Ephesus to remind them of their condition before they came to faith in Christ. The death Paul refers to is not physical but spiritual, a separation from God based on the presence of sin, IN which all people reside when born into this world. "For all have sinned and fall short of the glory of God." (Romans 3:23) And "The wages of sin is death, but the gift of God is eternal life in Christ Jesus our Lord." (Romans 6:23)

Paul also describes the lifestyle of the "walking dead". He writes, "IN (sin) which you used to live when you followed the ways of this world and of the ruler of the kingdom of the air, the spirit who is now at work in those who are disobedient. (Ephesians 2:2) People who are spiritually dead follow the ways of this world. In the Bible, the term *world* can refer to the earth and physical universe (Hebrews 1:2; John 13:1), but it most often refers to the humanistic system that is at odds with God.

1 John 2:15-16 says, "Do not love the world or anything in the world. If anyone loves the world, love for the Father is not in them. For everything in the world—the lust of the flesh, the lust of the eyes, and the pride of life—comes not from the Father but from the world." When we as Christians are told not to love the world, it does not mean the people, the Bible is referring to the world's corrupt value system. Satan is the god of this world and he has his own value system contrary to God's. This system is grounded in the basis for all sin and rebellion against God, which is "the lust of the flesh, the lust of the eyes, and the pride of life."

Just like in the TV show and other zombie movies, the "walking dead" tend to gather and rally around others like themselves and follow wherever the crowd leads them. "…For wide is the gate and broad is the road that leads to destruction, and many enter through it." (Matthew 7:13) The "ruler of the kingdom of the air" refers to Satan and those who are SPIRITUALLY DEAD actually have his spirit influencing their thoughts and actions. They think they are alive but they are not! They think they are free to live but they actually are in bondage to sin and death. 2 Timothy 2:26 says, "and they (walking dead) may come to their senses and escape from the snare of the devil, having been held captive by him to do his will."

Paul reminds the Ephesian Christians and us that we were once among the "walking dead" following the desires of this world. He writes, "All of us also lived among them at one time, gratifying the cravings of our flesh and following its desires and thoughts. Like the rest, we were by nature deserving of wrath." (Ephesians 2:3) The "walking dead" crave after sin, much like the zombies in the TV shows crave to eat the flesh of the living. Ironically, the Bible refers to these sinful cravings as "the flesh", which is referring to the sin nature each person is born with.

It is only through the finished work of Jesus Christ on the cross that the "walking dead" can be rescued from death and be made alive! Ephesians 2:4-5 says. "But because of his great love for us, God, who is rich in mercy, made us alive with Christ even when we were dead in transgressions—it is by grace you have been saved." God's grace is his undeserved favor towards us. God took the form of a man, Jesus Christ, lived a sinless life and proved His deity by His miracles and by rising from the dead. Thus, Jesus overcame sin and death for us and through Him we can be made alive in this life and for all eternity!

John 3:16 says, "For God so loved the world (walking dead) that He gave His only begotten Son, that whoever believes in Him shall not perish but have eternal life." And John 3:36 says, "He who believes in the Son has eternal life; but he who does not obey the Son will not see life, but the wrath of God abides on him."

There are only two spirits at work in this world. The Holy Spirit of the Living God and the spirit of the anti-christ, Satan, which leads to spiritual death. This world is nearing the end of human history. Many signs and prophecies have been fulfilled and Jesus Christ is coming for His church, those who have placed their faith in Him. Satan has been defeated and he knows his time is short. If you have not placed your faith in Jesus Christ, then I pray you will "come to your senses and escape the snare of the devil". If you have placed your faith in Christ, then live for Him with all your heart, mind, soul, and strength! Reach out to the lost with the truth of the gospel and stand firm in your faith!

"And this world is fading away, along with everything that people crave. But anyone who does what pleases God will live forever." (1 John 2:17) May God bless you all!

FOCUS QUESTIONS

Who is the god of this world?

What does following the "ways of this world" refer to?

How are the "walking dead" made alive?

A Message of Change

Politicians love to use a message of change to get votes. Their campaigns are often centered on the idea that aspects of the government and society are lacking or failing in some way and in need of reform. And of course, they are the ones who have the knowledge and answers to change it all and make it right. They have the answers we so desperately need.

This message of change resonates with voters and people in general because the world we live in is broken. There are so many problems that need to be fixed; poverty, crime, injustice, political corruption, health care, unemployment, education, and terrorism, just to name a few. The humanistic, secular philosophy of the world believes that mankind has the power and ability to fix all these problems. Man has the answers. It is just a matter of time before the evolution of human society reaches a state of perfect harmony and cooperation. Science and reason will rule the day and religious superstition will be cast away to the ash heap of history.

There are those who believe that human knowledge of science, medicine, and technology will eventually reach a level that one day all disease and even death can be cured. There are even people who have had their dead bodies frozen and preserved in anticipation of one day being revived and able to live again. Wow! Talk about believing in the power of man!

The idea that mankind has the power to fix the problems of this world is a lie. It is a lie spun from the "father of lies", Satan, and it is the same lie he used to deceive the first human beings. He tricked them into believing they can be god of their own lives and not depend upon the one true God who had created them. You see, MANKIND IS THE PROBLEM, not the solution.

Because of Adam and Eve's disobedience, sin and death entered God's good creation and there is nothing within the power of human effort that can change that. There are no social services, government programs, or self-help seminars that can take away the power of sin to corrupt people's thoughts and actions, or take away the sting of death.

In order for true change to occur, people must be fundamentally made new from the inside out. The power of sin over the human heart must be dealt with because it the source of the problems in this world. Mark 7:21 says, "For it is from within, out of a person's heart, that evil thoughts come—sexual immorality, theft, murder, adultery, greed, malice, deceit, lewdness, envy, slander, arrogance and folly."

So how can this happen? How can people change their nature? How can people overcome the evil that dwells within the human heart and learn to love others more than themselves?

The answer is no one can truly change their nature by their own efforts. True change can only come from God. God sent His Son Jesus Christ into the world for that very reason. Jesus came to earth to defeat sin and death once and for all and to provide a way for all people to experience true, meaningful change. It is only by God's grace through faith in the finished work of Jesus Christ that a person can change their destiny from certain death to certain eternal life.

Romans 8:1-2 says, "Therefore, there is now no condemnation for those who are in Christ Jesus, because through Christ Jesus the law of the Spirit who gives life has set you free from the law of sin and death." And Galatians 2:20 says, "I have been crucified with Christ and I no longer live, but Christ lives in me. The life I now live in the body, I live by faith in the Son of God, who loved me and gave Himself for me."

When a person places their faith in Christ they experience a spiritual rebirth. God considers them as having shared in Christ's death on the cross and also His resurrection from the dead to an eternal life. That is what being "In Christ" means. We are no longer the same person because God sends His Spirit to live within us. Romans 6:3-4 says, "Or don't you know that all of us who were baptized into Christ Jesus were baptized into his death? We were therefore buried with him through baptism into death in order that, just as Christ was raised from the dead through the glory of the Father, we too may live a new life."

After a person places their faith in Christ, they must change from relying on the futility of human philosophy to guide their lives to instead relying on the living word of God. Romans 12:2 says, "Do not conform to the pattern of this world, but be transformed by the renewing of your mind. Then you will be able to test and approve what God's will is—his good, pleasing and perfect will." And 2 Timothy 3:16-17 says, "All Scripture is God-breathed and is useful for teaching, rebuking, correcting and training in righteousness, so that the servant of God may be thoroughly equipped for every good work."

When a person places their faith in Christ, not only do they pass from death to life, they receive the Holy Spirit. The Holy Spirit gives us insight into the word of God, the bible, to understand it and to allow God to work within us, changing our thinking and actions. This change of attitudes and actions from sinful desires to Christ-like character is called the fruit of the Spirit. Galatians 5:22-23a says, "But the fruit of the Spirit is love, joy, peace, forbearance, kindness, goodness, faithfulness, gentleness and self-control."

God's word is living and active, and it is able to change our thoughts and desires to conform to the image of our Lord Jesus Christ. Hebrews 4:12 says, "For the word of God is alive and active. Sharper than any double-edged sword, it penetrates even to dividing soul and spirit, joints and marrow; it judges the thoughts and attitudes of the heart." Therefore, as Christians you and I must commit to reading the bible as often as possible. Filling our minds with God's word is how we renew our minds and produce the fruit of the Spirit.

In closing, true change comes only through faith in Jesus Christ. Christians look forward to the Day when our Lord will return and make all things new, fixing this broken world once and for all. Until then, we live each day by faith and look to God's word to guide us, because relying on human wisdom will prove to be futile. The words of King Solomon remind us of this sobering truth. "What has been will be again, what has been done will be done again; there is nothing new under the sun." (Ecclesiastes 1:9) May God bless you all!

FOCUS QUESTIONS

What is the source of the problems in this world?

What is the solution to changing this broken world?

What is Truth? Part 1

"What is truth?" These three words are the reply given by the Roman Governor Pontius Pilate when Jesus said to him, "You say that I am a king. In fact, the reason I was born and came into the world is to testify to the truth. Everyone on the side of truth listens to me." (John 18:37) Pilate had the authority (given by God) to release Jesus. The Jewish leaders had brought Jesus to him demanding that he be executed because he claimed to be God. Pilate questioned Jesus and concluded, "I find no basis for a charge against him (Jesus)." (John 18:38) Yet, pressured by the Jews and worried about his own political future, Pilate reluctantly handed Jesus over to the Roman soldiers to be crucified. Pilate's actions are an example of many people's response when confronted with the truth of Jesus as the Son of God, and as the One through whom our redemption to God is made whole.

The phrase "what is truth?" can imply there is no real truth, that there is no God and therefore no purpose to human existence. The universe and all life as we know it is simply the result of random chance and all things are simply matter and energy being acted upon by undirected forces. There is no absolute truth and therefore no basis for moral judgment. This view is the logical conclusion if there really is no truth and everything is meaningless. This belief is the heart of a secular worldview.

American society is growing to be more secular and atheism is more common than it used to be, but most Americans still profess to believe in God and that heaven does exist. But when pressed on the question of how does one get into heaven, or what we must do for God to let us into heaven, people will give many different responses. This happens because people will pick up bits and pieces of truth from Christian sources, along with mountains of misinformation from secular sources (schools, science, workplace, etc...). Then they will mix them together with opinions from pop culture (movies, television, music, social media, etc...), and form their own philosophy about god, heaven and how to get there.

This is why a message that says there are many paths to heaven and that all roads lead to God is so readily accepted. This resonates with people because it does not contradict the varied philosophies formed by those who have not heard and accepted the truth of the gospel, but instead have embraced a form of religion that supports their self-serving lifestyles. It is much more palatable for people to hear that living a good life basically consists of not harming others or daring to question others on their lifestyle choices. Be tolerant of others, "give back" by supporting charitable causes (unless those causes promote an intolerant message like that of the bible), and don't question reasoning based on science.

However, truth does not change. Truth does not bend with the winds of popular opinion, nor does it retrofit its foundation on which it is built and supported. It is this unshakable foundation that allows certain inalienable truths to exist and cannot be altered by the hollow and deceptive philosophies of a world opposed to it.

In this essay I will attempt to present the truth of the gospel message as is recorded in the bible. I will explain what I and many other Christians believe to be an accurate interpretation of God's word and I hope to answer questions you may have concerning various points of doctrine. My prayer is that these words will be exactly what God wants you to read and that His Holy Spirit will guide you to the truth of their meaning.

Let's begin with the foundation of all Christian belief.

Isaiah 28:16 says, "So this is what the Sovereign Lord says: 'See, I lay a stone in Zion, a tested stone, a precious cornerstone for a sure foundation..." And 1 Corinthians 3:11 says, "For no one can lay any foundation other than the one already laid, which is Jesus Christ." Thus Jesus is the foundation upon which the entire Christian faith is built. There is no other. Any attempt to remove or to reshape this "precious cornerstone" will result in a faith that cannot stand up to the forces opposed to it.

Jesus said, "Therefore everyone who hears these words of mine and puts them into practice is like a wise man who built his house on the rock. The rain came down, the streams rose, and the winds blew and beat against that house; yet it did not fall, because it had laid its foundation on the rock. But everyone who hears these words of mine and does not put them into practice is like a foolish man who built his house on sand. The rain came down, the streams rose, and the winds blew and beat against that house, and it fell with a great crash." (Matthew 7:24-27)

Jesus is the rock, the cornerstone on which all truth is built. Not science, not philosophy, not any other religious figure. If we do not place our faith in Jesus as the cornerstone of what we believe, then we are building our philosophy of life on the sand. Jesus warned us the results of that "foolish" choice will be a "great crash". This may not happen to all people during this life on earth. Many who do not profess faith in Jesus Christ live good lives and do not experience a high degree of suffering. They may have wealth, good marriages, fulfilling careers and good health. But one day all people will have to stand before Almighty God and face His Holy judgment. Each person will have to give an account of their life and be judged on their worthiness to enter heaven. It is at that moment when each one of us will need Jesus Christ, the Savior of the world, as the rock on which we have placed our faith.

Why is this? Because God is holy and righteous, sinless and perfect in every way. He cannot allow sin to enter into heaven, a place of perfection which awaits all who love Him and have placed their trust in His Son Jesus Christ. And the truth is that there is not one person who does not sin. Romans 3:23 says, "For all have sinned and fall short of the glory of God." And Ecclesiastes 7:20 says, "Indeed, there is no one on earth who is righteous, no one who does what is right and never sins." So what is a person to do? If God cannot allow sin into heaven and everyone sins, then how do we get in? Please return for our next post to learn more. May God bless you all!

FOCUS QUESTIONS

Why is the "all roads lead to heaven" philosophy readily accepted by so many people?

Why is Jesus called "The precious cornerstone"?

What is Truth? Part 2

In part one we learned that many people mix bits of truth with false ideas they get from secular and popular sources to form their own beliefs about God and heaven. We also established that Jesus Christ is the foundation upon which all truth is built. A person who builds their beliefs upon Jesus can withstand the forces opposed to their faith, but the person whose faith is not built upon Jesus is doomed to destruction. This is so because all people will one day have to face judgment by a holy, righteous God, who cannot allow sin to enter into His perfect heaven. It is at that moment when all people have a serious problem because "...all have sinned and fall short of the glory of God." (Romans 3:23)

This is a harsh but bitter truth that many people refuse to accept. The secular worldview preaches that all people are basically good and that many of the shortcomings we see in people are the product of an imperfect society. If only our education system was better, then we would not have so many dropouts and people in poverty. Education and counseling can eliminate drug and substance abuse by teaching people about their dangers and attending to their psychological needs. If only our society was not so unfair and biased, then those disadvantaged people would not have to resort to crime and violence to get what they want. These beliefs about society have an element of truth, and education and social programs can and do help many people. But they do not address the core issue that is at the root of these and all other problems people face.

The core issue is the spiritual condition of mankind, which is selfish and opposed to God. Romans 3:11 says, "There is no one who understands; there is no one who seeks God." And Jesus said, "For out of the heart come evil thoughts—murder, adultery, sexual immorality, theft, false testimony, slander." (Matthew 15:19) So you see, social reforms and humanistic approaches to changing people's behavior cannot solve our problems because they don't address this issue of sin and unrighteousness.

A person who holds a secular worldview might say, "Stop right there! You Christians say people are sinners and against God. First of all, I don't believe in God, and second of all, you can't prove people are sinners. That is just a religious word to describe people's actions." Okay, let us address this. First of all, evil is defined as morally wrong, wicked, or bad (among many other words). So let us ask ourselves the question, "Does evil exist?" Is it wrong for a person to commit rape and murder? Is it wrong for a person to steal? Is it wrong for someone to molest a child, or physically abuse another person? We could go on and on with many other examples, and any rational person who has the slightest understanding of morality must answer YES, EVIL EXISTS!

At this point the humanist may return to blaming society as the cause of evil, not the human condition of a sinful heart opposed to God. Okay, let us then examine our human hearts under the light of God's law, the Ten Commandments. Galatians 3:24 says, "Wherefore the law was our schoolmaster to bring us unto Christ, that we may be justified by faith." God has given us His commandments in order to teach us what sin is and to show us His standard for living a righteous life. This is the standard He will use to judge every person's life to determine if they are fit to enter into His perfect heaven. Let's see then how we measure up to this standard.

Have you ever told a lie? If yes, then you have broken the 9th commandment and you are a liar. Have you ever stolen anything, no matter how small or inexpensive? If yes, then you have broken the 8th commandment and you are a thief. Have you ever used God's name in vain? If yes, then you have broken the 3rd commandment by committing blasphemy, which is taking God's name and dragging it through the mud as a cuss word. Have you ever lusted after another person? Jesus said to lust after someone is equivalent to committing adultery (Matthew 5:27-28). If yes, then you have broken the 7th commandment and you are an adulterer. Have you ever hated another person? 1 John 3:15 says, "Anyone who hates a brother or sister is a murderer, and you know that no murderer has eternal life residing in him." If yes, then in God's eyes you have broken the 6th commandment and are guilty of murder.

We could go on and look at the other commandments, but hopefully you are getting the point. People are not basically good, not when examined under the light of God's law. We all are guilty! Even the best of us who have tried so hard not to break His commands have stumbled, and James 2:10 says, "For whoever keeps the whole law and yet stumbles at just one point is guilty of breaking all of it." This is why if we are placing our hope of entering heaven on our own works, then we are in big trouble! Romans 3:20 says, "Therefore no one will be declared righteous in God's sight by the works of the law; rather, through the law we become conscious of our sin."

Evil exists in all of us, and the only way to truly change people's actions is to change their hearts and minds from the inside out. That is exactly what God can do when a person comes to believe in Jesus Christ and allows Him into their heart. This is a supernatural occurrence which transcends all human understanding. We will continue to develop this point in our next post. May God bless you all!

FOCUS QUESTIONS

What is the secular answer to the cause of all problems?

What is the bible's answer to the cause of all problems?

What is the purpose of God's law, the Ten Commandments?

What is Truth? Part 3

To this point we have established that Jesus is the foundation, the "precious cornerstone", upon which all truth is built. We have also made the case that all people by nature are opposed to God and evil stems from within people's hearts. God's word, the bible, calls this sin and clearly states that God will not allow sin to enter into his perfect heaven. Therefore, in order to remedy this problem, true change must come from within a person. In other words, people must be fundamentally made new from the inside out. So how can this happen? How can someone change their nature?

The answer is no one can truly change their nature by their own efforts. True change can only come from God. God sent His Son Jesus Christ into the world for that very reason. Jesus came to abolish sin and death and to take the punishment of our sin so that you and I can come before God and be declared righteous. So what must you and I do to obtain this new nature?

It begins by admitting our guilt before Holy God. When we examine ourselves under the light of God's law and admit that we are guilty of breaking it, then we have taken the first step towards true change. <u>This first step is being humble and recognizing that we are not worthy to enter heaven on our own merit</u>. When we honestly reflect on the evil thoughts that course through our minds on a daily basis, we recognize that we fall short of God's standard of righteous perfection. We understand that if we have to stand before God and give an account of ourselves, we will undoubtedly be found guilty of breaking His law and we will be judged accordingly.

Many people cannot get past this first step. Their natural inclination is to resist being humble and to allow their pride to stand in the way of true reform. Proverbs 11:2 says, "When pride comes, then comes disgrace, but with humility comes wisdom." And Proverbs 16:18 says, "Pride goes before destruction, a haughty spirit before a fall." Selfish pride is the enemy of all people. It keeps us from humbling ourselves before God and from admitting we are sinners in need of redemption. But humility brings wisdom, because it allows a person to see the truth about their sin and to respect God's position as the creator and righteous judge of all people.

Once a person completes the first step of humbling themselves before God, then they can move on to the <u>second step which is repentance</u>. 2 Corinthians 7:10 says. "Godly sorrow brings repentance that leads to salvation and leaves no regret, but worldly sorrow brings death." When a person sees the truth about their sin, and understands that that they are in need of forgiveness, the gravity of their unrighteousness weighs heavy on their heart. They become remorseful and contrite to the point of sorrow. It is important to note that this "Godly sorrow" is directed at the wrong they have committed, as opposed to the "worldly sorrow" which is directed at the consequences of their transgressions. For example, there is a difference between the person who is sorry for the crime they have committed because they recognize it is wrong and hurtful to others, and the person who is sorry for their crime because they were caught and they now must pay a fine and go to jail.

Furthermore, repentance includes a person's desire to turn away from their old ways and to start a new direction in life. In other words, a person who repents does a 180 degree turn and begins a new journey in the opposite direction they had been going. This is exactly what happens when a person humbly comes to God seeking His forgiveness. We will revisit this point later.

The third step toward true change is believing the truth about Jesus Christ.

The apostle John begins his gospel by introducing us to the person of Jesus Christ. John 1:1-3 says, "In the beginning was the Word, and the Word was with God, and the Word was God. He was with God in the beginning. Through Him all things were made; without Him nothing was made that has been made." The "Word" in Greek is logos, which the Greeks used to refer to not only to the spoken word but also to the unspoken word still in the mind—the reason. When applied to the universe it means the rational principle that governs all things. The Jews used it to refer to the "word of God" by which He created the world and governs it. Thus, John is presenting Jesus Christ as the reason, the rational thought by which all things have been created. In addition, Jesus is seen as distinct from God the Father and at the same time in possession of full deity as God. His divine creative power is affirmed as the One through whom all things have been made.

This is an astounding statement about Jesus! So many people marginalize Jesus by saying that "he was a good teacher", or that he was a "prophet" who taught us many good things about living. This is patronizing garbage! Jesus claimed to be God in the flesh! He said many times that He was God and that he would suffer and die, then rise again from the dead. Therefore, he must be accepted as God, or he must be labeled a raving lunatic! Each person must believe one or the other, because he did not leave us any other choice. We will continue this point in the next post. Thank you for reading this and may God bless you all!

FOCUS QUESTIONS

What is the first step toward true change?

What is repentance?

Who is Jesus? What are the only two logical conclusions a person can have about him?

What is Truth? Part 4

In our last post we ended by looking at the truth about Jesus as revealed in the bible. We read in John 1 which states that Jesus is the Word, meaning He is the rational thought by which all things have been created. We also saw that Jesus is distinct from God the Father and is fully God himself. Therefore, a person must accept Jesus for who he claims to be, or they must reject him as a lunatic. Jesus did not leave us any other choice.

We also began to outline the steps towards true change, which is salvation that comes from accepting the gospel of Jesus Christ. The first step is humbling ourselves before God and admitting we are sinners in need of forgiveness. The second step is repentance, a sorrowful attitude about our sin and a desire to turn away from it and start a new direction in life. The third step is believing Jesus to be who He claimed to be, the Son of God who came to earth to die on the cross for our sins so that we might be saved.

So why did Jesus allow himself to be killed and then rise again from the dead? If he is God, then why can't he simply fix what he made? Why all this drama? That is a very long answer, but it basically comes down to two words; love and freedom. God is love and He created us to be in a love relationship with Him. However, genuine love requires freedom of choice. <u>God wants our love for Him to be genuine; therefore, He places an extremely high value on freedom.</u> This is contrary to what Satan wants you to believe. He wants people to think God is a stern old man who demands that we live our lives according to His set of rules: A set of rules which are meant to hold us back from being everything we want to be and to prevent us from enjoying life. This is the oldest lie ever told! (Genesis 3:4-5)

God created Adam in his own image, with an eternal soul that has the capacity to reason, create, and to have fellowship with him. God made both Adam and Eve perfectly good, free from all that is evil, including freedom from sin and death. He demonstrated his love for them by providing everything they needed. He provided for their physical needs by providing them food, shelter, and each other as mates in the Garden of Eden. He also provided for their spiritual needs with His presence as their companion. And He gave them freewill, the right to choose for themselves whether or not they would love him in return.

How does a person demonstrate love for God? By their obedience. I John 5:3 says, "In fact, this is love for God: to keep His commands…" When a person chooses to follow God by obedience to His commands, we are demonstrating love for Him because we are giving Him His rightful place as our Lord and Creator. Our obedience is a demonstration that we trust He knows what is best for us and we want to please Him with our choices. It is very much like the relationship between children and parents. A loving parent sets boundaries for their children because they know what is best for them and they want to protect them. And a child shows love and respect for a parent by their obedience.

Unfortunately, Adam and Eve's choice to disobey God brought sin and death into the world, and it has been passed on to all people, including you and me. Thus, people are not born into spiritual freedom like God intended in the beginning. We are all born into bondage to sin and our fate is certain death. Romans 5:12 says, "Therefore, just as sin entered the world through one man, and death through sin, and in this way death came to all people, because all sinned." This is why Jesus Christ came into the world. He came to rescue us and to set us free from our slavery to sin and a certain death!

Remember what we already learned about Jesus, that He is fully God and that through Him all things were made. (John 1:3) Jesus is God! And He came into this world to die in our place that we might be set free from our certain fate, which is death and eternal separation from our Lord and Creator. That is love! God not only says that He loves us; He proved it by shedding His blood on the cross! Romans 5:18-19 says, "Consequently, just as one trespass resulted in condemnation for all people, so also one righteous act resulted in justification and life for all people. For just as through the disobedience of the one man the many were made sinners, so also through the obedience of the one man the many will be made righteous."

Therefore, God did fix His creation, and he has given each of us a way back to him. He has provided exactly what we needed to be set free from a life of slavery, slavery to sin. This happens when we complete <u>the fourth step towards true change, which is accepting the salvation offered to us through Jesus Christ.</u> Jesus said, "Very truly I tell you, no one can see the kingdom of God unless they are born again." (John 3:3) And Romans 10:9 says, "If you declare with your mouth 'Jesus is Lord' and believe in your heart that God raised Him from the dead, you will be saved."

Thus, a person can receive God's gift of salvation by praying to God, humbly admitting they are sinners, having a repentant attitude, believing Jesus is God who died and rose again and accepting Jesus into their heart as their Lord and savior. Specific words are not required, just a sincerity of the heart which God will see. When a person does this they become reborn spiritually and we are no longer under the condemnation of sin. They also become fundamentally a new person on the inside. God changes them and He gives them a new nature, one which begins to transform them into the image of His Son Jesus Christ. This is a supernatural occurrence beyond all human understanding. We will continue to explore this amazing process in our next post by looking at what God's word says about it. May God bless you all!

FOCUS QUESTIONS

Why does God give people freewill?

What are the necessary steps to receive salvation?

What is Truth? Part 5

We finished part 4 by reviewing the necessary steps to receiving salvation. You can receive God's gift of salvation by praying to God, humbly admitting that you are a sinner, having a repentant attitude, believing Jesus is God who died and rose again, and accepting Jesus into your heart as your Lord and Savior. Specific words are not required, just a sincerity of the heart which God will see.

When you do this something supernatural occurs. First, you become reborn spiritually and are no longer under the condemnation of sin. Romans 8:1-2 says, "Therefore, there is now no condemnation for those who are in Christ Jesus, because through Christ Jesus the law of the Spirit who gives life has set you free from the law of sin and death." God takes the righteousness of our Lord Jesus Christ and imputes it to you, in other words, you receive credit for what Christ has done. In Christian theology this is known as justification. 2 Corinthians 5:21 says, "God made Him(Jesus) who had no sin to be sin for us so that in Him we might become the righteousness of God." And Romans 4:24-25 says, "…God will credit righteousness—for us who believe in him who raised Jesus our Lord from the dead. He was delivered over to death for our sins and was raised to life for our justification."

You see, God cannot ignore your sins and still be the holy righteous judge that He is. The penalty of sin is death and it must be paid. Jesus took that punishment for you and all people on the cross, He paid your fine of death and God can accept it as payment on your behalf. This allows God to forgive you and set you free from the penalty of sin without compromising justice. This is what many have referred to as "amazing grace"!

When a person receives salvation they also become fundamentally a new person on the inside. Ephesians 1:13-14 says, "And you also were included in Christ when you heard the message of truth, the gospel of your salvation. When you believed, you were marked in him with a seal, the promised Holy Spirit, who is a deposit guaranteeing our inheritance until the redemption of those who are God's possession—to the praise of his glory." The moment we accept Christ as our Savior the Holy Spirit of God comes to dwell within us. We belong to God and our redemption is guaranteed because God is the One who gives it to us. We did not earn it or buy it for ourselves, it is the gift of God given by His grace and received by faith (Ephesians 2:8-9), and nothing can change that.

Does this mean we are now free to live however we want, because our salvation is secure? Absolutely not! Remember a key step to salvation is repentance, a godly sorrow for our trespasses and a sincere desire to change and start on a new path of living for God. God knows our hearts and He is not fooled. If we are not truly repentant, then the Holy Spirit will not come into our heart. But if we are sincere, then God seals us with His Spirit and begins to renew us, changing us from the inside out.

His Spirit gives us new desires for righteous living and has the power to transform us into the image of His Son Jesus Christ. This is known as sanctification, meaning we become set apart for God and begin the process of becoming more and more holy in our living for Him. It is a life-long process that results from our daily choice to follow the example of our Lord Jesus Christ. Jesus said, "...Whoever wants to be My disciple must deny themselves and take up their cross daily and follow Me." (Luke 9:23)

<u>Thus, being a Christian is not a one-time commitment you make to escape condemnation, but rather it is an everlasting relationship with the living God.</u> And like any relationship, it requires effort on our part to maintain and grow it. We should pray daily, attend a church to fellowship with other Christians and get encouragement, begin to serve within the church and our community, read the bible regularly and share the gospel with others. All of these activities are important in growing our faith and renewing our attitudes to be more like Jesus. Because of limited time I am going to elaborate on only one of these today.

Reading the bible is essential for us to grow in our faith and strengthen our relationship with God. Hebrews 4:12 says, "For the word of God is living and active, sharper than any two-edged sword, piercing to the division of soul and of spirit, of joints and of marrow, and discerning the thoughts and intentions of the heart." And 2 Timothy 3:16-17 says, "All Scripture is breathed out by God and profitable for teaching, for reproof, for correction, and for training in righteousness, that the man of God may be competent, equipped for every good work."

God's word is not ordinary; it is supernatural because it comes from the mind of God. Therefore, it has the power to discern our hearts and to identify the sins we struggle with the most. The Holy Spirit convicts us of our need to abandon that sin and to ask forgiveness from God through prayer. 1 John 1:9 says, "If we confess our sins He is faithful and just and will forgive us our sins, and purify us from all unrighteousness."

You see, even though we are sealed with the Holy Spirit who dwells within us, and we have been set free from the penalty of sin, we still have our old nature, the flesh, which is sinful and opposed to the ways of God. Galatians 5:13 says, "You, my brothers and sisters, were called to be free. But do not use your freedom to indulge in the flesh; rather, serve one another humbly in love." And verses 16-17 says, "So I say, walk by the Spirit, and you will not gratify the desires of the flesh. For the flesh desires what is contrary to the Spirit and the Spirit what is contrary to the flesh. They are in conflict with each other, so that you are not to do whatever you want."

<u>To walk by the Spirit means to daily surrender our lives to God.</u> It is not trying harder to live for God on our own strength, rather it is filling our minds with God's word, praying, and allowing

the Holy Spirit to renew the way we think. Then we begin to desire less and less of the things of this world and more and more of the things of God, and our lives produce fruit of the Spirit, which is love, joy, peace, patience, kindness, gentleness and self-control. (Galatians 5:22-23)

Thank you for reading this and I pray God will fill you with His love, joy, and peace. God bless you all!

FOCUS QUESTIONS

What is justification?

Why is reading the bible important for our living for God?

S.C.O.T.U.S.

It is now official. The culture of the United States of America is no longer predominantly Christian, but is now modern secular. It has been confirmed by the decision of the Supreme Court of the United States to legalize same sex marriage in all 50 states. Pile this on top of legalized abortion, which has been on the books for more than 40 years, and America stands defiant to the God in which she supposedly trusts.

Yes, it is true most people in America believe in God. Yes, it is true most people pray. Yes, it is true that most people attend church at least once a year. But it is also true that most people do not stand up for the Christian faith in their speech, action, and voting. Too many Christians have compromised their beliefs so as not to appear "intolerant" or "bigoted", the derogatory terms of the political correctness crowd, which attack the character of anyone who dares to disagree with their secular view of the world.

In addition, the senses of many Christians have been numbed by the continuous onslaught of electronic entertainment, the vast majority of which propagates a secular worldview. Movies, television, social media on computers and cell phones, music, and even our automobiles with the Bluetooth and satellite radios keep many plugged in to the message of the enemy and distracted from the words of our Lord. But it does not have to be this way. Christians can choose to use these things to help spread the gospel and to grow in our faith. After all, that is the purpose of this Facebook page.

Fellow Christian, all is not lost, because our hope is not in the government or in the culture of this world. Our hope is in Jesus Christ, the King of Kings and Lord of Lords. He has risen from the tomb and conquered sin and death, and no decision of man can change that immutable truth! We who belong to Him are His brothers and sisters (Matthew 12:50), and heirs of His kingdom which draws nearer each day! (Galatians 4:7) This world is not our home and we look forward to the Day when He will judge the world in righteousness and make all things new! (Revelation 21:4-5) (Acts 17:31)(John 5:22)

Notice that Christ will judge the world, not you and me. Therefore, we must be careful not to show contempt or hate towards those who support same sex marriage or those who act upon this statute by marrying. <u>They are not the enemy! They are victims of the enemy!</u> Christ died on the cross for their sin too and it is up to us to continue to spread this good news. Let's not lose focus on what really matters and has always been the most important characteristic of Christian living; LOVE.

"Love is patient, love is kind. It does not envy, it does not boast, it is not proud. It does not dishonor others, it is not self-seeking, it is not easily angered, it keeps no record of wrongs. Love does not delight in evil but rejoices with the truth. It always protects, always trusts, always hopes, always perseveres." (1 Corinthians 13:4-7) Notice that it is correct for us to not delight in evil but to rejoice in the truth. So it is right for Christians not to agree with this decision because it clearly violates God's word. Yet we are called to persevere in our love for God and for all people, no matter what they may believe.

Finally, it is important for Christians to remember that Jesus warned us these things would happen during the end times, just before His return. (Read Matthew 24) In addition, Acts 17:26 says, "From one man He (God) made all the nations, that they should inhabit the whole earth; and He marked out their appointed times in history and the boundaries of their lands." God has determined that you and I should live and stand for Him during this point in history. Therefore, He has a divine purpose for each one of us. Let us rise to the occasion and draw near to Him, fulfilling all the good works He has ordained for us to do. (Ephesians 2:10)

Finally, let's finish with a couple of passages from scripture. Romans 12:1-2 says, "Therefore, I urge you, brothers and sisters, in view of God's mercy, to offer your bodies as a living sacrifice, holy and pleasing to God—this is your true and proper worship. Do not conform to the pattern of this world, but be transformed by the renewing of your mind. Then you will be able to test and approve what God's will is—his good, pleasing and perfect will." And 1 Thessalonians 5:16-18 says, "Rejoice always, pray continually, give thanks in all circumstances; for this is God's will for you in Christ Jesus."

Each generation of Christians has had challenges to face. Our generation is no different. And the answer to our struggles is also no different. The answer is Jesus. It always has been and always will be. May God bless you all!

FOCUS QUESTIONS

How can you use technology to grow in your faith and spread the gospel?

List the characteristics of love.

How can we live and stand for Jesus?

Chapter 3

Skeptics and Hard Questions

"Faith does not eliminate questions. But faith knows where to take them." — **Elisabeth Elliot**

Calling All Skeptics!

Have you ever flown in a commercial airliner? Most people have at least once in their life and many do on a regular basis. For those who have flown before, I'd like to ask you some questions. First question: Before you board your flight do you investigate every aspect of that airplane? For instance, do you interview the pilots to make sure they are competent to fly, or to check if they are rested and alert? Do you personally inspect the plane to ensure it is good working order? Do you insist on an explanation on how each part works and why it is needed before placing your trust in that flight?

I think it is safe to say your answer to all of these questions is no. Why? <u>Because no one can know everything and many things in life we must accept by faith,</u> like flying in airplanes, or allowing doctors to operate on us and to give us drugs.

This is not to say we throw reason to the wind when we fly or receive treatment from doctors. Nor is it to say we engage in these actions with 100% confidence. I know I have some doubts when I board an airliner, but it is not enough to keep me off the plane. Why is this? Because I understand the "big picture" about airline travel. I know that flying has been developed and tested innumerable times in the last 110 years. I know millions have placed their trust in these flights before me and had good results. And I know the preponderance of the evidence shows that flying is safer than other forms of travel and it is the best choice available for me to get to where I want to go.

When I fly I place my faith in the expertise of the people who built the airliner and who maintain it. I trust that the pilots have been well-trained, have experience and are dedicated to their jobs. And I don't need to comprehend the aerodynamics of how a plane flies in order for it to get me to my destination. I also place a similar trust in the doctors and nurses who care for me in a hospital because I am unable to diagnose myself and get better on my own. Sometimes my best and only choice is to receive their prescribed treatment in order to make me well.

When it comes to the question of whether or not God exists and if His word the bible can be trusted, it is very similar to these examples of flying in airplanes and receiving treatment from doctors. Concerning God, you and I can look at the wonder and complexity of our world and know that someone or something intelligent must have been at work (Romans 1:20). We don't have to comprehend every detail of how life works to understand that it is precious, fragile, and not within our control. We did not give life to ourselves and we are unable to keep it for ourselves. That alone should be enough to draw each person to seek the truth about the cause of all life. And reason should lead us to conclude that cause must be extremely powerful, intelligent, and have purpose to its actions.

As for the bible, many people will pick out passages that are difficult to explain or understand as evidence the bible is not true. However, just like the workings of an airplane, I don't need to understand every passage in the bible in order to be convinced that it is true and reliable. Instead, I can look at the "big picture" and know that the central theme of its text is about the One who came to save me, Jesus Christ, and that the salvation He offers to me is by grace through faith. (Ephesians 2:8-9)

The bible clearly explains to me my condition as a sinner (Romans 3:23), and I know within my heart that it is true because I live with myself each day, and I know the thoughts that course through my mind. And God knows them too. He has shown me in His word why I am this way, and why Jesus Christ willingly paid the penalty for my lawlessness, so I can be set free from death. (Romans 6:23) Just like trusting in a doctor to treat my sickness, I can trust in my Lord Jesus Christ, the Great Physician, to fix my condition of sinfulness, because I am unable to fix it myself (Mark 2:17).

Looking at the big picture of the bible, it explains the origin of all life; the history of how sin and death entered the world; the existence of evil forces which are opposed to God and harmful toward man; the history of Israel, the nation from which the Messiah would come; the birth, life, death, and resurrection of Jesus Christ; the history of the church; the future events that will occur on earth; and the ultimate fate of all people, those who place their trust in God and those who are opposed to God.

Revelation 21:6-8 says, "He said to me: "It is done. I am the Alpha and the Omega, the Beginning and the End. To the thirsty I will give water without cost from the spring of the water of life. Those who are victorious will inherit all this, and I will be their God and they will be my children. But the cowardly, the unbelieving, the vile, the murderers, the sexually immoral, those who practice magic arts, the idolaters and all liars—they will be consigned to the fiery lake of burning sulfur. This is the second death."

You and I must decide whether or not to place our trust in the God of the bible. Millions have gone before us because they knew and understood their condition as sinners and thirsted for the righteousness found by faith in Jesus Christ. They also recognized the bible as the best explanation of our existence and the best (and only) choice to get to where they want to go. To be in paradise with our Lord for all eternity, fulfilling the purpose for which they were created, to be children of God. Unfortunately, many refuse to accept the truth about God and the bible.

Jesus said, "For you are the children of your father the devil, and you love to do the evil things he does. He was a murderer from the beginning. He has always hated the truth, because there is no truth in him. When he lies, it is consistent with his character; for he is a liar and the father of lies." (John 8:44) Jesus spoke these words to the religious leaders of Israel who witnessed

His grace and truth as evidenced by the many miracles He performed. They did not even dispute his resurrection from the dead; rather they attempted to cover it up (Matthew 28:11-15). These men refused to place their trust in Jesus because they hated the truth.

It is the same with many people today, who can see the truth that God is real yet still reject Him and will not give Him His rightful place in their lives. They refuse to place their trust in Jesus Christ out of love for their own sin and their hatred for God. Thus, they prove themselves to be like their father, the devil, and they will spend all eternity with him and the fallen angels in the lake of fire. (Revelation 20:10-15)

If you are a skeptic about God and the bible, I urge you to consider the ideas expressed in this essay. Please get a bible and read the referenced passages for yourself. If you are a Christian, hopefully this essay has ideas to help you share your faith with your non-Christian friends and family. May God bless you all!

FOCUS QUESTIONS

How is airline travel an example of having faith?

What are some of the "big picture" truths expressed in the bible?

Did Man Invent God?

The most challenging obstacle you and I face as finite human beings is understanding who or what God is. All people throughout history have sought to define God and have demonstrated an innate desire to worship him or her or whatever it is to them. Why is this? Why has virtually every culture that ever existed had a god or many gods that they worshipped?

Perhaps you've heard it said by skeptics that god is the invention of man? One basis for this argument is that human beings exhibit many behaviors that fit nicely with a belief in God. Since a belief in God meets human psychological and social needs, God can be explained simply as something invented to meet those needs. Therefore, God does not exist. Atheists point out human behaviors that we all observe, but then draw an arbitrary and unsupported conclusion from those commonly observed behaviors: that man invented God. I'm always amazed that atheists, who advertise themselves as practitioners of reason, are always making arguments that logically don't hold water.

It is true that human beings are hard-wired to give and receive love, to be affectionate to their parents, and to categorize people as friends or outsiders. They are also wired to interpret what happens to them as not merely random. Leaping beyond logic, this argument goes from observed behaviors (so far, so good) to suggesting that those behaviors fit with a belief in God (still logically on target) to therefore, God does not exist. Wait a minute! How does that follow? Logically it does not. Just because you and I exhibit psychological needs that fit with a belief in God does not disprove God's existence. That is simply a matter of opinion derived from the atheist's worldly beliefs.

A theistic explanation of those human behaviors flips the equation. If God exists, then it is equally plausible that God created human beings with those "God friendly" psychological needs we observe. <u>In other words, God gave man the need for Himself.</u> Ecclesiastes 3:11 says, "He (God) has made everything beautiful in its time. He has also set eternity in the human heart; yet no one can fathom what God has done from beginning to end." And Psalm 42:2 says, "My soul thirsts for God, for the living God. When can I go and meet with God?"

In the absence of knowledge of the true God, mankind will create all manner of false gods in order to fill this void within themselves, so in that sense, the atheist is correct. Pagan cultures throughout history have created and worshipped many false gods. This is one reason the God of the bible chose a people group, the nation of Israel, through whom He would reveal Himself to all mankind.

God's promise of a coming Redeemer to reconcile a lost world to Himself required that God would one day become a man. Thus, He would have to be born into a particular nation and people. Such a nation would have to be prepared, both by divine revelation and national experience, to be the nation through which the Savior would come. All of the nations formed as a result of the judgment at Babel (Genesis 11) were already in rebellion against God and unsuitable for this purpose. God, therefore, chose one man, Abraham, to establish a new nation through which "all peoples on earth will be blessed…" (Genesis 12:1-3)

A person needs only examine the nation Israel to see there has been divine intervention throughout its history and it continues today. Why else would such a tiny, seemingly insignificant nation, continually be the focal point of world affairs? This people group has survived 400 years of slavery in Egypt and complete annihilation in war in which their survivors were exiled to Babylon. They miraculously returned to rebuild their nation only to be conquered and occupied by the Romans.

Eventually, their temple would be destroyed and they would be dispersed from their homeland to foreign countries all over the globe. Six million of them would be imprisoned and murdered by Hitler's army and yet they still survived to return to their homeland to reform their nation, despite being dispersed for 2000 years! They have persisted and survived numerous wars and attacks despite being outnumbered by their enemies. Is all this incredible history of survival just dumb luck? Not according to God's promise to Israel which was prophesied more than 3000 years ago. Deuteronomy 30:4-5 says, "Even if you have been banished to the most distant land under the heavens, from there the Lord your God will gather you and bring you back. He will bring you to the land that belonged to your ancestors, and you will take possession of it."

Rather than looking to psychology to explain God, an investigation of the bible is much more fruitful. That text is the place a rational man would evaluate the evidence for God. First of all, the bible itself is a marvel of authenticity and of divine inspiration (2 Timothy 3:16-17). In it we find there exists a God who doesn't operate according to man's wisdom. He's not bound by our puny concepts that we ascribe to deity. Isaiah 55:8-9 says, "For my thoughts are not your thoughts, neither are your ways my ways," declares the Lord. "As the heavens are higher than the earth, so are my ways higher than your ways and my thoughts than your thoughts." The God who has revealed Himself to us in the bible has provided everything we need to know about Him for now, but there exists far more about Him than our finite minds can understand.

If man truly invented the God of the bible, then he would never come up with the idea of man's inability to gain salvation through good deeds (Ephesians 2:8-9), or the idea of God sending His Son to die for hostile men to provide that salvation. (Romans 5:8) Those ideas are counter-intuitive to how man thinks. 1 Corinthians 1:27 says, "But God chose the foolish things of the world to shame the wise; God chose the weak things of the world to shame the strong." And 1 Corinthians 1:18 says, "For the message of the cross is foolishness to those who are perishing, but to us who are being saved it is the power of God."

In closing, mankind has invented many false gods, but man did not invent the one true living God. This is the God who has revealed Himself to us through the nation of Israel and the Holy Bible. All manner of human thought cannot change this immutable truth. John 1:18 says, "No one has ever seen God, but the one and only Son, who is himself God and is in closest relationship with the Father, has made Him known." In order to find God a person needs only to look at Jesus Christ. But that is for another time. May God bless you all!

FOCUS QUESTIONS

How does the skeptic argue that man created god?

Why did God raise up the nation of Israel?

Where should a rational person look to see if God is real?

Why does God allow suffering? Part 1

When God created man He chose to give man the option of not choosing Him in return. This is known as freewill. You see, God could have created man without freewill, much like a machine that has no other option but to carry out its intended purpose. But true love and fellowship requires reciprocation between the parties involved. If man had no choice but to obey God and to follow Him, then is that love real? Is that devotion genuine? I think not.

How often have you heard it said that if you love something you must set it free and let it return to you? Therefore, God in His desire to have a genuine love relationship with mankind gave you and me the freedom to choose for ourselves. Thus, God endowed us with the ability to reject Him and that is exactly what happened in the garden with Adam and Eve. They chose to break fellowship with God by disobeying Him and therefore brought sin and death into God's good creation. That sin permeates all of mankind and is the source of human suffering.

Our sinful condition and bad choices has an impact on others. When an innocent person is killed by a drunk driver they are the victim of another person's sinful action. Diseases and tragic deaths by natural disasters are the result of creation being corrupted by sin. Romans 8:20-22 says "For the creation was subjected to frustration, not by its own choice, but by the will of the one who subjected it, in hope that the creation itself will be liberated from its bondage to decay and brought to freedom and glory of the children of God."

Did God realize this would happen? Of course He did. God is Omniscient (all-knowing). But He had a plan. That plan was He Himself would take the form of a man, the man Jesus Christ, and live the life that He intended us to live. Then, He would allow Himself to be put to death on a cross and become the ultimate sacrifice for our sin. He would thus become our Savior from death and reconcile us to Himself. Jesus said in John 15:13, "Greater love has no one than this: to lay down one's life for one's friends." How true! God not only says He loves us, He proved it on the cross!

Christians can look forward to the day when God will renew His Creation and make it prefect once again. Except this time, it will be populated by multitudes of people from throughout history who have made the choice to love God in return. Satan, demons, sin, death, and those who choose to reject God will be forever banished in a place created for evil; a place called hell. This should motivate us to share the gospel and warn people of their fate without Christ!

FOCUS QUESTIONS

Why does God give people freewill?   What is the source of human suffering?

Why does God allow suffering? Part 2

Let's continue our discussion on human suffering by making this point: <u>No person has all of the answers.</u> 1 Corinthians 13:12 says, "Now we see things imperfectly, like puzzling reflections in a mirror, but then we will see everything with perfect clarity. All that I know now is partial and incomplete, but then I will know everything completely, just as God now knows me completely." And Isaiah 55:9 says, "As the heavens are higher than the earth, so are my ways higher than your ways and my thoughts higher than your thoughts."

These verses remind us that we cannot stand in the shoes of God and explain every tragic event that takes place. <u>We don't have God's mind and we don't see with God's eyes.</u> Our finite perspective doesn't allow us to understand His thoughts, nor do we have the right to stand in judgment of His ways. He is God and we are not. But we can examine the Bible to help us find insight about the human condition, which can lead us to a point of restful assurance that <u>God can be trusted to put things right in the end, even if we can't see that far ahead right now.</u> Here are 4 points Christians can look at to help us deal with the painful circumstances we face.

First of all, God is not the cause of our suffering. God loves us and He endows all people with the freedom to either love Him or reject Him in return. But unfortunately, we humans have abused our freewill by rejecting God and walking away from Him. We prefer to live our lives according to our own agendas, rather than to give God His rightful place in our lives. We are all guilty of breaking His commandments by lying, stealing, lusting, hating, blaspheming His name, etc...This is known as sin. <u>Sin permeates all of mankind and is the cause of all human suffering.</u> God may allow suffering to enter into our lives, like with Job, but the next point offers us comfort for this.

Second, God is able to produce something good out of any circumstance we (Christians) may face. Romans 8:28 says, "And we know that in all things <u>God works for the good of those who love Him</u>, who have been called according to His purpose." Because of our finite perspective we may not see it during this life on earth. But God makes the solemn pledge that He will take the bad circumstances that befall us and cause good to emerge for those who are committed to following Him.

Consider this: God took the very worst thing that has ever happened in history, the death of Jesus Christ on the cross — and turned it into the very best thing that has happened in history: the opening up of heaven to all who follow Jesus. If God can take the worst circumstance imaginable and turn it into the best situation possible, then He is able to take the worst circumstances of your life and create something good from them.

In addition, suffering can help us mature in our faith. James 1:2-3 says, "Consider it pure joy, my brothers and sisters, whenever you face trials of many kinds, because you know that the testing of your faith produces perseverance." And in verse 12 James wrote, "Blessed is the one who perseveres under trial because having stood the test, that person will receive the crown of life that the Lord has promised to those love Him." We can rest in the goodness of our God who knows our troubles and promises to be with us and reward us for trusting Him.

Third, the day is coming when suffering will end and God will judge evil. For human suffering to end, sin and evil must be judged and removed from God's creation. The day will come when sickness and pain will be eradicated and people will be held accountable for the evil they've committed. Justice will be served in a perfect way. Thus, God created a place to put evil. The bible tells us God created the lake of fire (hell) for Satan and his fallen angels. But it also says that those people who reject His offer of salvation through Jesus Christ will join them. Revelation 20:15 says, "Anyone whose name was not found written in the book of life was thrown into the lake of fire." That day will come, but not yet. Second Peter 3:9 says: "The Lord is not slow in keeping His promise, as some understand slowness. He is patient with you, not wanting anyone to perish, but everyone to come to repentance." God is delaying the consummation of history as long as possible so that people will choose to place their trust in Jesus Christ for the salvation of their souls. He's delaying everything out of His love and desire for all people to spend eternity in heaven with Him.

The 4th and final point is that our suffering will pale in comparison to what God has in store for His people.
This is not to trivialize the trials we face in this life, or to minimize the pain people endure. But Christians can look forward to an eternity without the pain and suffering this life offers. Revelation 21:4 says, "He (God) will wipe every tear from their eyes. There will be no more death or mourning or crying or pain, for the old order of things has passed away."
The Apostle Paul experienced hunger, poverty, being stoned and left for dead, shipwrecked, imprisonment, and 3 times received 39 lashes. Finally, he was beheaded. Yet, he wrote in Romans 8:18 "I consider that our present sufferings are not worth comparing with the glory that will be revealed in us." And in Second Corinthians 4:17 he wrote, "For our light and momentary troubles are achieving for us an eternal glory that far outweighs them all." Light and momentary troubles? Seriously? Paul could not have written these words without the

inspiration of the Holy Spirit giving him the firm knowledge that his (our) destiny as followers of Jesus is an eternity of splendor beyond his (our) ability to imagine!

Consider this: Jesus said, "…I go and prepare a place for you, I will come back and take you to be with me…" (John 14:2) God (Jesus) created the entire universe in just six days. He has been gone 2000 years! Can you imagine what He has prepared for you? No you can't! It is beyond all human comprehension! Remember this fellow Christian: whatever trials and suffering you must face in this life, <u>our gracious Lord has all of eternity to make it up to you</u>! Don't forget this! May God bless you all.

FOCUS QUESTIONS

Who or what is the source of human suffering?

What does God promise to do with the difficulties His people face?

What hope does God offer for all eternity to those who love Him?

How Can a Loving God Send People to Hell?

The answer to this question is closely related to the question "Why does God allow suffering?" There are two other posts in this book which address this question and I encourage you to read them so you can get a more detailed answer. But the bottom line answer is twofold: 1) Sin is the cause of human suffering, including the need for the creation of hell. 2) God gives each person the freewill to choose their own eternal destiny.

God is love and He created all people with the freewill to love Him in return. However, freewill means people also have the option to reject God and to violate the laws He has established. And that is exactly what happened in the garden with Adam and Eve. They chose to break fellowship with God by violating the one and only law He gave them and therefore brought sin and death into God's good creation. That sin permeates all of mankind and is the source of human suffering. You may ask, "Why did God create people He knew would reject Him?" Again, please refer to the posts on suffering for that answer.

Many people will question God's love because He promises to judge sin. Yes God is love, but He is also holy, just and perfect. As our Creator and righteous judge, He establishes the laws by which we are to live, and if we break those laws, then we must pay the consequences. For example, if you jump off a high building and shout out "God is love!" all the way down, although you are yelling truth, you are still going to splatter when you hit the pavement! If you break the law of gravity, it will break you! Similarly, you can love your child to the moon and back, but if he sticks his little finger into the flame on your gas stove, then he is going to get burned! You can say, "God is love, God is love, God is love," until you are blue in the face, but fire will burn you and gravity will kill you.

In the same way our sin will condemn us to hell no matter how much God loves us. Sin is transgression of God's moral law, the Ten Commandments. If you think you have not sinned, then ask yourself the following questions: Have you ever lied, or stolen anything? Have you ever taken God's name in vain (blasphemy)? Have you ever lusted for another person (adultery) or hated another person (murder)? These are only five of the Ten Commandments and if you are honest with yourself then you know you have violated them because everyone does. The bible says, "For all have sinned and fall short of the glory of God." (Romans 3:23)

Because God cannot allow sin and evil into heaven for all eternity He had to create a place for them to go. Think about it, if God allowed liars, thieves, blasphemers, adulterers, murderers, etc…into heaven, then it would no longer be heaven, it would be hell! Therefore there must be a place for God to put evil so that it remains separate from Him and from those who choose to love Him.

The Bible says God prepared the lake of fire (hell) for the devil and his fallen angels (Matthew 25:41). It also says that those unrepentant people who freely reject His offer of salvation through His Son Jesus Christ will join them. Revelation 20:15 says, "Anyone whose name was not found written in the book of life was thrown into the lake of fire." This is a harsh truth which many pastors will not mention out of fear of offending people, but Jesus spoke often of it and Christians need to be honest about the Bible's teachings. But we may rest assured that no one will suffer in hell who could by any means have been won to Christ in this life.

God leaves no stone unturned in His attempts to rescue all who would respond to the convicting truth of His gospel message. God is constantly reaching out to the lost through the prayers of Christian parents, friends, and co-workers. God has richly blessed Americans with religious freedoms and has given us more opportunities to accept His plan of salvation than most people in the world. He gives us the freedom to read His word (the bible) and to attend churches. We have freedom of speech and access to vast amounts of information about the Bible and the Christian faith.

Furthermore, God has given each person the innate ability to know right from wrong (conscience) so that His laws are understandable to us. And He has made His existence clear to every person through what He has made. Romans 1:20 says, "For since the creation of the world God's invisible qualities—His eternal power and divine nature—have been clearly seen, being understood from what has been made, so that people are without excuse." God also delays His coming judgment of the world to allow all people the opportunity to receive salvation and eternal life. 1 Peter 3:9 says, "…He (God) is patient with you, not wanting anyone to perish, but everyone to come to repentance."

Along the road to destruction (hell) God has placed the bridge to life through the atoning sacrifice of His one and only Son. John 3:16 says, "For God so loved the world, that He gave His only begotten Son, that whoever believes in Him should not perish, but have eternal life." Even though "the wages of sin is death," the Bible says "the gift of God is eternal life in Christ Jesus our Lord" (Romans 6:23). God did more than say He loves us. He proved it by becoming a man and taking our punishment for sin on the cross!

Sometimes God allows difficult circumstances to come into your life in order to wake you up, to stop you from continuing along your selfish path and to bring you back to Him. While breath remains in your body it is not too late to respond to God. You can respond to Him by admitting to Him that you have broken His law and by repenting (turning away from your sin). Believe Christ died for you and rose again, and place your trust in Him as your Lord and Savior. Do this and He will eagerly forgive your sins and give you a new heart with new desires to live for Him. You will become a child of God and receive the hope of eternal life God grants to everyone who will call upon His name. God can forgive every sin you have ever committed or will commit, except one: The sin of rejecting His Son Jesus Christ and the salvation found in His name.

In conclusion, God is doing everything possible to save you from that terrible, terrible place and still leave you as a person with freewill, not just a robot. That is the way He made you--after His image, after His likeness, with the freedom to say "yes" or the freedom to say "no," the freedom to reject Him as your own Creator. If you do not want God in your life here on earth, then you will not want Him for all eternity. In the end, God will not overrule the deliberate choices of those who consciously and willfully turn away from Him. <u>God does not send anyone to hell. People choose to send themselves there.</u>

"Whoever believes in Him is not condemned, but whoever does not believe stands condemned already because they have not believed in the name of God's one and only Son. This is the verdict: Light has come into the world, but people loved darkness instead of light because their deeds were evil." John 3:18-19

FOCUS QUESTIONS

Why must God judge sin?

Why is hell necessary?

What has God done to keep people from being condemned to hell?

Is There Only One Way to God?

Many people criticize Christians as being narrow-minded because we believe Jesus Christ is the only way to salvation. They point to the numerous other religions of the world and say, "How can your way be the only way?" This implies that all the religions in the world are basically the same. But that simply is not true. For example, Christians, Jews, and Muslims believe in a personal God who has revealed Himself to mankind. Buddhists and Hindus believe God is impersonal and unknowable. But God cannot be both personal and impersonal -- both concepts cannot be correct.

Christianity is unique from all other religions of the world in one vitally important concept -- the idea that God has reached out to man to save him because man is helpless to save himself. Every other religion in the world is based on man's efforts to reach God. These world religions teach that man must do righteous deeds or perform religious service in order to become good enough for God.

To gain favor with God a person must pray a certain number of times, in a certain manner, facing a certain direction. Some require wearing a religious garment and a particular way of worship. Some require pilgrims to crawl on their knees a certain distance in prayer in order to earn righteous points with God. Some religions require worship on Friday; others on Saturday; and others on Sunday. Some religions require sacrifice and even the infliction of pain upon a believer in order to become holy in the sight of God. But in all of this, the striving after righteousness is based on the religious works of the person.

Christianity teaches that man is a sinner and could never earn salvation by doing works. As the Scriptures say, "There is no one is righteous, not even one." (Romans 3:10) and "For by grace you have been saved through faith, and that not of yourselves; it is the gift of God, not of works, lest anyone should boast." (Ephesians 2:8-9) No matter how good you are; no matter how religious you are; no matter what you do for God, you can never be good enough to earn your salvation. Any plan of salvation that is based on your own human effort will fall short.

The Bible clearly states that salvation is available only through the sacrifice that Jesus Christ made when He carried the sins of the world on the cross. It says, "For God made Christ, who never sinned, to be the offering for our sin, so that we could be made right with God through Christ."(2 Corinthians 5:21) Jesus never sinned and He is the only one able to pay the price for the sins of all people who have ever lived. This salvation comes only by the grace of God toward mankind and we can only receive it by faith.

Consider this illustration: Imagine you are found guilty before a judge for a serious crime. The fine is $100,000 and you can't pay it. You are about to be led away to prison when suddenly a man comes into the court and walks up to the judge. He says, "I love (your name) and I am going to pay (your name) fine." The judge can accept the payment on your behalf and let you go free without compromising justice because your fine has been paid. Ephesians 1:7 says "In Him (Christ) we have redemption through His blood, the forgiveness of sins, in accordance with the riches of God's grace…" That is what Jesus did for you on the cross. He paid your fine for sin, which is death, so that God can set you free without compromising His justice. Wow! That is amazing love! What makes it even more amazing is this: Jesus is God Himself!

This is another unique aspect of Christianity, that Jesus Himself declared to be God in the flesh. Jesus said, "I and the Father are one." (John 10:30) and "He who has seen Me has seen the Father… (John 14:9) The great British writer, C. S. Lewis, explained in his well-known book, *Mere Christianity*, "A man who was merely a man and said the sort of things Jesus said would not be a great moral teacher; he'd either be a lunatic -- on a level with a man who says he's a poached egg -- or else he'd be the devil of hell. You must make your choice. Either this man was, and is, the Son of God; or else a madman or something worse." Since Jesus claimed to be God, we must judge his statements about himself as either true or false, there is no middle ground.

You may accept Jesus' claims as true and think you are saved because you believe in Him, but that is not enough! Even the demons believe in Jesus and shudder (James 2:19). To receive salvation, you must accept Jesus' payment on your behalf. This means that you need to admit your sin and turn away from it (repentance) and place your trust in Jesus as your Lord and Savior. The following scenario is a good illustration of this principle: Imagine you have to jump out of an airplane 25,000 feet in the air and there is a parachute available to you. You believe the parachute can save you, but if you jump without it you will certainly die. You must put on the parachute for it to save you. It is the same with Jesus. Believing He can save you is not enough, you must put Him on by trusting in Him as your Savior. This is done by humbly admitting your sin and asking Him into your heart. When you do He promises to send the Holy Spirit to dwell within you and make you a new person, with new desires to live for Him. 2 Corinthians 5:17 says, "Therefore, if anyone is in Christ the new creation has come: the old has gone, the new is here!"

In closing, virtually all religions claim exclusive path to God. Just ask a Muslim or a Hindu if a Christian is one of them. Different religions have differing requirements and not all teach there is a heaven or hell or life after death. So the issue of exclusive truth, that is to say "there is one way of salvation", cannot be brushed aside by statements like, "There are many paths to God."

Jesus said, "I am the way and the truth and the life. No one comes to the Father except through me." (John 14:6) In the end, you must choose. May God richly bless you!

FOCUS QUESTIONS

What vitally important concept makes Christianity unique from other world religions?

On what concept do all world religions base their salvation or getting right with God?

Who did Jesus claim to be and what did He do for all people?

That is a Big If!

If there is no God, then all life is meaningless! Everything that we hold dear is really not worth cherishing. The people we love, the relationships we count on to fill our lives with meaning, the acts of kindness and charity we show to others really amount to nothing more than fleeting moments of feeling good about ourselves. Because if it is true that when we die we simply cease to exist, then everything we do has no eternal meaning with no lasting consequences, whether good or bad.

The act of stepping in front of a bullet to save an innocent child's life has no more eternal value than the act of pulling the trigger that shoots the bullet towards the child. I say eternal value because the ultimate fate of each person and the ultimate consequence of each act are the same. Nothingness. A person simply ceases to exist and is no longer a conscious being. This philosophy of life has Adolf Hitler and Mother Teresa sharing the same ultimate fate! Nothingness!

Of course, there are temporary consequences in this life for our actions. The person who pulls the trigger may suffer loss of privilege by going to prison. Maybe. The person who steps in front and takes the bullet may become paralyzed and not walk again for the rest of their temporary life on this earth. In this case, the person is probably better off being killed by the bullet, because again, they will not know the difference and they will be spared a lifetime of suffering. This is the basis for the humanistic philosophy that killing can be justified for those who are incurably ill or suffer from disabilities.

If God is not real and if we all cease to exist after we die, then where is the motivation to do anything that does not maximize our self-gratification right now? Think about it. You and I could die at any moment. We don't know when death will come, but we do know that it will come. That is certain! And when death comes, if we will no longer exist then we had better make the most of life today! Right now!

When I say make the most of life right now I am talking about doing whatever makes me feel good. Why not party it up while I have the chance? Why not enjoy whatever gives me pleasure while I still can, before it is too late? What is my motivation to sacrifice my precious time to work, other than earning money to fulfill my pleasures? And since time is so precious, why spend years working and saving when I can earn a bundle in a short time by engaging in illegal activity?

After all, if I get killed doing them, I won't know the difference and there is no Holy God waiting to judge my actions. There is no eternal place of punishment where I will have to pay for my crimes. The biggest risk is again a temporary punishment in prison here on earth. Therefore, a life of crime, if done right, can be a benefit to me.

So why in the world does anyone ever do anything self-sacrificing and altruistic? Because there is a God! If God was not real, then you and I would not know the difference between good and evil. There would be no reference point to measure whether an act was right or wrong because all actions would simply be the result of natural extinct. After all, evolution makes no moral claims. Rather it is the mindless, purposeless interaction of matter and energy through random mutation and natural selection that governs our physical existence.

Because God is real and because God is truly good, all people have been shown the difference between right and wrong. You can go to the most remote parts of the earth and meet people from the most uncivilized tribes, and they know that it is wrong to steal, lie, and commit murder. All people have the inner knowledge of right and wrong because God has implanted it into each person. It is the conscience. The word "con" means with and the word "science" means knowledge. Every person has it and evolution theory cannot explain its existence.

Because God is real and He has made Himself known to mankind, you and I can know what we do in this life does truly matter and does have eternal consequences. Acts of self-sacrifice for the good of others can be truly celebrated because we know they have real meaning. When we honor the courage and sacrifice of the men and women who serve in the military and who have given their lives to protect our freedoms, we know their actions serve a greater purpose.

Because God is real people can do acts of kindness and give freely to others in need without expecting any reward in this life. We do it to serve the God who has shown us by His own actions that He will reward us for all eternity for doing good in His name. Psalm 62:12 says, "and with you, Lord, is unfailing love"; and, "You reward everyone according to what they have done."

Because God is real we also understand that all people must give an account of their actions to a holy, righteous judge. Acts 17:31 says, "For he has set a day when he will judge the world with justice by the man he has appointed. He has given proof of this to everyone by raising him from the dead." Jesus Christ will judge the world and we are assured that justice will be carried out.

"For God so loved the world that he gave his one and only Son, that whoever believes in him shall not perish but have eternal life. For God did not send his Son into the world to condemn the world, but to save the world through him. Whoever believes in him is not condemned, but whoever does not believe stands condemned already because they have not believed in the name of God's one and only Son. This is the verdict: Light has come into the world, but people loved darkness instead of light because their deeds were evil." John 3:16-19

Karl Marx called religion the "opiate of the masses". But the philosophy of atheism that claims the fate of all people is nothingness is the "opiate of the unrepentant wicked", those who love darkness instead of light!

Fellow Christian, we have the hope of eternal life and the assurance that we will not be condemned, because we have Jesus Christ as our Savior. We also know that the injustice people suffer in this world will ultimately be accounted for by a holy God who will set it all right in the end.

Proverbs 24:19-20 says, "Do not fret because of evildoers or be envious of the wicked, for the evildoer has no future hope, and the lamp of the wicked will be snuffed out." Thus, the fate of people like Adolph Hitler and Mother Teresa are not the same! People's actions do matter and Jesus Christ will judge them! May God bless you all!

FOCUS QUESTIONS

Why do all people know right from wrong?

Why do our actions in this life matter?

Is the Bible Reliable? Part 1

There are many who would ask "**How do we know the Bible is not just a myth made up over time?**"

To answer this question we must first determine if the Bible we have today is the same as the original. There are two essential criteria for establishing authenticity (accuracy of translation and copying) of ancient documents.

1. The number of copies

2. The gap in years between the original writings and the earliest copies of those writings.

Looking at the number of copies, we find that the number of New Testament manuscripts far exceeds the number of classical ancient manuscripts available today. According to New Testament scholars, there are more than 5600 Greek manuscripts. In addition, there are over 19,000 copies in the Syriac, Latin, Coptic, and Aramaic languages. Thus, the total number of New Testament manuscripts is over 24,000! Among classical manuscripts, Homer's Iliad is first with only 643 copies.

Looking at the second criteria, the gap in years between the original writing and earliest copies, we find the classical works of antiquity has a range of 400 - 1400 years. However, the New Testament writings have a range of only 50-225 years. Thus, no other ancient texts are as well preserved as the New Testament. If critics want to disregard the New Testament, then they must also disregard other ancient writings by Plato, Aristotle, and Homer. This is because the New Testament documents are better-preserved and more numerous than any other ancient writings. And because they are so numerous, they can be cross checked for accuracy, and they are very consistent. The internal consistency of the New Testament documents is about 99.5% textually pure. That is an amazing accuracy!

In his book *Evidence that Demands a Verdict,* Josh McDowell writes, "It can be empirically verified that, the text of the Bible has been transmitted accurately. In fact, there is more evidence of the reliability of the text of the New Testament as an accurate reflection of what was initially written than there is for any ten pieces of classical literature put together. We may rest assured that what we have today is a correct representation of what was originally given."

Okay, so the question as to the authenticity of the Bible we read today is put to rest. The Bible you hold in your hand is an accurate copy of the original writings.

Going further, even if we had no copies of the New Testament, it was so often quoted by the early church fathers in the 1st and 2nd centuries, the entire New Testament can virtually be reconstructed from their quotations alone! There are more than 36,000 quotations from the gospels, the letters of Paul, the books of Acts and Revelation! Dear Christian, understand that GOD HAS PROTECTED AND PRESERVED HIS WORD AND MADE SURE WE HAVE RECEIVED IT IN ITS ENTIRETY.

The skeptic says "Okay, the text is accurate, but how do we know the writers did not make up the stories?

There are several secular sources that corroborate details written in the New Testament concerning Jesus and the newly established Christian church. We will look at one of them. The Roman historian Flavius Josephus wrote, "At this time there was a wise man who was called Jesus. And his conduct was good and (he) was known to be virtuous. And many people from among the Jews and other nations became his disciples. Pilate condemned him to be crucified and to die. And those who had become his disciples did not abandon his discipleship. They reported that he had appeared to them three days after his crucifixion and that he was alive; accordingly he was perhaps the Messiah concerning whom the prophets have recounted wonders."

The significance of Josephus is we have a secular source verifying Jesus to be an authentic historical figure. It also verifies there was a Roman named Pilate who sentenced Jesus to die. In addition, it corroborates aspects of Jesus' impact on the world at that time, including the claim of His disciples that He had risen from the dead!

Again the skeptic says, "Okay, so the Bible text is accurate and it is corroborated by secular sources, but did the writers use primary sources?

Primary sources provide first-hand testimony or direct evidence concerning a topic under investigation. They are created by EYEWITNESSES or recorders who personally experienced the events being documented.

The Apostle Peter wrote, "For we did not follow cleverly devised stories when we told you about the coming of our Lord Jesus Christ in power, but we were eyewitnesses of his majesty." (2 Peter 1:16) And the Apostle John wrote, "That which was from the beginning, which we have heard, which we have seen with our eyes, which we have looked at and our hands have touched—this we proclaim concerning the Word of life." (1 John 1:1)

Peter and John, along with many others, lived side by side with Jesus. They heard His teachings, they witnessed firsthand His miracles, such as the feeding of thousands, walking on water, healing the sick, deaf, mute, and crippled, and even raising the dead to life! All of Jesus' disciples died martyrs deaths, except John who was exiled in prison. They endured prison, torture, beatings, ridicule, poverty, and excommunication from Jewish society! And for what? For a lie? For stories they made up?

Consider these facts as well. The Bible - Old and New Testaments - was written by 40 different authors, ranging from poor to wealthy and from many different walks of life, in 3 languages, over a 1500 year period. And yet, the Bible is amazingly unique in its "unity". The books of the New Testament continually refer back to and fulfill the prophetic writings of the Old Testament. There are more than 300 prophecies written in the Old Testament concerning the Messiah that Jesus fulfilled and were recorded in the New Testament!

In closing, we have learned that the New Testament is authentic, more than any other ancient writing. There are secular sources which corroborate its details, and the writings were based on primary sources, EYEWITNESSES who were there. Fellow Christian, even though most of us did not need these facts to believe and accept Jesus as our Lord, ours is not a blind faith. There are these and many other evidences which support the truth of the Bible and the gospel message. At the end of the day the condition of a person's heart determines their willingness to accept the truth. Understand this and pray for those who don't know Christ as their Savior. May God bless you all!

FOCUS QUESTIONS

How does the authenticity of the New Testament compare to other ancient documents?

What corroborates the details of the New Testament?

What are primary sources?

Is the Bible Reliable? Part 2

In part one we learned the bible is the most well-preserved ancient writing in the world. And we learned there are secular historical sources which corroborate details of its content. Finally, we learned that the accounts were written using primary sources, in other words, eyewitnesses who were there. Almost all of these eyewitnesses were followers of Jesus who were persecuted and killed for their faith. The claim by skeptics that they made up the stories is illogical to the point of absurdity. People will hardly choose to die for the truth, much less a lie they made up!

Consider these facts as well. The Bible - Old and New Testaments - was written by 40 different authors over a 1500 year period by a variety of writers, from poor to wealthy, from many walks of life. And yet, the Bible is amazingly unique in its "unity" - the Old Testament prophecies the coming of the Messiah documented in the New Testament! The books of the New Testament continually refer back to and fulfill the prophetic writings of the Old Testament. There are more than 300 prophecies written in the Old Testament concerning the Messiah that Jesus fulfilled and were written in the New Testament. (See "A True Story of Epic Proportion! Part 5")

The Bible is not a science book but it contains many references to scientific facts that are accurate and were unknown when it was written. Here a just a couple examples. Job 38:16 says, "Have you journeyed to the springs of the sea or walked in the recesses of the deep?" The ocean is very deep. Almost all the ocean floor is in total darkness and the pressure is enormous. It would have been impossible for Job to have explored the "springs of the sea." Until recently, it was thought that oceans were fed only by rivers and rain. Yet in the 1970s, with the help of deep diving research submarines that were constructed to withstand 6,000 pounds-per-square-inch of pressure, oceanographers discovered springs welling up on the ocean floor! Who would have known this 3500 years ago?

Isaiah 40:22 says, "It is He who sits above the circle of the earth, and its inhabitants are like grasshoppers, who stretches out the heavens like a curtain, and spreads them out like a tent to dwell in." The word translated "circle" here is the Hebrew word *chuwg* which is also translated "circuit," or "compass". That is, it indicates something spherical, rounded, or arched—not something that is flat or square. The book of Isaiah was written sometime between 740 and 680 BC. This is at least 300 years before Aristotle suggested that the earth might be a sphere in this book *On the Heavens*. This brings up an important historical note related to this topic.

Many people are aware of the conflict between Galileo and the Roman Catholic Pope, Paul V. After publishing *A Dialogue on the Two Principal Systems of the World*, Galileo was summoned to Rome, where he was forced to renounce his findings. (At that time, "theologians" of the Roman Catholic Church maintained that the Earth was the center of the universe, and to assert otherwise was deemed heretical.) As a result, cynics often reference this incident to paint Christians as ignorant bigots who believe a book of fairy tales. This is not true. There is no verse in the Bible that claims the Earth is flat, or that it is the center of the universe. History shows that this conflict, which took place at the time of the Inquisition, was part of a power struggle, not a conflict about biblical doctrine.

Since the Bible is a religious book, many scholars take the position that it is biased and cannot be trusted unless we have corroborating evidence from extra-Biblical sources. In other words, the Bible is guilty until proven innocent and any lack of outside evidence places the Biblical account in doubt. This standard is far different from that applied to other ancient documents, even though many, if not most, have a religious element. They are considered to be accurate, unless there is evidence to show that they are not. Although it is not possible to verify every incident in the Bible, since the mid-1800s many discoveries in archaeology have demonstrated the reliability and plausibility of the Bible narrative.

For example, it was once claimed there was no Assyrian king named Sargon as recorded in Isaiah 20:1, because this name was not known in any other record. Then, Sargon's palace was discovered in Khorsabad, Iraq. The very event mentioned in Isaiah 20, his capture of Ashdod, was recorded on the palace walls. What is more, fragments of a stela memorializing the victory were found at Ashdod itself! This is just one of many discoveries which reveal the bible to be historically accurate.

In closing, we've seen evidence that the Bible has been accurately copied and passed down from generation to generation. Secular sources have corroborated historical references found in the text, which was written using primary sources, in other words, the people that were there. There is the fulfillment of prophecies concerning the Messiah that defy staggering probabilities of being coincidental. The bible contains references to science that were not known until recent history, and many archeological evidences support the historical accuracy of the Bible accounts.

The most prolific book in all of history, written by 40 authors over 1500 years. Is it just a myth formed over time, or is it what it claims to be? God's communication to mankind answering all of the essential questions concerning our existence. Where we came from, where we've been, where we are headed? Looking at the preponderance of the evidence, what makes the most sense? What is the best explanation? It's really an open and shut case. A reasonable answer is the Bible is true! It is reliable and it follows that we can believe its contents to be reliable.

FOCUS QUESTIONS

How does the bible demonstrate unity in its content?

What evidences do we have today that support the bible as being accurate and reliable?

Got Faith?

Everyone exercises faith in life. Have you ever flown in a jet airliner? If so, do you get nervous when you do? I know I do! Intellectually, I know statistics say flying is safer than driving a car. But that doesn't matter, because I also know that things can go wrong. Why? Because they have gone wrong before and they will again. And when they do go wrong, the results are often devastating!

When I enter that airliner I am placing my confidence and trust that I will safely arrive at my destination. I am placing my faith in the pilot's ability to navigate any and all obstacles that may present themselves. And I am trusting that this incredibly complex machine is not going to malfunction to the point where it is impossible for the pilot to keep it in the air and safely land it.

Why do I do this? Because the preponderance of the evidence clearly shows me that this is the best way to go. And I need to take a step of faith in order to get to where I want to be. Is my confidence 100% certain? No. But it is "beyond a reasonable doubt". I hope you take this to heart and understand that having faith is not such an incredible leap. And that all life, your life, is incredibly complex, much more than a jet airliner. You need to put your trust in Jesus Christ, the One who made you and made all things and allow Him to pilot your life.

What does the bible say about faith? Hebrews 11:1-2 says, "Now faith is confidence in what we hope for and assurance about what we do not see. This is what the ancients were commended for." Notice the word hope is in linked with faith. Faith and hope go together. So I ask you, do you have hope for your future? When things go wrong in this life, and you know they do, who or what are you placing your faith in to guide you through? Where is your hope? Is it in modern medicine? Science? Your 401k?

Jeremiah 29:11 says "For I know the plans I have for you," declares the LORD, "plans to prosper you and not to harm you, plans to give you hope and a future." When a person puts their confidence and trust in the ability of the One who made them, who has a plan for them, and who loves them more than can be measured, then that person has genuine hope. The opposite is also true. If you have not put your trust in Jesus Christ, then you have no lasting or real hope.

The bible lists many examples of ordinary people like you and me who responded with faith to God's calling, and by doing so accomplished extraordinary things. Hebrews 11:7 says, "By faith Noah, when warned about things not yet seen, in holy fear built an ark to save his family. By his faith he condemned the world and became heir of the righteousness that is in keeping with faith."

Noah's faith triumphed over all the corrupt reasoning of his culture. Surely he was laughed at and ridiculed. The prevailing wisdom of his time said floodwaters were impossible. Building the massive ark would take 100 years and require all of his resources. But Noah believed God's warning and he feared the coming destruction. God had graciously provided an escape and Noah put his faith into action and was saved in the end.

We can learn a lot from Noah. Noah's holy fear condemned the security and vain confidence of a wicked generation; his faith condemned their unbelief; his obedience condemned their contempt for God's warning and their rebellion against God. The bible tells of a yet another coming destruction, when heaven and earth will be destroyed by fire and all people will be judged by God. Again, God has graciously provided an escape. Jesus Christ, through His obedience and by His sufferings on the cross, has prepared a spiritual ark for us, one which we must choose to enter by faith.

"By faith Abraham, when called to go to a place he would later receive as his inheritance, obeyed and went, even though he did not know where he was going." (Hebrews 11:8) By putting his faith into action, Abraham allowed God to establish the nation of Israel, through whom the Messiah, Jesus Christ would be born.

"By faith Moses, when he had grown up, refused to be known as the son of Pharaoh's daughter. He chose to be mistreated along with the people of God rather than to enjoy the fleeting pleasures of sin. He regarded disgrace for the sake of Christ as of greater value than the treasures of Egypt, because he was looking ahead to his reward." (Hebrews 11:25-26)

As the adopted son of Pharaoh's daughter, her only child, Moses was faced with tremendous temptation. He stood to inherit the riches and privileges of the kingdom of Egypt. But by doing so, he would be forced to renounce his relation to God's people Israel and thus to God Himself. Moses chose to suffer with God's people rather than to enjoy the pleasures of sin for a season. He understood that temporary suffering on earth with God's people far outweighs eternal suffering and separation from God.

Jesus said, "Therefore everyone who hears these words of mine and puts them into practice is like a wise man who built his house on the rock. The rain came down, the streams rose, and the winds blew and beat against that house; yet it did not fall, because it had its foundation on the rock. But everyone who hears these words of mine and does not put them into practice is like a foolish man who built his house on sand. The rain came down, the streams rose, and the winds blew and beat against that house, and it fell with a great crash." (Matthew 7:24-27) So let me ask you again, "Got Faith?"

Jesus said, ""Very truly I tell you, whoever hears my word and believes him who sent me has eternal life and will not be judged but has crossed over from death to life." (John 5:24) If you have not placed your trust in Jesus as your Savior I urge you to take that step of faith today. Your life on this earth is a fragile gift from God and you must be prepared for the day it will end.

For those of us who have already taken that step we must nurture and grow our faith. Colossians 2:6-7 says, "Therefore as you have received Christ Jesus the Lord, so walk in Him, having been firmly rooted and now being built up in Him and established in your faith, just as you were instructed, and overflowing with gratitude." Brothers and sisters in Christ, let us continue to walk in Him and live each day for Him, as we look forward to that glorious day when she shall meet Him face to face! May God richly bless you all!

FOCUS QUESTIONS

How is faith and hope related?

How has God provided us an escape from the coming destruction?

Evidence for the Resurrection Part 1

Is the resurrection of Jesus Christ a historical event that really happened, or is it only a myth, as many skeptics claim? This is a crucial question because Jesus claimed to be the Son of God, the promised Messiah who was to bring hope, justice, the promise of eternal life, and restoration to a world marred by sin and death. <u>This is the most important event in human history.</u> It is what you and me and all Christians who have ever lived believe to be true. For if it is not true, then our faith is in vain.

The apostle Paul wrote to the following passages to the believers in Corinth: **"if Christ has not been raised, our preaching is useless and so is our faith."** (1 Corinthians 15:14) And in verses 17-19 he wrote, **"If Christ has not been raised, your faith is futile: you are still in your sins. Then those who have fallen asleep in Christ are lost. If only for this life we have hope in Christ, we are of all people most to be pitied."** So you see, the resurrection is the pillar on which our faith is supported and held firmly true, or it is a quicksand of lies in which we sink to our destruction.

In our study we are going to answer the following question to help us substantiate the truth of the resurrection: Does the evidence concerning the resurrection story support a verdict that is beyond a reasonable doubt?

Whether your answer to this question is yes or no, it is an expression of faith, because you are expressing something that can't be proven. Therefore, for a question such as this, the right way to come to an answer is the same as in a court of law. Evidence must be examined, as much as possible that pertains to the case. Then a conclusion must be reached, one that is based upon the preponderance or "weight" of the evidence and is "beyond a reasonable doubt." In other words, we are looking for the best explanation.

Evidence comes in many forms. Evidence can be physical. Evidence can be documentary or written. It can be testimonial: What a person has seen or heard. While no one witnessed the actual resurrection, <u>many people swore they saw the risen Christ after his death and their lives were never the same.</u>

An examination of the resurrection requires that we examine the reliability of the Bible itself because it is the primary source of our evidence. Please refer to the two previous posts in which we learned about the reliability of the bible. In those posts we found out the Bible we have today is an accurate copy of the original writings. And we learned there are many secular and archeological sources which corroborate the truth and accuracy of its contents. We also discovered it contains many eyewitness accounts and testimonies of people who were there, who witnessed the risen Jesus Christ in the flesh. So let us start examining proofs for the resurrection.

The Resurrection Proof #1: The Empty Tomb of Jesus

The empty tomb may be the strongest proof Jesus Christ rose from the dead. One of the most common theories presented by skeptics to refute this proof is to claim the disciples merely stole the body of Jesus and hid it. Then they lied to people telling them Jesus rose from the dead. Let's examine this theory and see if it stands the test of scrutiny and logic by asking a few simple questions.

If Jesus did not actually rise from the dead, then why did the disciples go from frightened, timid followers of Jesus before his death, to bold evangelists willing to die preaching his resurrection, if they made the whole thing up?

Remember, before Jesus was crucified, the disciples were, for the most part, cowards. When the soldiers came to arrest Jesus in the garden of Gethsemane the disciples ran away! Peter denied that he knew Jesus 3 times before the crucifixion. What event changed Peter and the others from being cowards to courageous preachers willing to die? Answer: **THEY MUST HAVE ACTUALLY SEEN THE RISEN JESUS!**

Why were the disciples willing to be tortured and killed for a known lie?

You don't need a degree in psychology to know that people do not die for a cause they *know* to be false. People do certainly die for false beliefs all the time, but they *think* they are dying for the truth. If the disciples faked the resurrection, they would know Christianity is a lie. History records they were tortured and killed for their faith, and not one of them said under torture "okay, okay, we made the whole thing up!" Why is that? Answer: **THEY MUST HAVE ACTUALLY SEEN THE RISEN JESUS!**

Why would the disciples make up the resurrection story if Jesus was a fraud?

Remember, Jesus told them he would rise after 3 days. If he was still dead on day four, that means he wasn't who he claimed he was, he wasn't the Messiah and certainly wasn't God after all! So why would the disciples worship a dead guy who lied to them and was exposed as a fraud? Answer: **THEY MUST HAVE ACTUALLY SEEN THE RISEN JESUS!**

What would be their motive for lying?

Lies or deceptions are typically done for some selfish motive. Preaching the resurrection of Jesus would not bring the disciples wealth, fame, status or popularity. It would only cause them to be hated, scorned, persecuted, excommunicated, imprisoned, exiled, beheaded, tortured and crucified. So again, what could possibly be their motive? Just to save face? That's certainly not logical. No one is going to go through what the disciples went through just because they're too embarrassed to say "I guess we were wrong". So what was their motive? Answer: **IT WAS THE TRUTH. THEY MUST HAVE ACTUALLY SEEN THE RISEN JESUS!**

How could the disciples even steal the body in the first place?

The body was encased in a tomb with a 24-hour watch by Roman guards trained to kill. The punishment for breaking a Roman grave seal, or attempting to steal a body or overpowering a Roman soldier was death! So how did the timid, cowardly disciples muster up the courage to try this? And as stated before, for what motive? That's a big risk for absolutely no payoff!

Some will say "maybe the guards were asleep?" I don't think so! Dereliction of duty brought certain death to a Roman soldier! In addition, the stone covering the tomb weighed 2 tons and was rolled into a stone groove flush against the stone opening of the grave. Think about how loud a 2 ton stone scraping against the stone wall would be as several disciples tried to move it. So, how could the disciples have stolen the body? Answer, they didn't. **JESUS ACTUALLY ROSE FROM THE DEAD!**

Please return next time when we examine more proofs of the resurrection. May God bless you all!

FOCUS QUESTIONS

Why is the truth of the resurrection crucial to the Christian faith?

Give three rebuttals to the claim the disciples stole the body of Jesus.

Evidence for the Resurrection Part 2

In part one we began to look at the evidence concerning the resurrection story. The first resurrection proof we discussed was the empty tomb and we answered the questions skeptics have posed to refute it. Let's continue.

The Resurrection Proof #2: The Holy Women Eyewitnesses

The holy women eyewitnesses are further proof that the Gospels are accurate historical records. If the accounts had been made up, no ancient author would have used women for witnesses to Christ's resurrection. Women were second class citizens in Bible times; their testimony was not even allowed in court! Yet the Bible says the risen Christ first appeared to Mary Magdalene and other holy women (Matthew 28) (Luke 24). Even the apostles did not believe Mary when she told them the tomb was empty (Luke 24:11). Jesus, who always had special respect for these women, honored them as the first eyewitnesses to His resurrection. The male Gospel writers had no choice but to report this embarrassing act of God's favor because that was how it happened!

The Resurrection Proof #3: Jesus' Apostles' New-Found Courage

After the crucifixion, Jesus' apostles hid behind locked doors, terrified they would be executed next. But something changed them from cowards to bold preachers. Anyone who understands human character knows people do not change that much without some major influence. That influence was seeing their Master alive, raised from the dead. Christ appeared to them in the locked room (John 20:19-23), on the shore of the Sea of Galilee (John 21), and on the Mount of Olives (Luke 24:50-51) (Acts 1:9-12). After seeing Jesus alive, Peter and the others left the locked room and preached the risen Christ, unafraid of what would happen to them. They quit hiding because they knew the truth. They finally understood that Jesus is God incarnate who saves people from their sin.

The Resurrection Proof #4: Changed Lives of James and Others

Changed lives are yet another proof of the resurrection. James, the brother of Jesus, was openly skeptical that Jesus was the Messiah. Later James became a courageous leader of the Jerusalem church, even being stoned to death for his faith. Why? The Bible says the risen Christ appeared to him (1 Corinthians 15:7). What a shock to see your own brother, alive again, after you knew he was dead. James and the apostles were effective missionaries because people could tell these men had touched and seen the risen Christ. With such zealous eyewitnesses, the early church exploded in growth, spreading west from Jerusalem to Rome and beyond. And for 2,000 years encounters with the resurrected Jesus have continued to change people's lives.

The Resurrection Proof #5: Large Crowd of Eyewitnesses

It is recorded that after the crucifixion, Jesus appeared alive over a span of 40 days and to "500 brethren" at the same time. (Back then, only men were counted in crowd totals, so factoring in women and children, Jesus most likely appeared to at least 1500 to 2000 people at one time). The Apostle Paul records this event in 1 Corinthians 15:6. He states that most of these men and women were still alive when he wrote this letter around 55 A.D. Undoubtedly, they must have told others about this miracle.

Skeptics may claim it was a hallucination, but modern psychologists say it would be impossible for a large crowd of people to have had the same hallucination at once. Smaller groups also saw the risen Christ, such as the apostles, and Cleopas and his companion on the road to Emmaus (Luke 24:13-35). They all saw the same thing, and in the case of the apostles, they touched Jesus and watched him eat food (Luke 24:42). The hallucination theory is further debunked because after the ascension of Jesus into heaven, sightings of him stopped.

Why would thousands of people immediately convert if Jesus didn't actually rise from the dead?

Think about it. History records that thousands upon thousands were instantly and immediately mass converting to be followers of Jesus, as many as 3000 in a single day (Acts 2). If that many people saw Jesus alive, it would explain how so many were converting because even the most hardened skeptics would have crowds and crowds of former skeptics saying "yes, it's true, we all have seen him too!." But if no one saw him alive and the crowds had only the words of the disciples to go by, why would thousands convert? Remember, the disciples were preaching to many who didn't want to believe Jesus was the Messiah, so what words could they speak to hostile crowds to convince them Jesus really did rise from the dead? "Trust us"? That might convince some of the disciple's closest friends, but not thousands upon thousands of skeptics. So why did thousands convert? Answer: **CROWDS MUST HAVE ACTUALLY SEEN THE RISEN JESUS!**

The Resurrection Proof #6: The Conversion of Paul

The conversion of Paul records the most drastically changed life in the Bible. As Saul of Tarsus, he was an aggressive persecutor of the early church. When the risen Christ appeared to Paul on the Damascus Road (Acts 9) Paul became Christianity's most determined missionary. He endured five floggings, three beatings, three shipwrecks, a stoning, poverty, and years of ridicule. Finally the Roman emperor Nero had Paul beheaded because the apostle refused to deny his faith in Jesus. What could make a person willingly accept—even welcome—such hardships? Logically, if Jesus didn't really rise from the dead, Saul would just gloat in his victory, exposing Jesus as a fraud who couldn't conquer death after all. So what event could have caused him to convert? Answer: **He must have actually encountered the risen Jesus.**

The Resurrection Proof #7: They Died for Jesus

Countless people have died for Jesus, absolutely certain that the resurrection of Christ is a historical fact. Tradition says ten of the original apostles died as martyrs for Christ, as did the Apostle Paul. Hundreds, perhaps thousands of early Christians died in the Roman arena and in prisons for their faith. Down through the centuries, thousands more have died for Jesus because they believed the resurrection is true. Even today, people suffer persecution because they have faith that Christ rose from the dead. An isolated group may give up their lives for a cult leader, but Christian martyrs have died in many lands for nearly 2,000 years, believing Jesus conquered death to give them eternal life.

<u>Taking the preponderance of the evidence concerning the resurrection story, the most reasonable conclusion, the best explanation is that it was virtually impossible that the apostles could have persisted in spreading the gospel had not Jesus Christ actually risen from the dead!</u>

When you come down to it, people reject Jesus not because of a lack of evidence. It is fundamentally a condition of the heart that keeps a person from coming to Christ. It is a hardened heart, a selfish pride. Selfish pride is the enemy of all of us. It keeps us from admitting we are guilty of sin. It keeps us from humbling ourselves before almighty holy God. And it keeps us from repentance, the turning away from our own agenda to follow God's agenda.

Jesus said, "I am the way and the truth and the life. No one comes to the father except through me." (John 14:6). Read Acts 3:19, Romans 10:9, and John 1:12. May God bless you all!

FOCUS QUESTIONS

Why would the testimony of women not be put in a made-up story?

Give reasons why the apostles could not have made-up the resurrection?

Seeing is Believing?

"On the evening of that first day of the week, when the disciples were together, with the doors locked for fear of the Jewish leaders, Jesus came and stood among them and said, "Peace be with you!" After he said this, he showed them his hands and side. The disciples were overjoyed when they saw the Lord." (John 20:19-20)

This scene occurred on Sunday evening, the day of our Lord's resurrection from the tomb. Just three days before (by Jewish reckoning) Jesus' disciples had witnessed his brutal crucifixion and burial. They were hiding out, fearing the Jewish leaders would be coming for them next. What joy and encouragement the disciples must have experienced, to see the risen Jesus in person and realize their faith had not been in vain! Fellow Christian, this is a joy we also look forward to, the day when we shall meet our Lord and know for certain that our faith has also not been in vain! I say this because it is natural for even the strongest Christians to sometimes struggle with their faith.

You see, it is human nature to have doubts. It is not unusual to be skeptical of things we do not fully understand. What better example of this fact than the disciples of Jesus? The disciples traveled and lived with Jesus, witnessing countless miracles (John 21:25). They received His teaching and took part in His earthly ministry for three incredible years! Jesus even told them ahead of time of His pending death, yet they did not comprehend what he was telling them. (Luke 18:31-34) Even John the Baptist, praised by Jesus as the greatest man born of women (Matthew 11:11), showed his humanity by expressing doubt about Jesus being the Messiah! (Luke 7:20-22)

Let us return to the scene that Sunday evening when the risen Jesus appeared to the disciples. "Now Thomas (also known as Didymus), one of the Twelve, was not with the disciples when Jesus came. So the other disciples told him, "We have seen the Lord!"But he said to them, "Unless I see the nail marks in his hands and put my finger where the nails were, and put my hand into his side, I will not believe."

"A week later his disciples were in the house again, and Thomas was with them. Though the doors were locked, Jesus came and stood among them and said, "Peace be with you!" Then he said to Thomas, "Put your finger here; see my hands. Reach out your hand and put it into my side. Stop doubting and believe." Thomas said to him, "My Lord and my God!" Then Jesus told him, "Because you have seen me, you have believed; BLESSED ARE THOSE WHO HAVE NOT SEEN AND YET HAVE BELIEVED." (John 20:24-29)

Thomas was skeptical. He would not believe that Christ had risen unless he could see and touch Him. This brings us to the main point of this essay: IT IS OKAY TO BE A SKEPTIC, ONLY BE OPEN TO THE EVIDENCE GOD GIVES YOU. God knows all things. He knows about our doubts. As we have noted, even those who were closest to Jesus experienced these feelings. Jesus will meet you where you are at and He can give you what you need; the key is YOUR HEART MUST BE READY TO RECEIVE IT.

Look at the way Jesus dealt with Thomas. Instead of rebuking Thomas, Jesus appeared to him with the evidence that Thomas needed. Jesus' compassion and humility brought Thomas to a place of surrender. Jesus will meet any and all skeptics exactly where they are at if they are open to look at the evidence that He gives them. He can turn anyone's doubt into belief, including a Christian who is struggling with their faith. As far as the evidence that God is real, there is a mountain of it, too much to describe in detail for one essay. But consider the following: No one has ever seen an atom.

As this essay has pointed out, humans like to see something before they believe in it. However, it is impossible for humans to see atoms. There are also many things much, much larger than an atom that humans can't see. People can't even see ordinary cells, which are six orders of magnitude larger than an atom. Atoms can't be resolved even with a microscope, because light is far bigger than the atom itself.

Even though no one has directly observed an individual atom, we have seen so much evidence of their existence that most of us believe in them. Thus, the Atomic theory is accepted as true and not discarded as a myth. This prevailing theory about the structure and behavior of atoms allows us to make predictions about the structure and behavior of the molecules that are made up of them. And all of our observations and tests agree with and support what atomic theory predicts. So, without directly seeing atoms, we infer their existence by observing their effects - effects that could not be explained by any other (better or more likely) theory.

It is the same with God. It is impossible to for humans to literally see God because it is beyond our ability. Speaking of God, 1 Timothy 6:15-16 says,"… He who is the blessed and only Sovereign, the King of kings and Lord of lords, who alone possesses immortality and dwells in unapproachable light, whom no man has seen or can see." And in Exodus 33:20 God declares, "You cannot see my face, for no one may see me and live." No one has ever seen God revealed in all His glory, because if God were to fully reveal Himself to us, we would be consumed and destroyed.

Despite the fact it is impossible for humans to see God, just like atoms, we can infer His existence by observing the world and the universe He has created. These observations, when examined closely, cannot be explained by any other (better or more likely) theory than God.

Romans 1:20 says, "For since the creation of the world God's invisible qualities—his eternal power and divine nature—have been clearly seen, being understood from what has been made, so that people are without excuse."

Going further, God not only has revealed Himself by what He has made, He also took a form in which we could "see" Him. John 1:18 says, "No one has ever seen God, but the one and only Son, who is Himself God and is in closest relationship with the Father, has made Him known." Jesus was God in the flesh (John 1:1, 14) so when people saw Him, they were seeing God. Jesus came to save mankind and in the process left evidence of His deity, including the eyewitness testimonies and first-hand accounts of those who were there, who witnessed His grace and truth.

There is much more that can be said but for now let us finish with these scriptures. 2 Peter 1:16 says, "For we did not follow cleverly devised myths when we made known to you the power and coming of our Lord Jesus Christ, but we were eyewitnesses of His majesty." And John 20:30-31 says, "Jesus performed many other signs in the presence of his disciples, which are not recorded in this book. But these are written that you may believe that Jesus is the Messiah, the Son of God, and that by believing you may have life in His name."

Dear Christian, if you are struggling with your faith, come to Jesus and allow Him to minister to your needs. Dear skeptic, if you have yet to believe, I pray the Spirit of God would soften the hardness of your heart and prepare you to receive the truth of His love and grace. May God bless you all!

FOCUS QUESTIONS

Why is it impossible for humans to see God?

How has God revealed Himself to mankind?

Chapter 4

Sharing the Gospel

"I used to ask God to help me. Then I asked if I might help Him. I ended up by asking God to do His work through me."

Hudson Taylor

Tips for Sharing the Gospel

The message of the gospel by itself is a simple message:

1) All people have broken God's law and must be punished.

2) Jesus Christ took the punishment Himself so that we could be set free.

3) People must respond to God of their own freewill by repenting (turning away from their sin), believing Christ died for them and rose again, and by placing their trust in Him as their Lord and Savior. There are many verses to support these steps. John 3:16, John 1:12, Romans 10:9, and 1 John 1:13 to name a few.

However, people will come up with all kinds of questions and arguments to refute the gospel. It is helpful for us to prepare a response to as many as we can, but no one can have all of the answers. And at the end of the day, it is the Holy Spirit who brings a person to the point of surrender before Almighty God. 1 Thessalonians 1:5 says "…our gospel came to you not simply with words but also with power, with the Holy Spirit and deep conviction." <u>You and I as Christ's disciples are simply the messengers. God does the saving.</u> In addition, we must remember that the message of the cross is foolishness to those who are perishing (1 Corinthians 1:18). So how do we proceed?

First we must learn to overcome our fear. WE MUST PRAY! Remember, the Holy Spirit is the One who convicts a person of the truth, we are simply messengers.

Next is to have mindset of HAVING FUN. Don't think of it an arduous task you must do out of obligation. It is true that Jesus commanded us to preach the Gospel, but we need to approach it with a positive attitude. When I witness on the street I stand tall and smile, I have a friendly disposition, and if a person does not want to talk with me I just let them go by. You will not have to engage someone if they do not wish to respond to you.

Finally, WE MUST BE PREPARED. I carry around gospel tracts that are icebreakers, something interesting that allows me to spark up a conversation. I bought mine from "The Way of the Master" evangelism course, but there are many others you can get. If you are on the street, these tracts help attract people's attention. I've discovered once a person stops and begins talking they will usually listen and engage me openly. Often during our conversation they will be laughing because they are relaxed and I am not preaching at them. I am simply sharing with them.

God has given all people a conscience. Con means "with" and science means "knowledge". The conscience is that inner knowledge of right and wrong, which is independent of ethnicity, education, religious upbringing, etc... Therefore, the most effective approach for presenting the gospel is usually to address a person's conscience instead of their intellect. In previous posts we have learned that God's law, the Ten Commandments, teaches people that they are sinners in need of forgiveness. (Galatians 3:24)

Here is a good principle to follow when talking to someone: Give the law to the proud, and give grace to the humble. A person is proud if they think they are a "good person". Almost everyone believes this. They must be presented with God's law to show them they are not. You only need to present a few commandments. Ask them if they have ever lied, stolen, used God's name in vain (blasphemy), or looked at another person with lust in their heart (adultery). This will personalize their sin and you will not be judging them because they will be admitting their guilt with their own words. I will often identify with them by admitting I've done the same things.

Many people think they are saved because they believe in Jesus, but that is not enough! Even the demons believe in Jesus and shudder (James 2:19). Be sure to emphasize their need for repentance from sin and placing their trust in Jesus as their Lord and Savior. (1 Peter 2:6) The following scenario is a good illustration of this principle: Imagine you have to jump out of an airplane 25,000 feet in the air and there is a parachute available to you. You believe the parachute can save you, but if you jump without it you will certainly die. You must put it on in order for it to save you. It is the same with Jesus. Believing He can save you is not enough, you must put Him on by trusting in Him as your Savior. This is done by humbly admitting your sin and asking Him into your heart.

Some people think God should just forgive them and let them into heaven just as they are. They think because they are sorry for their sin and try not to do it that God should just forgive them. The following scenario is a good illustration for helping them understand their guilt before a holy God:

Imagine a murderer standing before a judge who is 100% guilty. The evidence is clear and he has confessed to the crime. The murderer says to the judge, "Your honor, I am truly sorry for what I've done and I've tried very hard not to do it again. It's been 10 years since I've killed anyone. Can't you just forgive me and let me go?" The judge will say "Of course you should be sorry!" and "Of course you shouldn't do it again!" "You must receive the consequences for what you have done!" Only a corrupt judge would let the murderer go free. God is righteous and holy. He is a good judge and therefore He must punish sin. Again, a person must put on the Lord Jesus Christ in order to be set free from sin's punishment.

Once a person admits they are guilty of sin and that a Holy God will judge them based on His law, then they can understand their need for forgiveness. At this point some people will be humble and ready to hear about God's grace. Now you can share what Jesus did for them on the cross and it will make sense. Be sure to mention repentance (turning from their sin), believing and accepting Christ's payment on the cross for them, and placing their trust in Jesus as their Lord. Tell them once they do this God will give them a new heart with new desires to live for Him. Most people will not make a commitment on the spot and that is okay. You have prepared the soil and planted the seed. God will continue the work.

In closing, emphasize there is nothing more important to them than their soul. You are not asking them for money, or to join a church, you are simply trying to warn them about what happens when they die. Tell them 150,000 people die every day and you can bet almost all of them did not expect it. Most people own a bible. Ask them to look at it when they get home and to think about what you've shared with them. Then encourage them to get right with God before they go to sleep tonight. Finally, be sure to thank them for talking with you and give them a tract to take with them.

Remember to pray for boldness to reach out to the lost and may God bless you all!

FOCUS QUESTIONS

What is the very first step we must take to overcome our fear?

How is jumping out of an airplane without a parachute relatable to the gospel message?

Why can't God just forgive people for sin without involving Jesus?

Beware the "Modern Gospel" Part 1

"God loves you and He has a wonderful plan for your life." How many times have you heard this said by well-meaning Christians trying to witness to the lost? Perhaps you have said it yourself. I know I have. The implication is that accepting Jesus as our Lord and Savior will bring prosperity and happiness to our lives and solve all of our problems. It is true that God loves us and it is true that He has a wonderful plan. But His plan is to rescue us from the wrath to come on the Day when He will judge the world in righteousness. However, <u>Jesus did not promise His followers prosperity and a problem-free life on this earth!</u>

In fact, you and I as Christians can expect persecution and suffering for following after Him. Speaking to His disciples, Jesus said "Then you will be handed over to be persecuted and put to death, and you will be hated by all nations because of me." (Matthew 25:9) And in Luke 9:23 Jesus says "...Whoever wants to be my disciple must deny themselves and take up their cross daily and follow me." Christians in America have not seen much of this persecution, which is the norm for Christians living in other parts of the world. Think of what it must be like to be a Christian in China, North Korea, or the Middle East! However, even in America there is a growing tide of secularism which is opposed to the Christian faith. Christians in America must be prepared for increased opposition to our faith, and we are seeing that already in our schools, courts, and mass media.

<u>What Jesus does promise His followers is peace despite our circumstances.</u> In John 16:33 Jesus says "I have told you these things, so that in me you may have peace. In this world you will have trouble. But take heart! I have overcome the world." And in Philippians 4:6-7 the Apostle Paul wrote, "Do not be anxious about anything, but in every situation, by prayer and petition, with thanksgiving, present your requests to God. And the peace of God, which transcends all understanding, will guard your hearts and minds in Christ Jesus."

So you see, our approach to reaching the lost must not focus on the temporary things of this world. Everyone desires good health, successful marriages, financial stability, etc... but that is not why Jesus died on the cross! He gave His life to pay the debt for our trespasses, our violations of God's law, our sin! Romans 5:9 says, "Since we have now been justified by his blood, how much more shall we be saved from God's wrath through Him (Jesus)!" And 1 Thessalonians 1:10 says, "and to wait for his Son from heaven, whom he raised from the dead-- Jesus, who rescues us from the coming wrath."

Jesus' death and resurrection conquered sin and death once and for all! As Christians we place our trust in Christ so that in the Day of Judgment we will be declared righteous, and God can let us into heaven without compromising His holiness and justice. Therefore, people must respond to Jesus Christ by faith because they need His righteousness, not because they need their lives on this earth improved! This is why it is so difficult to witness to successful, happy people. When someone has all this life has to offer, they will not see their need for Jesus if we tell them "God has a wonderful plan for their life." Their life is already wonderful.

Similarly, when the "God has a wonderful plan" message is preached to those who are going through hard times, their motivation for coming to Jesus is life improvement, not to be made righteous. Thus, when trouble comes and difficulties arise, they feel God has let them down. They believe they were lied to and duped into following Christianity. Often they will fall away from the faith and become bitter towards Christianity.

Many atheists were at one time professing Christians who became disenchanted with the faith. They concluded God must not exist, because if He does exist, then how could He allow human pain and suffering? Many atheists will claim they've gained knowledge and become awakened to the way the real world works, but they have simply shifted their worldview. The same evidence that once did not affect their Christian faith they now cite as proof of God's non-existence.

The key which allows a person to come to a genuine, lasting Christian faith is the Ten Commandments. When a person understands that they have broken God's law and are under condemnation for doing so, they will begin to thirst for righteousness. Their motivation for coming to God through the Savior is salvation from the wrath to come. They will appreciate God's mercy and grace and look forward to the eternal life that awaits them in heaven, not the improved life many seek on earth. And when trouble comes into their life they can come to God for help without blaming Him for their circumstances, or questioning His existence.

In closing, we must beware using the modern gospel message of "God loves you and has a wonderful plan for your life". Instead, we should use the law of God, the Ten Commandments, when we witness to the lost. May God bless you all!

FOCUS QUESTIONS

Why did Jesus die on the cross?

How can the "God has a wonderful plan" message mislead those who hear it?

What is the key to bringing others to a lasting faith in God?

Beware the "Modern Gospel" Part 2

"Using the Law of God to Lead a Person to the Foot of the Cross"

In our first lesson, we learned that the "God loves you and has a wonderful plan for your life" message can be misleading. It is true that God is love and He does have a wonderful plan for all who call on His name, who accept Jesus Christ as their Savior. But this message implies that becoming a Christian will improve your life and remove all of your problems. This simply is not true! All people desire good health, successful marriages, and financial stability. But a person's motivation for coming to God through Christ should be their desire to be made righteous, not life improvement here on earth. God may choose to bless his children, and He does promise to provide for our needs, but He does not guarantee us prosperity in this life. In fact, our Lord guarantees that we can expect to suffer for His name.

A person's need to be made righteous is an aspect of the modern gospel message that is often neglected, because it is much more palatable to talk about God's love and forgiveness than to talk about sin, judgment, and hell. However, in order for a person to truly understand the depth of God's mercy and grace, he or she must first be confronted with the stark reality of what awaits the unrepentant sinner who must stand before Almighty God and be judged on their righteousness. Of course, no one will be justified before God and allowed to enter into heaven based solely on their righteousness. Romans 3:23 says "For all have sinned and fall short of the glory of God." And Romans 3:10 says "…There is no one righteous, not even one…"

However, people have difficulty understanding the gravity of their sins. This is where the Law of God, the Ten Commandments, is necessary for showing a person the reality of their sin and falling short of God's standard. It is the key to a person's heart to prepare them for the amazing grace which our Lord has provided for us. Psalm 19:7 says "The law of the Lord is perfect converting the soul." And Galatians 3:24 says "The law has become our tutor to lead us to Christ, so that we may be justified by faith." Therefore, it is crucial for a person to hear the Law of God and to be made conscious of their dire need for a savior! Let's look at an example from civil law to help us understand how the presence of the law of God works in a sinner's heart.

When there is no visible sign of the law on a freeway, motorists often transgress the speed limit. Apparently each speedster says to himself that the law has forgotten to patrol this part of the freeway. He says to himself that he is only breaking the speed limit by 15 miles per hour, and besides, he isn't the only one doing it. Suddenly, a highway patrol car enters the fast lane with lights flashing! The speedster's heart skips a beat! He is no longer secure in the fact that others are speeding too. He knows he is personally guilty of transgressing the law and he could be pulled over for it. The fact that there are others doing it is now irrelevant! It is very much the same with people and their sin.

If you ask someone if they consider themselves to be a "good" person, they will almost always say yes. However, if you present the law of God to them by asking if they have ever lied, or stolen, or blasphemed God's name, or lusted in their heart, it will be made very apparent to them that they have transgressed the law. Their conscience has done its job. You see, <u>when a person says they consider themselves to be a "good" person, what they really mean is they are no worse a lawbreaker than everyone else who also is guilty of doing the same things</u>. But that fact will become irrelevant to them when they recognize and admit their own personal guilt, just like the speedster. Now they are ready to learn of sin's consequences and what God has done to save them by asking three questions.

First, ask them "If God were to judge you based on His law, would you be guilty or innocent?" If they are honest they must say guilty. If they say they don't believe in God just respond by saying it is a hypothetical question, "IF God were to judge you…" and ask them again. Next, ask them "Would you go to heaven or hell?" Again, if they say they don't believe in hell just remind them it is hypothetical. Most people will admit they would go to hell, but some might say heaven. Their reasons are many and varied for this, but the bottom line is if God is a good and righteous judge He must punish sin, just like a good judge must sentence a murderer even if the murderer is sorry and has reformed his ways. Finally, ask them "Does that concern you?" You have now led them to the point where God's grace and mercy can be presented and it should make sense to them because they can see their need for forgiveness.

They can now be told what God has done to save them through Jesus Christ and the punishment He received on their behalf. Yes, God loves them and He proved it by what He did on the cross. They can see how His grace can be imparted to them and it is not by their own works or righteousness. Their motivation for coming to faith in Christ will be repentance and forgiveness of sins, not life improvement. When difficult times come, as they do for all of us, they can look to God for peace and comfort, instead of blaming Him and falling away from their faith. Thank you for reading this and may God bless you all!

FOCUS QUESTIONS

When someone says they are a "good" person, what are they really saying?

What questions can you ask to show someone their true condition as a sinner, a transgressor of God's law?

At what point in your conversation with a person are they ready to hear about God's grace?

Faithful are the Wounds of a Friend

Life passes by us very quickly and in our haste of living we often don't take the time to stop and appreciate it. We seldom take the time to tell our spouses, kids, parents, and friends that we love them and we are thankful for having them in our life. We also fail to drink in the times we are blessed to spend with them and to savor each and every drop.

Because time passes by so quickly, our lives tend to be marked by milestones, some joyful and some painful. Examples of joyful milestones might be the birth of a child, a marriage, a graduation, or a birthday. Examples of painful milestones may be the loss of a child, a divorce, dropping out of school, or the death of friend.

Many of us have known non-Christian friends for many years, yet we have scarcely mentioned the very thing that is most important in our life; our faith. We often shy away from sharing with our family and friends about what we truly believe because we fear rejection and damage to our relationships.

It is true that we can and should be a testimony of our faith by how we live our lives. There is no doubt that love, kindness, and integrity of character go a long way to showing others our faith is real. Nevertheless, we can't assume that our friends and family know the gospel message, because there is so much misinformation out there about who Jesus is and how a person becomes saved.

A wise king by the name of Solomon once wrote "Faithful are the wounds of a friend, but the kisses of an enemy are deceitful." (Proverbs 27:6)
Question: Who would prefer a friend's wounds to an enemy's kisses? Answer: The one who carefully considers the source.

A friend who has your best interests at heart may have to give you unpleasant advice at times, but you know it is for your own good. An enemy, by contrast, may whisper sweet words to you and happily send you on your way to destruction. People also tend to listen to what they want to hear and the enemy, Satan, will use that against them.

One of the enemies favorite lies is secularism, which basically says that all life is meaningless. This philosophy says that people's lives are an accident, the product of random chance (Evolution). Your life and mine have no real purpose because they are governed by the laws of matter and energy without any freewill of our own, and when we die we simply cease to exist, end of story. This belief system demands that there are no absolute truths or standards by which we should live. Morality is just a matter of personal opinion, and good and evil do not really exist.

As Christians, you and I know that people's lives are not accidents. We believe there is an intelligent mind behind the creation of the universe, which includes you, me, and all people. Because of this our lives do have real meaning and what we do in this life does matter. There are absolute truths and good and evil do exist. The choices we make have eternal consequences and we have been given the freewill to choose our own destiny beyond this temporary life on earth.

Other lies of the enemy are the multitudes of false religions which mislead people away from the only way to salvation, which is through faith in Jesus Christ (John 14:6). People are saved by God's grace through faith in Jesus, not by works, so that no one can boast. (Ephesians 2:8-9) It is not our righteousness which saves us; it is Jesus' righteousness which saves us. (2 Corinthians 5:21) Thus, our salvation is not a matter of going to church, giving money, or doing good works. It is all about Jesus!

You and I must be bold and trust in our Lord to help us share this monumental truth with our friends and family. We can't assume they know and we must tell them out of our love for them and our concern for their eternal destiny. I know this is difficult! But how can we not do this and say that we love them? Pray for courage and determine a time soon to humbly approach them. We don't know how long any of us have to live, so we must act now!

One way you can start is to say to them "Today I am taking a risk of telling you what I believe to be true, even though you may disagree and think me a fool. It is worth that risk to me because I can't stay silent about it and say I am your friend." Then share your faith with humility and sincerity and the Holy Spirit will do the real work in their hearts. May God bless you all!

FOCUS QUESTIONS

Why is it so difficult to share our faith with friends and family?

Why must we take the risk of sharing our faith with our friends and family?

Who will give us courage and work on the hearts of those we share with?

The Parable of the Sower

This parable is found in 3 of the gospels: Matthew, Mark, and Luke. We will read the account in Matthew and reference the other two accounts as needed.

"Then He (Jesus) told them many things in parables, saying: 'A farmer went out to sow his seed. As he was scattering the seed, some fell along the path, and the birds came and ate it up. Some fell on rocky places, where it did not have much soil. It sprang up quickly, because the soil was shallow. But when the sun came up, the plants were scorched, and they withered because they had no root. Other seed fell among the thorns, which grew up and choked the plants. Still other seed fell on good soil, where it produced a crop—a hundred, sixty or thirty times what was sown. Whoever has ears, let them hear." (Matthew 13:3-9)

Our word "parable" comes from the Greek word parabole which means "a placing beside", in other words a comparison or illustration. Parables are stories meant to illustrate spiritual truth using nature and human life. Jesus seldom interpreted His parables, but here He does. Let us read it and break down each of the four scenarios.

Scenario #1: "Listen to what the parable of the sower means: When anyone hears the message about the kingdom and does not understand it, the evil one comes and snatches away what was sown in their heart. This is the seed sown along the path." (Matthew 13:18-19)

Here we read that the seed represents "the message of the kingdom", and Mark 4:14 and Luke 8:11 also tell us the seed represents the "word of God". Since the intention of the scattering of God's word is for the listeners to understand it and for it to take root in their hearts, the word is the gospel message meant to bring salvation to lost souls. The evil one, Satan, is active in his efforts to prevent people from understanding the message and being saved. Therefore, it is reasonable to conclude that Satan will work at keeping this person from thinking about the message they heard and even bring circumstances to cause them to forget it.

Scenario #2: "The seed falling on rocky ground refers to someone who hears the word and at once receives it with joy. But since they have no root, they last only a short time. When trouble or persecution comes because of the word, they quickly fall away." (Matthew 13:20-21)

The rocky ground is a thin layer of soil that covered solid rock. Any moisture that fell there would soon evaporate and the germinating seed would wither and die. This person has a hard heart which does not allow the gospel message to penetrate to a depth that would allow for true change to occur. It is clear that this person did not really understand the gospel message, or only heard what they wanted to hear. Thus, this person's belief is superficial and does not save. When troubles or persecution comes because of the gospel, they fall away.

Scenario #3: "The seed falling among the thorns refers to someone who hears the word, but the worries of this life and the deceitfulness of wealth choke the word, making it unfruitful." (Matthew 13:22)

The Luke account also adds "life's pleasures", and the Mark account adds "the desires for other things". The result of these "thorns" is an unfruitful faith. Luke 8:14 refers to this unfruitfulness with the phrase "...and they do not mature." This scenario raises interesting questions concerning salvation and the role of works.

Our Lord Jesus said, "I am the vine; you are the branches. If you remain in me and I in you, you will bear much fruit; apart from me you can do nothing. If you do not remain in me, you are like a branch that is thrown away and withers; such branches are picked up, thrown into the fire and burned." (John 15:5-6) And in John 15:8 Jesus says, "This is to my Father's glory, that you bear much fruit, showing yourselves to be my disciples." In addition, James 2:17, 20 says faith without works is "dead" and "useless". James also points out that deeds are an indication of a genuine faith. James wrote, "...I will show you my faith by my deeds." (James 2:18)

These passages are very clear that genuine believers will produce fruit. Thus, the seed sown among the thorns describes a person whose faith is not real because it is not producing fruit due to the worries of this life and the pursuit of riches and pleasures. However, this does not mean that salvation is earned by doing good works! These passages tell us that works (deeds, fruit) are the RESULT OF GENUINE FAITH IN CHRIST, but they do not say works save us!

Ephesians 2:8-9 says, "For it is by GRACE you have been saved through FAITH—and this is not from yourselves, it is the GIFT OF GOD—NOT BY WORKS, so that no one can boast." Therefore, Christians are saved by God's grace through faith and our faith will produce fruit as the result of God's word changing our hearts (good soil). This is accomplished by the working of the Holy Spirit, which connects us to Jesus (vine) and gives us the power to we need to bring glory to God by our deeds. "For we (Christians) are God's handiwork, created in Christ Jesus to do good works, which God prepared in advance for us to do." (Ephesians 2:10)

This point is driven home by the fourth and last scenario: "But the seed falling on good soil refers to someone who hears the word and understands it. This is the one who produces a crop, yielding a hundred, sixty or thirty times what was sown." (Matthew 13:23)

Notice Jesus points out this person "understands" the message and the result is a change in their heart attitude and in their actions. What is it the person with the good soil (heart) understands that the other three do not? Most likely it is the role of repentance which softens the sinner's hard heart, allowing the gospel message to penetrate and take root, bringing them to a point of surrender before Holy God.

2 Corinthians 7:10 says, "Godly sorrow brings repentance that leads to salvation and leaves no regret, but worldly sorrow brings death."

Please return next time when we begin to explore the meaning of repentance. May God bless you all!

FOCUS QUESTIONS

What does the seed represent in this parable?

Can works (deeds, fruit) save us? Explain.

Prepare Ye the Way!

All four gospels have an account of John the Baptist, who preached "a baptism of repentance for the forgiveness of sins." (Mark 1:4) Even though our Bible seems to have little to say about John, he conveys to us a simple but important message that still applies today about the repentance of sins. The scriptures say that John was sent to "PREPARE THE WAY" for the coming of our Lord Jesus Christ (Mark 1:2-3), but what exactly did John do in preparing the way?

Luke 3:3-4 says, "He (John)went into all the country around the Jordan, preaching a baptism of repentance for the forgiveness of sins; As it is written in the book of the words of Isaiah the prophet: A voice of one calling in the desert, prepare the way for the Lord, make straight paths for Him." And Matthew 3:1-2 says, "In those days John the Baptist came preaching in the Desert of Judea, and saying, Repent, for the kingdom of heaven is near." What does it mean to "prepare the way"?

It means to create a favorable environment or to make it easier for one to come to you and operate in your life. Luke 3:5 says, "Every valley shall be filled, and every mountain and hill shall be brought low; and the crooked shall be made straight, and the rough ways shall be made smooth." Thus, the ministry of John the Baptist created a favorable environment and made it easier for Jesus to enter into and operate in the lives of the people who heard His message.

So what did people need to do in order to respond to John in preparing the way for Jesus? THEY REPENTED OF THEIR SINS. They confessed their sins and were baptized as a sign that they have turned from their sins. Matthew 3:6 tells us, "Confessing their sins, they were baptized by him in the Jordan River." An important principle we can learn from John's ministry is REPENTANCE IS ESSENTIAL in order to "prepare the way" for the Gospel message of Jesus Christ.

You see, before the Gospel message can take root in a person's heart, their heart must be made ready, just like the good soil in the parable of the sower. A sinner's hard heart must be softened by the truth of their sin nature and their guilt for breaking God's laws. Only then can they experience remorse for their sins and recognize their need for forgiveness. A person with a repentant heart will begin to thirst for righteousness and appreciate the sacrifice made for them by the Lord Jesus Christ.

Matthew 5:6 says, "Blessed are those who hunger and thirst for righteousness, for they will be filled." A person may acknowledge they have sin, but without repentance a person's understanding of the gospel message is incomplete or misguided. We see this today in many churches, in which people make professions of faith in Christ without repenting of their sin.

Simply acknowledging our sins is not enough and John rebuked the Pharisees for not living up to their professions of faith.

Matthew 3:7-8 says, "But when he (John) saw many Pharisees and Sadducees coming to be baptized, he denounced them. 'You brood of snakes!' he exclaimed. 'Who warned you to flee God's coming judgment? Prove by the way you live that you have really turned from your sins and turned to God." And Proverbs 28:13 says, "He who conceals his sins does not prosper, but whoever confesses and renounces them finds mercy." These passages make it clear that repentance requires people not only to acknowledge their sins, but also to forsake or turn away from them.

Many pastors today avoid preaching about sin, punishment and hell because those are not popular messages people like to hear, but people need to hear them! Just like the people who heard the message of John the Baptist were made ready to hear the gospel, people today need to hear that same message. Otherwise, their motivation for coming to Christ is for Him to fix all of their problems and bless their lives with riches and health, etc…But they have not been taught the key reason why Jesus died on the cross!

Each person needs to be confronted with the reality of their spiritual bankruptcy before the Holy God who created them. They must understand they are guilty of violating God's laws, be remorseful and desire to please God by changing their actions. They also must understand they are powerless to receive forgiveness for sins by earning righteousness through good works. THEY NEED THE RIGHTEOUSNESS OF JESUS CHRIST!

Jesus died on the cross to pay the penalty of sin, which is death, so that by placing our faith in Him we can be forgiven of our sins and set free from death. Romans 6:23 says, "For the wages of sin is death, but the gift of God is eternal life in Christ Jesus our Lord." And 2 Corinthians 5:21 says, "For our sake He (Father) made Him [Jesus] who knew no sin to be sin for us, so that in Him we might become the righteousness of God". Our motivation for coming to Jesus must be to receive His righteousness, which is what every person needs to enter heaven. This is the gospel message. Hebrews 12:14 tells us, "... without holiness no man shall see the Lord."

It is important to note that confessing sins and being baptized with water is not enough to save people from their sins! John PREPARED THE WAY for people to receive Jesus' message by preaching repentance and baptizing them for the remission of their sins. Thus, people still needed to receive Jesus after they repented in order to be saved. John's message was, "…After me will come one more powerful than I, the thongs of whose sandals I am not worthy to stoop down and untie. I baptize you with water, but HE (JESUS) WILL BAPTIZE YOU WITH THE HOLY SPIRIT." (Mark 1:7-8) May God bless you all!

FOCUS QUESTIONS

How did John prepare the way for Jesus?

Is acknowledging our sin enough to save us? Explain.

Why did Jesus die on the cross and how does repentance prepare our hearts to receive this message?

What is Repentance?

In the previous post we learned John the Baptist prepared the way for the coming of our Lord Jesus Christ through preaching repentance and baptism for the remission of sins. By doing so He created a favorable environment for Jesus to enter and operate in the lives of the people who heard his message.

Repentance begins when a person comes to understand their true spiritual condition before the Holy God who made all things. The true spiritual condition of all people is complete unrighteousness, a spiritual bankruptcy due to the breaking of God's law. This is known as sin and everyone, no matter how good they may appear to be before other people, have this condition. The bible is very clear about this fact. Romans 3:23 says, "For all have sinned and fall short of the glory of God." And Romans 3:10 says, "As it is written: 'There is no one righteous, not even one.'" Once a person recognizes and admits they are guilty of sin and in need of forgiveness, how should they respond to this disturbing news?

2 Corinthians 7:10–11 says, "Godly sorrow brings repentance that leads to salvation and leaves no regret, but worldly sorrow brings death. See what this godly sorrow has produced in you: what earnestness, what eagerness to clear yourselves, what indignation, what alarm, what longing, what concern, what readiness to see justice done."

Godly sorrow, also translated "godly grief," is an acute sense of sadness we experience as a result of the sins we have committed. We not only understand and admit we are guilty but we long to make it right before God. We are in agreement with God that His ways are right and we humble ourselves before Him seeking His forgiveness and mercy. Many understand the term repentance simply to mean "turning from sin." Certainly this is part of it, but there is more to the biblical definition of repentance.

In the Bible, the word repent means "to change one's mind." In Peter's sermon on the day of Pentecost, he concludes with a call for the people to repent (Acts 2:38). Repent from what? Peter is calling the people who rejected Jesus to change their minds about Him, to recognize that He is indeed "Lord and Christ" (Acts 2:36). Peter is calling the people to change their minds from rejection of Christ as the Messiah to faith in Him as both Messiah and Savior. Thus, in this passage we see that repentance preceded coming to faith in Jesus, just as we saw in John the Baptist's ministry that repentance "prepared the way" for people to receive Jesus.

Repentance and faith can be understood as "two sides of the same coin." It is impossible to place your faith in Jesus Christ as the Savior without first changing your mind about who He is and what He has done. Whether it is repentance from willful rejection or repentance from ignorance or disinterest, it is a change of mind. Thus, biblical repentance in relation to salvation is admitting you are a sinner, humbling yourself before God, and changing your mind from rejection of Christ to faith in Christ. "Repent, then, and turn to God, so that your sins may be wiped out, that times of refreshing may come from the Lord." (Acts 3:19)

However, some people have been taught that they must perform religious ceremony and do good works in order to receive God's forgiveness. This is not true. Ephesians 2:8-9 says, "For it is by grace you have been saved through faith—and this is not from yourselves, it is the gift of God—NOT BY WORKS SO THAT NO ONE CAN BOAST." Those who rely on their religion rather than on the finished work of Jesus Christ demonstrate a prideful heart and lack of humility before God, relying on their own efforts to gain righteousness. Jesus warned us about this religious mindset.

Luke 18:9-14 says, "To some who were confident of their own righteousness and looked down on everyone else, Jesus told this parable: "Two men went up to the temple to pray, one a Pharisee and the other a tax collector. The Pharisee stood by himself and prayed: 'God, I thank you that I am not like other people—robbers, evildoers, adulterers—or even like this tax collector. I fast twice a week and give a tenth of all I get.' "But the tax collector stood at a distance. He would not even look up to heaven, but beat his breast and said, 'God, have mercy on me, a sinner.' "I tell you that this man, rather than the other, went home justified before God. For all those who exalt themselves will be humbled, and those who humble themselves will be exalted."

It is equally important we understand repentance is not a work we do to earn salvation. No one can repent and come to God unless God pulls that person to Himself. John 6:44 says, "No one can come to Me (Jesus) unless the Father who sent me draws them…" Acts 5:31 and 11:18 indicate that repentance is something God gives—it is only possible because of His grace. All of salvation, including repentance and faith, is a result of God drawing us, opening our eyes, and changing our hearts.

While repentance is not a work that earns salvation, repentance unto salvation does result in works. It is impossible to truly and fully change your mind without that causing a change in action. In the Bible, true repentance results in a change in behavior. That is why John the Baptist called people to "produce fruit in keeping with repentance" (Matthew 3:8). A person who has truly repented from rejection of Christ to faith in Christ will give evidence of a changed life. (2 Corinthians 5:17; Galatians 5:19-23; James 2:14-26)

In conclusion, repentance, properly defined, is necessary for salvation. The full biblical meaning of repentance is a "Godly sorrow" about the sins we have committed and a desire to make it right with God and a "change of mind "that believes and accepts Jesus as the Messiah and

Savior. This is "repentance that leads to salvation and leaves no regret". The evidence of a person's faith in Christ will be a change in behavior in which the person turns from their sins and produces good works for the glory of God.

Each day our culture in America is growing more and more hostile to our Christian faith and there are many wolves in sheep's clothing sowing false teaching. Dear brothers and sisters in Christ, cling to the truth of God's word and do not be led astray! Pray constantly and never forget that you belong to the King! May God bless you all!

FOCUS QUESTIONS

What is "Godly sorrow"?

Can a person do good works to earn salvation?

Chapter 5

Men's Leadership

"The ultimate measure of a man is not where he stands in moments of comfort and convenience, but where he stands at times of challenge and controversy."   - **Martin Luther King Jr.**

Men's Leadership Part 1

2000 years ago in the land of Israel, on a mountaintop near Jerusalem, Jesus spoke the following words to His disciples: "All authority in heaven and on earth has been given to me. Therefore go and make disciples of all nations, baptizing them in the name of the Father and the Son and the Holy Spirit, teaching them to obey everything I have commanded you. And remember, I am with you always, to the end of the age." (Matthew 28:18-20) This is known as the "Great Commission".

Notice the first sentence, Jesus said *"All authority in heaven and on earth has been given to me."* Just a few weeks before, Jesus was arrested and taken to the Roman authorities who sentenced Him to die. Jesus' disciples watched Him suffer and die a painful and humiliating death on a cross. Jesus had willingly submitted Himself to this shame in order to pay the penalty of sin for you and me and for all people who have ever lived.

But Jesus did not stay dead! God raised Him on the third day and He appeared to hundreds of eyewitnesses over a period of 40 days! This proved He was the Son of God and His death and resurrection conquered sin and death once and for all. Thus, Jesus has made it possible for all people to be set free from certain spiritual death, which is separation from God for all eternity. In addition, Jesus reclaimed God's creation from the clutches of Satan and He alone has supreme authority over all things.

On this mountaintop Jesus commissioned His disciples, much like a general in the army would commission his officers. Only the war they are told to fight is not a physical war, but a spiritual war for the souls of people. Instead of commanding that His enemies be destroyed, Jesus commanded His disciples to go rescue His enemies by making them also His disciples. In doing so, Jesus' enemies would be set free from the evil ranks of Satan and certain spiritual death. Instead they would be added to the ranks of Almighty God, made righteous by faith in Jesus Christ. This is a mission of the upmost urgency!

Notice Jesus said **"make disciples of all nations"**. And a short time before this, Jesus also said to His disciples; "But you will receive power when the Holy Spirit comes on you; and you will be my witnesses in Jerusalem, and in all Judea and Samaria, and to the ends of the earth." (Acts 1:8) Here we read Jesus told the disciples to be His witnesses **"to the ends of the earth"**. Thus, the battlefields on which this spiritual war, this "Great Commission" would be fought encompasses the entire earth. This war is still going on right now, this very day, and you, me, and all of people are a part of it.

Since this is spiritual warfare, it must be fought with spiritual weapons. The apostle Paul wrote about them in the book of Ephesians. These weapons are called **"The Full Armor of God"**. Ephesians 6:11-13 says, "Put on the full armor of God, so that you can take your stand against the devil's schemes. For our struggle is not against flesh and blood, but against the rulers, against the authorities, against the powers of this dark world and against the spiritual forces of evil in the heavenly realms. Therefore put on **the full armor of God**, so that when the day of evil comes, you may be able to stand your ground, and after you have done everything, to stand."

In these verses Paul reaffirms to us that we are in a spiritual war. Also notice who we are fighting against. Is it other people here on earth? No! It is against the "spiritual forces of evil in the heavenly realms." Thus, the battles we fight are meant to free people from the enemy!

Next, Paul lists spiritual weapons we need to use to fight this war.

Ephesians 6:14-18 says, "Stand firm then, with **the belt of truth** buckled around your waist, with **the breastplate of righteousness** in place, and with your feet fitted with the readiness that comes from **the gospel of peace**. In addition to all this, take up **the shield of faith**, with which you can extinguish all the flaming arrows of the evil one. Take **the helmet of salvation** and **the sword of the Spirit**, which is the word of God. And pray in the Spirit on all occasions with all kinds of prayers and requests. With this in mind, **be alert and always keep on praying** for all the Lord's people."

We are not going to explain all of these today (see chapter 6), but I wanted to us to see that we Christians need to have these weapons ready so that we can stand against the evil forces opposed to our faith.

So far we have seen that our Lord Jesus has commissioned us to make disciples of all nations, and that we are in a spiritual war of good against evil. Let's stop and think about something. When a war is being fought, who is placed on the front lines? Who is expected to do the hand to hand combat? Is it the women? Is it the children? No, of course not! It is the men! It would be crazy for an army to go to war putting women and children on the front lines of battle and leave the men back home! But that is exactly what is happening today in the Christian church. Christian men in the United States are not rising up and stepping forward to take their place as leaders.

Let's be clear about one thing, Jesus calls all of His disciples, both men and women, to carry out this "Great Commission". But our enemy is clever. Satan knows if he can keep Christian men off the front lines of this spiritual battle, then he can trick more people into following him rather than following God. And guys, some of those he tricks could be our own children and our own family members. Therefore, it is critical for Christian men in America to rise up, equip themselves with the Armor of God and take their positions as spiritual leaders, as spiritual warriors for Jesus Christ!

Men, it does not matter what age or stage in life you are in now. ALL ARE CALLED by God to lead. If Godly men don't rise up and lead, then someone else will, and the consequences to our families and churches can be disastrous for generations. And we are already seeing that happen in American culture today. My prayer is that each man who reads this will open his heart and embrace who God has called him to be. So what kind of leaders has God called His men to be?

Authentic leadership has been taught and modeled for us by Jesus. His example was emulated by Paul, Peter, and the courageous men who started the first-century church. In Matthew 20:28 Jesus said of Himself, "…the Son of Man did not come to be served, but to serve, and to give His life as a ransom for many." Contrary to the secular worldview of leadership, the heart of biblical Christian leadership is being a servant.

This series of posts will focus on five leadership qualities that make up a true man of God. They are obedience to God, dependence on God, humility, integrity and self-discipline. These are attributes we Christian men must develop if we are to serve with faith, confidence, strength, courage, and endurance. Please return next time when we look at the first leadership quality which is **obedience to God.** May God bless you all!

FOCUS QUESTIONS

What is the Great Commission?

What kind of war are we fighting and who is the enemy?

What is the heart of Christian leadership?

Men's Leadership Part 2

In our first post we learned that there is a spiritual war raging right now and that Christian men in America must answer the call to be spiritual warriors for Jesus Christ. We also noted that the heart of Christian leadership is being a servant. There are five qualities Christian men must work on developing to help us lead our families and to protect them from the spiritual forces of evil opposed to our faith.

The first leadership quality we need to have is **Obedience to God.** Obedience begins by recognizing that God does not give commands because He wants restrict our freedoms. God does not want to take away our joy or to keep good things away from us. That is the oldest lie ever told! When God created the first man, Adam, God placed Adam in a garden, and God gave Adam only one command. Genesis 2:16-17 says, *"And the LORD God commanded the man, "You are free to eat from any tree in the garden; but you must not eat from the tree of the knowledge of good and evil, for when you eat from it you will certainly die."*

Notice three things: First, God gave the command to the man Adam, for God had not yet created woman. Second, the command was meant to protect Adam. It was for Adam's own good, *"...for when you eat from it you will certainly die."* Third, notice God gave Adam the freedom to eat from all the other trees in the garden. It is clear that Adam's need for food and variety was abundantly provided for by God. But God established a boundary for Adam not to cross. Remember, God is the Creator and He required Adam to give Him His rightful place, just as He requires that we give Him His rightful place in our lives.

Let us continue with the story... Genesis 2:20-22 says, *"So the man gave names to all the livestock, the birds in the sky and all the wild animals. But for Adam no suitable helper was found. So the LORD God caused the man to fall into a deep sleep; and while he was sleeping, He took one of the man's ribs and then closed up the place with flesh. Then the LORD God made a woman from the rib He had taken out of the man, and He brought her to the man."* And verse 25 says, *"Adam and his wife were both naked, and they felt no shame."* Again, the LORD God provided for Adam's needs by creating a woman to be his wife and helper, and both of them lived together in complete innocence, free from sin.

Now enter Satan, the father of lies. In Genesis 3:1-5 we read: *"Now the serpent was more crafty than any of the wild animals the LORD God had made. He said to the woman, "Did God really say, 'You must not eat from any tree in the garden'? The woman said to the serpent, 'We may eat fruit from the trees in the garden, but God did say, 'You must not eat fruit from the tree that is in the middle of the garden, and you must not touch it, or you will die.' You will not certainly die,"* the serpent said to the woman. *"For God knows that when you eat from it your eyes will be opened, and you will be like God, knowing good and evil."*

Notice Satan's strategy. First, he questioned if God actually gave the command not to eat of the tree. Then, he contradicts the consequences of disobeying God by telling Eve *"You will not certainly die"*. Next, he attacks God's character by accusing God of trying to keep something good from Eve. He tells Eve that God is holding her back from being like Him, knowing good and evil. Selfish pride is our biggest weakness as people. It is the desire to be God of our own lives and it is the main reason people rebel and disobey God's commands. Satan knows this and he targets it when he attacks us!

Continuing the story…*"When the woman saw that the fruit of the tree was good for food and pleasing to the eye, and also desirable for gaining wisdom, she took some and ate it." (Genesis 3:6a)*

Notice that the fruit had the appearance of goodness. So many temptations are pleasing to our eyes and pleasurable to our bodies, but the consequences can be devastating. Again, this shows we must depend on God and trust He knows what is best for us. So, where was the man Adam at this time? Was Eve acting alone? Let's read on…*"She also gave some to her husband, who was with her, and he ate it." Genesis 3:6b*

Adam was with her! He was there during the encounter with the serpent. And what did he do? He did nothing! As the man, as the spiritual leader, he failed to exercise faith and obedience to God's word! What was the result of their disobedience? Genesis 3:7 says, *"Then the eyes of both of them were opened, and they realized they were naked…"* And Romans 5:12 says, *"Therefore, just as sin entered the world through one man, and death through sin, and in this way death came to all people, because all sinned—"* The man and woman had lost their innocence. After this God banished them from the garden and sin and death had now entered the world.

LEADERS MUST PRACTICE OBEDIENCE. No one said this would be easy. There will often be times when obedience to God means saying no to our personal desires. The night before His death Jesus modeled such obedience for us in the Garden of Gethsemane. It was almost time for Jesus to be arrested and taken to the Roman governor to be executed, although Jesus had committed no crime and was sinless. Matthew 26:39 says, *"…He (Jesus) fell with his face to the ground and prayed, "My Father, if it is possible, may this cup be taken from me. Yet not as I will, but as you will."*

Jesus knew obeying His Father would lead Him to an agonizing death, and worse yet, an unimaginable separation from His Father. Jesus was fully aware of all this, yet He exercised faith and trust that His Father's will was best. This is precisely the opposite of Adam. Adam was in a garden of his own, and when temptation came Adam decided "My will God, not yours."

Here Jesus, the second Adam, is also in a garden at His moment of decision, but unlike Adam, Jesus chose to trust and obey His Father. Because of His obedience, Jesus was able to fulfill His glorious purpose to bring salvation to all people. *"...For just as through the disobedience of the one man the many were made sinners, so also through the obedience of the one man the many will be made righteous."* Romans 5:19

Although no human will ever know the depth of suffering Jesus faced, His words should be our response to our heavenly Father. *"Yet not as I will, but as you will."* This is the ultimate statement of obedience. We as men are called to follow Jesus' example. We must set our minds on obeying God, denying ourselves and surrendering our will to His. If we do, then we also can fulfill the glorious purposes God has for our lives.

Men, the ultimate test of our leadership is our willingness to obey the same Father to whom Jesus entrusted himself. That is all for now. Please return next time when we explore the next two qualities of leadership: dependence on God, and humility. God bless you all!

FOCUS QUESTIONS

Why does God give us commands to follow?

What does Satan target when he attacks us and tempts us?

Men's Leadership Part 3

In part 2 we learned about the first quality which is Obedience to God. Today, we continue with the second leadership quality which is **Dependence on God.**

Just as a small child is meant to depend on his father and mother for everything, we are also meant to depend on our heavenly Father for everything. This is a tricky concept to understand. First of all, I'm not saying men should act like children, nor am I saying we should sit around and do nothing waiting for someone else to do everything for us. My point is that most of us have been taught that men who lead don't need any help and can get things done on their own. This is not what the Bible teaches. Jesus said this to His disciples before He left them:

"I am the vine; you are the branches. If you remain in me and I in you, you will bear much fruit; apart from me you can do nothing." John 15:5

So you see we are always to depend on God for everything. Why? **Because He is God and we are not.**

When we try to live life based on our own knowledge and strength, we are saying we do not need God. But when we live life based on God's knowledge and strength, we are giving Him His rightful place in our lives and we are showing faith and trust in His ability to meet our needs. The Bible has many examples of men who lived this way. Abraham, Moses, Daniel, the Apostle Paul, and the early Christians whose lives are recorded in the book of Acts all lived this way. What they did could not have happened without their total dependence on God. They recognized their complete inability to live for God on their own strength. And they acknowledged God's complete ability to supply their each and every need.

Jesus said this to His disciples; *"So do not worry, saying, 'What shall we eat?' or 'What shall we drink?' or 'What shall we wear?' For the pagans run after all these things, and your heavenly Father knows that you need them. But seek first His kingdom and His righteousness, and all these things will be given to you as well." Matthew 6:31-33*

Here Jesus is telling us that we need to include God in all areas of our lives; In our family relationships, in our work, in our church, in our thoughts and behaviors. Jesus reminds us that our heavenly Father knows our needs and He is faithful in providing them.

So you see **God is most glorified in us when we are most dependent on Him.** This is the heart of living a Christian life. The good news of the gospel is despite our complete inability to live by God's standards, in other words to never sin, through faith in Jesus Christ and God's amazing grace, we receive salvation. We are rescued from the penalty of sin and death and our souls are held secure in God's hands, and He will never let go of us. That's how the Christian life begins and that is how the Christian life is meant to continue. This leads to our next leadership quality, which is **humility.**

The supreme biblical example of humility is Jesus. In Philippians 2, we learn about Christ's servant attitude;

"Your attitude should be the same as Christ Jesus: Who, being in very nature God, did not consider equality with God something to be grasped, but made Himself nothing, taking the very nature of a servant, being made in human likeness. And being found in appearance as a man, He humbled himself and became obedient to death – even death on a cross!" Philippians 2:5-8

And what was the result?

"Therefore God exalted Him to the highest place and gave Him the name that is above every name, that at the name of Jesus every knee should bow, in heaven and on earth and under the earth, and every tongue should confess that Jesus Christ is Lord, to the glory of God the Father." Philippians 2:9-11

Here we find an important principle in Scripture: before honor comes humility.

Jesus did not selfishly cling to His divinity. Instead, He took the form of a servant. The philosophy of this world is to exalt oneself through power and manipulation. We see this all the time when worldly leaders put themselves first and abuse their positions of power, ignoring the needs of the people they govern. It is through our willingness to serve that we avoid manipulating other people to get what we want.

Because of our identity in Christ, we can serve others without the need to be noticed or rewarded for it here on earth. Ephesians 6:7-8 says, *"Serve wholeheartedly, as if you were serving the Lord, not people, because you know that the Lord will reward each one for whatever good they do, whether they are slave or free."* God longs to bless and reward His people. When we understand that God always sees what we do and that He has promised to reward us in eternity, we can serve others without expecting anything from them in return.

Humility is also one of the keys to unity in our churches. The church in Philippi was experiencing tension, and Paul encouraged them to exercise humility so that they could stay focused on the same things. Philippians 2:3-4 says, *"Do nothing out of selfish ambition or vain conceit, but in humility consider others as better than yourselves. Each of you should not look only to your own interests, but also to the interests of others."*

To avoid disharmony in the body of Christ, we must all have "the same love" – the love of Jesus Christ. The more we love Jesus, the more we will love one another. Then we can serve others and share a common purpose as His disciples. But it isn't natural for us to consider the needs of others before our own. The only way can do it is to surrender ourselves to Christ. As the perfect model for godly leadership, Jesus set the perfect example of humility.

Please return next time when we will learn about the fourth quality of Christian men's leadership, which is integrity. God bless you all!

FOCUS QUESTIONS

What does John 15:5 teach us about leadership?

How did our Lord Jesus Christ model humility for us?

Men's Leadership Part 4

To this point we have learned that obedience to God, dependence on God, and humility are qualities a Christian man should be working on in order to be effective leaders. The fourth quality of leadership is **Integrity.**

After surveying thousands of people around the world and performing more than 400 written case studies, researchers James Kouzes and Barry Posner identified those characteristics most desired in a leader. In virtually every survey, honesty or integrity was identified more frequently than any other trait. That makes sense, doesn't it? If people are going to follow someone, they want to know that they can trust that person. One question we can answer to test the quality of our integrity as men is: "Are we men of our word?" In other words, do we keep our promises and follow through on our commitments?

The Bible makes it clear that promises are important to God. Throughout the Scriptures, God shows us He is a God who makes and keeps His promises. In Psalm 105:7-8 we read, *"He is the LORD our God; His judgments are in all the earth. He remembers His covenant forever, the promise He made, for a thousand generations".* God remembers His promises and is trustworthy to keep them. He expects the same from His disciples.

Our Lord also expects us to keep our commitments. Jesus said, *"Again, you have heard that it was said to the people long ago, 'Do not break your oath, but fulfill to the Lord the vows you have made.' But I tell you, do not swear an oath at all: either by heaven, for it is God's throne; or by the earth, for it is his footstool; or by Jerusalem, for it is the city of the Great King. And do not swear by your head, for you cannot make even one hair white or black. All you need to say is simply 'Yes' or 'No'; anything beyond this comes from the evil one"* (Matthew 5:33-37)

So you see, as men of God we should do what we say we are going to do. In fact, Jesus wants our integrity to be at such a high level that a simple yes or no answer from us will be as good as an oath or a binding contract.

A second question we can ask to test our integrity as Godly men is, "How do I live when no one is looking?"

Jesus said, *"Be careful not to practice your righteousness in front of others to be seen by them. If you do, you will have no reward from your Father in heaven. So when you give to the needy, do not announce it with trumpets, as the hypocrites do in the synagogues and on the streets, to be honored by others. Truly I tell you, they have received their reward in full. But when you give to the needy, do not let your left hand know what your right hand is doing, so that your giving may be in secret. Then your Father, who sees what is done in secret, will reward you."* (Matthew 6:1-4) When we do acts of kindness or charity, it should be done not to purposely attract attention to ourselves. If you desire the praise of men, then that alone will be your reward.

Men, it is easy to act like a person of integrity when people are watching, but how do we live our private lives, where no one can see us? Do we live with the same level of honesty and obedience to God's word as our public life? How do we treat our wives and children when no one is looking? Remember men, we are to follow Christ's example. Ephesians 5:25 says, *"Husbands, love your wives, just as Christ loved the church and gave Himself up for her."* Jesus gave His life for the church and for all people who choose to follow Him. Men, Jesus expects our love for our wives to be at that same level of commitment.

Living our lives for Christ begins at home. We can't show the love of Christ to other people if we are not showing it to our own families, especially to our own wives. There is no doubt that a man will risk his own life protecting his wife. It is in you because that is the way God made you. But we are not talking about that. We are talking about loving our wives in a self-sacrificial way, putting her needs ahead of our own desires. This means going out of our way to help her and to show her kindness and gentleness. This means being willing to listen to her. This is where the real challenge is for us as men, because we are wired so differently than our wives. We must ask the Holy Spirit to help us and we must daily surrender our hearts and minds to Christ!

What about our children? Ephesians 6:4 says, *"Fathers, do not exasperate your children; instead, bring them up in the training and instruction of the Lord."* Men, our children, perhaps more than anyone else, need us to be spiritual warriors; leaders willing to do the difficult work of training them to follow the Lord. And how are we to do it? The same way Jesus did, by example.

Our children are watching us. They hear what we say, they see how we act, and for good or bad, they will imitate our actions. Every little boy desires a hero to look up to. For those boys who are lucky enough to have a father living with them, the first person they will place on that hero pedestal is their daddy. A little girl will learn her value as a woman by the treatment her father shows her mother. And when they grow up they will typically seek out men like their father. So I ask you men, would you want your daughter to marry a man like you? Would you want her to be treated as you treat your wife? I know these are hard questions. It is very difficult to live up to such a high standard of conduct. But that is what godly men do!

God expects His men to accept the responsibility of leadership. He expects us to have courage to stand for His principles and to say no to the world's desires.   We are Christian men and we don't need to apologize for it! We live for the truth, not for a lie! We must recognize our Lord calls us to live as He did, and we must be humble enough to admit that we cannot do it on our own strength! We need His help, because it is not in our nature to be unselfish. It is not in our nature to love others more than we love ourselves. This is the key men. We must admit we need His power to live as He asks.

Jesus said, *"I am the vine; you are the branches. If you remain in me and I in you, you will bear much fruit; apart from me you can do nothing."* (John 15:5) Please return next time when we will learn about the fifth quality of men's leadership, which is self-discipline. May God bless you all!

FOCUS QUESTIONS

What does the Bible say about making promises?

How are men to be leaders in the home?

What steps can we take as Christian men to improve our ability to lead as Jesus did?

Men's Leadership Part 5

Finally, the 5th and last quality of leadership we will learn is **Self-Discipline.**

The apostle Paul understood the importance of self-discipline in living our lives for Christ. He used the analogy of athletic competition to help the believers in Corinth and to help us understand it too. In 1 Corinthians 9:24-25 we read, *"Do you not know that in a race all the runners run, but only one gets the prize? Run in such a way as to get the prize. Everyone who competes in the games goes into strict training. They do it to get a crown that will not last; but we do it to get a crown that will last forever."*

The crown first-century athletes won was a laurel wreath. This is a great example of the rewards in this world that we attempt to reach. A laurel wreath wilts in just a few hours so it can only be worn for one day. Likewise, the victories this world has to offer are temporary. We could earn all the riches and rewards our hearts desire, but when we die we must leave them behind. Therefore, Godly leaders must have an eternal perspective. We must fix our eyes on a prize that will not fade or wear out, one that will last forever and will be waiting for us when we meet our Lord.

As we spend time developing the disciplines of the spirit, Paul says we're to be like runners. During a race, runners do not stray from the course. They focus their attention on the finish line and run toward it. And we need to realize that living a life for God is not like a sprint, it is like a marathon. It requires patience and endurance, not a quick burst of energy that exhausts us after a short time!

Paul points out that everyone competing goes into 'strict training'. Paul trained for his daily spiritual journey like a world-class athlete. Godly leaders need to cultivate this same kind of spiritual fitness. If you want to be an effective leader, you must place a high priority on completing the daily tasks necessary for developing spiritual endurance, such as reading the Bible and praying. These spiritual habits will give you the momentum you need to not only move forward, but also to live your life for God with strength and purpose.

It is also important to recognize that runners do not slow themselves down by carrying unnecessary weight. Hebrews 12:1 says, *"Therefore, since we are surrounded by such a great cloud of witnesses, let us throw off everything that hinders and the sin that so easily entangles. And let us run with perseverance the race marked out for us."*

Just as a runner cannot compete carrying heavy burdens, neither can we compete if we try to carry our sins with us. There is no way we can effectively live for God if we continue to disobey

Him with our choices. We must let go of them and with a repentant attitude give them to God. Of course, there will be times when we fall down, you can count on it. Everyone makes mistakes. We all let Jesus down at one time or another. Thankfully, we have a God who is merciful and forgiving. 1 John 1:8-9 says, *"If we claim to be without sin, we deceive ourselves and the truth is not in us. If we confess our sins, He is faithful and just and will forgive us our sins and purify us from all unrighteousness."*

Spiritual endurance means when we fall down, we don't quit. It means that we get back up and continue running the race. At the start of a marathon race, all the runners are crowded together. But over time as they run they begin to spread out. And an interesting thing happens – fewer people finish the race than started it. Living our lives for Christ is similar to a marathon because it's not how you start, it's how you finish that matters most.

What can we do to help us finish the race? Hebrews 12:2-3 says,"*...fixing our eyes on Jesus, the pioneer and perfecter of faith. For the joy set before Him He endured the cross, scorning its shame, and sat down at the right hand of the throne of God. Consider Him who endured such opposition from sinners, so that you will not grow weary and lose heart."* Once again, we need to follow the example Jesus gave us.

Okay, so we recognize that leaders must have self-discipline. That is easy to say but very hard to do. Many people think self-discipline is simply a matter of trying harder. But the Bible speaks of self-discipline as a fruit of the Holy Spirit. Writing to the Galatians, Paul said *"But the fruit of the Spirit is love, joy, peace, patience, kindness, goodness, faithfulness, gentleness and self-control" (Galatians 5:22-23)* And in his letter to Timothy Paul wrote, *"God did not give us a spirit of timidity, but a spirit of power, of love and of self-discipline" (2 Timothy 1:7)*

It is true that some people without Christ can demonstrate self-control, but this quality finds its fullest expression as part of the spiritual fruit that only the Holy Spirit can produce. The Holy Spirit of God is the ultimate source of spiritual nourishment and power that allows us as Christians to live for God. Just like plants don't produce more fruit by trying harder, we can't produce these fruits of the Spirit by trying harder. Jesus told His disciples, *"Remain in me, as I also remain in you. No branch can bear fruit by itself; it must remain in the vine. Neither can you bear fruit unless you remain in me. I am the vine; you are the branches. If you remain in me and I in you, you will bear much fruit; apart from me you can do nothing." (John 15:4-5)* Jesus also said, *"Whoever wants to be my disciple must deny themselves and take up their cross daily and follow me." (Luke 9:23)*

Instead of trying harder, we must surrender to our minds and bodies to Christ. He is the source of our power to live for Him. It is a daily decision we must make as His followers. We live in an undisciplined world. All too often people seek freedom through self-pleasure and gratification, but instead they find bondage. Self-discipline, as a fruit of the Spirit, allows us as God's people to experience true freedom as we grow in our faith and walk in obedience to God's word.

In this series of posts we've learned five qualities Christian men need to develop to help them be effective leaders. We've also learned that our Lord Jesus Christ has commissioned His disciples to fight in a spiritual war for the souls of people. And we've noted that Christians need to equip themselves with the Armor of God in order to fight this war. If you are a Christian man and you agree with this message, if you want to be the leader our Lord Jesus calls you to be, then talk to your pastor or another brother in Christ and get going. Time is short! You are needed to help lead your families toward Christ and away from the lies of this world! May God bless you all!

FOCUS QUESTIONS

How is living for Christ similar to running a race?

Who or what is the source of power to help you live as you should?

What are your next steps in equipping yourself to be a spiritual leader?

Chapter 6

Christian Living

"We never grow closer to God when we just live life. It takes deliberate pursuit and attentiveness." — **Francis Chan**

The Armor of God Part 1

Ephesians 6

"Put on the full armor of God, so that you can take your stand against the devil's schemes. For our struggle is not against flesh and blood, but against the rulers, against the authorities, against the powers of the dark world and against the spiritual forces of evil in the heavenly realms. Therefore, put on the full armor of God, so that when the day of evil comes, you may be able to stand your ground, and after you have done everything, to stand." (Hebrews 6:11-13)

Paul tells us we must put on **the full armor of God** so that we may be able to make a stand for the truth of the gospel of Jesus Christ and for His church. Although Satan has already been defeated by Jesus at the cross, our Lord wants us to live victoriously for His name while we are here on earth. Paul reminds us that we are in a war against the spiritual forces of evil in the heavenly realms. We know Satan and his fallen angels (demons) are opposed to the spread of the gospel and the testimonies of Christians who have overcome sin and death by placing their faith in Jesus Christ.

1 John 5:4-5 says, "for everyone born of God overcomes the world. This is the victory that has overcome the world, even our faith. Who is it that overcomes the world? Only the one who believes that Jesus is the Son of God." To overcome the world means to come to a saving faith in Christ in spite of the deceptive philosophies of this world. Secularism and the many false religions that are opposed to the gospel have their foundation in the satanical forces of evil. This world system propagates lies intended to blind people to the truth.

Colossians 2:6-10 says, "So then, just as you received Christ Jesus as Lord, continue to live your lives in him, rooted and built up in him, strengthened in the faith as you were taught, and overflowing with thankfulness. See to it that no one takes you captive through hollow and deceptive philosophy, which depends on human tradition and the elemental spiritual forces of this world rather than on Christ. For in Christ all the fullness of the Deity lives in bodily form, and in Christ you have been brought to fullness. He is the head over every power and authority." (Colossians 2:6-10) Therefore, Christians must put on the full armor of God in order to make a stand against these worldly philosophies and reach people with the truth of the gospel.

1 Peter 5:8-9 says, "Be alert and of sober mind. Your enemy the devil prowls around like a roaring lion looking for someone to devour. Resist him, standing firm in the faith, because you know that the family of believers throughout the world is undergoing the same kind of sufferings." And Revelation 12:10 says, "He (Satan) is our accuser who stands before God in heaven accusing our brothers and sisters day and night."

Peter tells us to resist the devil. The term "to resist" is similar to the term used by Paul in Ephesians "to stand", meaning we are to take a position of defense against our adversary, not a position of offense. And our stand is to be taken wholly dependent upon Christ, not on our own strength. If we attempt to stand on our own we will fail. Our victory is found in Christ and in Him alone.

Our mindset is to be one of readiness, sober and alert, knowing that we are in a struggle against an evil adversary seeking to destroy. Satan knows he cannot take away our salvation, which is held for us in heaven and is eternally secure. But he can take away our joy and peace, and he can diminish our zeal for the gospel and our confidence to share our testimonies with others.

Notice Paul writes not if but "when the day of evil comes..." We can be sure there will be trials and tribulations in this life, especially if we are attempting to walk with Christ and live out the truth of the gospel. Our enemy will take notice and make an effort to limit our effectiveness as witnesses of the truth and to take away our peace. Jesus said, "I have told you these things, so that in me you may have peace. In this world you will have trouble. But take heart! I have overcome the world."(John 16:33) Jesus offers us comfort by His reassurance that He has gained victory for us who believe and we can find peace with Him.

Ephesians 1:18-23 says, "I pray that the eyes of your heart may be enlightened in order that you may know the hope to which he has called you, the riches of his glorious inheritance in his holy people, and his incomparably great power for us who believe. That power is the same as the mighty strength he exerted when he raised Christ from the dead and seated him at his right hand in the heavenly realms, far above all rule and authority, power and dominion, and every name that is invoked, not only in the present age but also in the one to come. And God placed all things under his feet and appointed him to be head over everything for the church, which is his body, the fullness of him who fills everything in every way."

The same power that raised our Lord from the dead and placed Him at the right hand of the Father is available to us. Jesus is the ultimate authority and all things have been placed under Him. There is nothing to fear for us who profess His name and belong to Him. However, it is our duty to put on our armor and to make a stand for Him. Please return next time when we break down the pieces of armor and their purpose. God bless you all!

FOCUS QUESTIONS

Who are the enemy opposed to the gospel?

What does it mean to overcome the world?

The Armor of God Part 2

Ephesians 6

In part 1 we learned that there is a spiritual war going on all around us. This war is for the souls of people and is being fought against the spiritual forces of evil opposed to the truth of the gospel. We learned that our Lord Jesus Christ has already won this war and gained victory for all eternity over Satan and his fallen angels. This was accomplished by the finished work of our Lord Jesus on the cross. We also noted that as Christians our salvation in Christ is secure, held in heaven for us and shielded by God. (1 Peter 1:3-5)

Nevertheless, there are still battles to be fought in this life on earth; battles for the salvation of those who have yet to hear the gospel and for those who have not received salvation through faith in Christ. As Christians, our walk with Christ is constantly under attack, and we must be ready to defend against the attempts of our enemy to steal away our peace and make us fearful of sharing our testimonies. Therefore, you and I must put on the full armor of God so that we can take a stand for the truth and gain victory in our day to day battles here on earth.

Let's look at the first piece of armor, the BELT OF TRUTH. Ephesians 6:14a says, "Stand firm then, with the belt of truth buckled around your waist..." One of Satan's primary weapons he uses are lies. He uses deceptions and falsehoods meant to weaken our faith and our resolve to stand for the truth of the gospel. Verse 11 refers to these lies as "the devil's schemes" and Ephesians 4:14 refers to the false doctrines and false religions as "the cunning and craftiness of people in their deceitful scheming." Thus, if we are going to stand against these schemes you and I must be armed with the truth.

However, this weapon is not referring to the content of truth found in God's word, which will come later when we discuss the SWORD OF THE SPIRIT (v.17). The belt of truth refers to having an ATTITUDE OF READINESS to fight in battle. In Paul's day, the Roman soldiers wore tunics—big pieces of square material with holes for the head and arms. The tunic hung low and loose over the body. Soldiers going into battle would not want their tunics flapping in the breeze, inhibiting their mobility and causing them to trip. So they would take a leather belt and cinch it around their waist, tucking in the tunic and giving themselves the flexibility they would need to fight effectively. Jesus said, "Be dressed ready for service and keep your lamps burning." (Luke 12:35) The King James Version says, "Let your loins be girded about..." This verse is also referring to tucking in your tunic and being prepared for battle.

In addition to preparing a soldier for mobility in battle, cinching the belt also refers to having an ATTITUDE OF COMMITMENT to the cause. 2 Timothy 2:4 says, "No one serving as a soldier gets entangled in civilian affairs, but rather tries to please his commanding officer." In other words, we should not be tangled up with the affairs of this life in a manner which takes away from our commitment to the battle. A good soldier must have a single-minded purpose, self-discipline, and unquestioned obedience to the commanding officer.

What does this look like in practical everyday life of a Christian? Do we disengage ourselves from the world and withdraw from friendships with non-believers? Are we not to have jobs and occupations in the secular business world? Do we isolate ourselves from our communities and only associate with other Christians? Of course not!

Our Lord calls us to be witnesses for Him by being in this world but not a part of this world. That is, we are not to conform to the same pattern of life as those who do not know Christ as Savior. Romans 12:2 says, "Do not conform to the pattern of this world, but be transformed by the renewing of your mind. Then you will be able to test and approve what God's will is—His good, pleasing and perfect will." And 1 Peter 2:12 says, "Live such good lives among the pagans that, though they accuse you of doing wrong, they may see your good deeds and glorify God on the day He visits us."

So you see, being committed to living for Christ changes our behavior, and we no longer live as we used to live. Our neighbors and co-workers see a change, and even though they may disagree with our beliefs and even mutter under their breath about us, over time our testimonies bring glory to God. Notice that the key for us to transforming how we live is the "renewing of our minds". This is done by the word of God.

2 Timothy 3:16-17 says, "All Scripture is God-breathed and is useful for teaching, rebuking, correcting and training in righteousness, so that the servant of God may be thoroughly equipped for every good work." You and I must commit ourselves to reading and studying the bible regularly in order to change our thinking. Changing our thinking will result in changing our behavior and give us the power not to conform to the world around us.

In addition, reading God's word will arm us with the truth. Our enemy is clever! There are non-Christian people, including many who practice false religion, who live good moral lives and also have testimonies. But they do not have the truth of the gospel to offer those who are watching them. That is why it is so important for us to know the gospel, to live according to it each day, and to be ready to share it with others!

In closing, having the belt of truth buckled around us is having a mindset of READINESS and total COMMITMENT to the battles we will face. A soldier's belt also was used to support his weapons, so we can see how the belt is the first piece of armor that we must put on in our preparation to stand against our enemy. We will continue our study on the pieces of armor in our next post. Thank you for reading this and may God bless you all!

FOCUS QUESTIONS

What does it mean to have the belt of truth around our waist?

What did Paul mean by a soldier not getting tangled in civilian affairs?

What is the key to renewing our minds?

The Armor of God Part 3

Ephesians 6

In part 2 we learned that the BELT OF TRUTH is having an attitude of readiness and commitment to living for Christ. We also learned that we must not conform to the pattern of this world but instead be renewed in our minds. This is done by reading and studying God's word regularly which results in a change of thinking and produces actions which bring glory to God. Reading God's word also arms us with the truth of the gospel which we must be ready to share to those who are watching how we live.

The next piece of armor we need to put on is the BREASTPLATE OF RIGHTEOUSNESS (v.14). No Roman soldier in his right mind would ever go into battle without wearing his breastplate. It protected his vital organs during hand to hand combat and also helped to defend against unseen arrows coming from other directions. All of the armor is important, but it seems the breastplate is the key piece. Righteousness is a right relationship with God. Without this in place you will not be able to utilize the other pieces and probably won't even try to put them on.

What is the righteousness Paul speaks of and how do we attain it? There are only 3 possibilities. The first is SELF-RIGHTEOUSNESS, in other words, relying on our own good works to save us from condemnation to hell and protect us from attacks by Satan. Let us consider the words of our Lord Jesus Christ concerning this issue.

Luke 18:9-14 says, "To some who were confident of their own righteousness and looked down on everyone else, Jesus told this parable: "Two men went up to the temple to pray, one a Pharisee and the other a tax collector. The Pharisee stood by himself and prayed: 'God, I thank you that I am not like other people—robbers, evildoers, adulterers—or even like this tax collector. I fast twice a week and give a tenth of all I get.'"But the tax collector stood at a distance. He would not even look up to heaven, but beat his breast and said, 'God, have mercy on me, a sinner.' "I tell you that this man, rather than the other, went home justified before God. For all those who exalt themselves will be humbled, and those who humble themselves will be exalted."

The Pharisees were considered the most religious and respected people in Israel. They strictly followed the Jewish laws, studied and taught the scriptures, prayed and worshipped God relentlessly. They did more good deeds than anyone and if righteousness could be earned, then they certainly would qualify. Yet in this story Jesus makes it very clear that the one forgiven and made righteous before God was the tax collector, not the Pharisee!

The apostle Paul himself was a Pharisee before his encounter with our risen Savior on the road to Damascus (Acts 9). In Philippians 3:4-9 Paul writes to us that if anyone could be made righteous by their works then he has the best case to offer. He writes, "If someone else thinks they have reasons to put confidence in the flesh, I have more: circumcised on the eighth day, of the people of Israel, of the tribe of Benjamin, a Hebrew of Hebrews; in regard to the law, a Pharisee; as for zeal, persecuting the church; as for righteousness based on the law, faultless.

But whatever were gains to me I now consider loss for the sake of Christ. What is more, I consider everything a loss because of the surpassing worth of knowing Christ Jesus my Lord, for whose sake I have lost all things. I consider them garbage, that I may gain Christ and be found in him, not having a righteousness of my own that comes from the law, but that which is through faith in Christ—the righteousness that comes from God on the basis of faith."

Paul makes it very clear that the righteousness we need to put on is not of our own working, it is gained only by placing our faith in Jesus Christ. Paul goes so far as to refer to his works as GARBAGE in comparison to what Christ has to offer him and us! Isaiah 64:6 says, "…all our righteousness are as filthy rags…", and Romans 3:10 says, "There is none righteous, no, not one."

The second possible type of righteousness is IMPUTED RIGHTEOUSNESS. When you become a believer by placing your trust in Jesus Christ as your Savior, His righteousness is imputed to us. In other words, His righteousness is credited to our account. 2 Corinthians 5:21 says, "God made him who had no sin to be sin for us, so that in him we might become the righteousness of God." This is the foundation of the gospel message and in fact the meaning of the word gospel is "good news!"

We already learned that the Pharisees were as righteous as a person can be on their own and still they fell short of God's standard. So what is God's standard? In His Sermon on the Mount, Jesus uttered these words: "You therefore must be perfect, as your heavenly Father is perfect" (Matthew 5:48). But who is able to meet that standard? No one! Praise be to God in the name of our Lord Jesus Christ who lived that perfect life for us and freely offered it up to God to pay the penalty of our sin! What great love He has for us! Not only does God tell us He loves us, He proved it by letting Himself be nailed to that cross, to purchase us back for Himself! Hallelujah!

Imputed righteousness is a marvelous truth in which we celebrate God's grace and mercy toward us! Yet, the meaning of the breastplate of righteousness is not referring to this. It is referring to the third possible meaning of righteousness which we will call PRACTICAL RIGHTEOUSNESS. <u>Practical righteousness is you and I as believers applying God's principles into our daily living.</u> Just because we are covered by the righteousness of Christ, this does not mean we will live each moment as we ought to—it only means we can.

We must surrender ourselves to leading of the Holy Spirit, which dwells within all true believers. The Holy Spirit gives us the power we need to walk with God (2 Timothy 1:7) and produce fruit in our lives (Galatians 5:22-23). Jesus said, "...Whoever wants to be my disciple must deny themselves and take up their cross daily and follow me." (Luke 9:23) So you see, PUTTING ON THE BREASTPLATE OF RIGHTEOUSNESS IS LIVING EACH DAY FOR GOD, NOT RELYING ON OUR OWN STRENGTH, INSTEAD, RELYING ON HIS HOLY SPIRIT WORKING IN US AND THROUGH US. That is all for now and may God bless you all!

FOCUS QUESTIONS

What is self-righteousness?

What is imputed-righteousness?

What is practical-righteousness?

The Armor of God Part 4

Ephesians 6

Today we will examine the next two pieces of armor, which are the GOSPEL OF PEACE and the SHIELD OF FAITH. Ephesians 6:15-16 says, "and with your feet fitted with the readiness that comes from the gospel of peace. In addition to all this, take up the shield of faith, with which you can extinguish all the flaming arrows of the evil one."

Shoes have become a major fashion item in modern American culture, but in Paul's day they were used to protect the feet against the rugged desert terrain of rocks, thorns, heat, and obstacles on the ground. They were especially important to a Roman soldier, who needed them in order to be able to stand firm and fight for their life. A soldier's shoe was specially designed to provide both protection and stability.

In the time of the Roman wars there was a common military practice of planting sticks in the ground. These sticks were sharpened to a razor point and concealed, much like a modern-day land mine. This was an effective tactic because if a soldier's foot was pierced, it made them virtually useless in battle. No matter how strong and skilled the soldier was, if they could not walk, then they could not fight. So in order to protect their feet, the roman soldier would wear a boot with a heavy sole that could not be pierced.

In addition to their thick soles, the boots also had small pieces of protruding metal on the soles, much like the cleats on modern-day athletic shoes. This provided the soldiers with grip on the soil, giving them traction and firm footing to stand during battle. Paul is using this illustration to teach us we must put on the protection and stability of the Gospel of Peace so that we can stand firm in battle against our adversary the devil.

Many have interpreted the meaning of this verse as a command to go preach the gospel (see Isaiah 52:7 and Romans 10:15), but that is not what Paul is saying here. Certainly, preaching the gospel is something we must do, but this particular passage is about believers standing firm in battle, holding our ground in a defensive position. It is about being prepared, committed, and not retreating in our daily struggles against the forces of evil opposed to our faith. So how does the gospel of peace apply here?

In Romans 5:1-11 Paul gives us a beautiful picture of the peace and hope we have in Christ Jesus. He writes, "Therefore, since we have been justified through faith, we have peace with God through our Lord Jesus Christ, through whom we have gained access by faith into this grace in which we now stand." (v.1-2) He goes on to remind us that before we came to know Christ as our Savior, we were powerless and unrighteous sinners, objects of God's wrath and God's enemies. The good news of the gospel of peace is that we are now reconciled to God!

We are no longer His enemies! And we are at peace with Him! This blessed reassurance of our right standing with God through Jesus Christ gives us the sure footing we need to stand firm against any and all attacks by the evil one. Hallelujah!

The next piece of armor is the SHIELD OF FAITH. Roman soldiers had different types of shields, but the Greek word Paul uses in this verse is thureon. The thureon was a large plank of wood, 4.5 feet tall by 2.5 feet wide. It was covered on the outside by metal and sometimes by thick leather that was specially treated to put out fire. When fiery arrows hit the shield they would be deflected by the metal or hit the leather and be extinguished. In those days people were much smaller, so the dimensions of the thureon shield were enough to provide total protection. When under attack a soldier would stick the shield on the ground and duck behind it and he would be fully protected from every fiery arrow coming his way.

You and I as Christians must be able to defend against the fiery arrows of Satan and his demons who are actively involved in an aggressive attack on the truth, on the character of God and His people. Satan fires arrows intended to tempt us to impurity, selfishness, doubt, fear, disappointment, lust, greed, vanity, covetousness, etc. All of these fiery arrows have their origin in the world. 1 John 2:16 says, "For everything in the world—the lust of the flesh, the lust of the eyes, and the pride of life—comes not from the Father but from the world." The world John wrote about refers to the "realm of sin" which is controlled by Satan and organized against God and righteousness.

Why is faith a shield against temptation? The term "faith" means "believing God". Faith is the foundation of the Christian life! We believe Jesus is the Son of God. We believe Jesus died on the cross for our sins and we believe He rose from the dead and is alive today. We believe Jesus' sacrifice conquered sin and death once and for all and we believe we have eternal life with Him. We believe the bible is the inspired word of God that He gave us to help grow our faith and live for Him.

Therefore, we must believe God and His word when temptation comes and we are under attack by the enemy. Psalm 18:30 says, "As for God, His way is perfect: The Lord's word is flawless; He shields all who take refuge in Him." And 1 John 5:4 says, "for everyone born of God overcomes the world. This is the victory that has overcome the world, even our faith." Like everything else in the Christian's life, it all depends on our relationship with God. The better we know Him the better we will trust and believe. God is on our side. He wants to give us victory in our daily battles, but we must do it His way by walking in obedience to His word.

Therefore, we must commit ourselves to reading and meditating on God's word each and every day! Proverbs 8:34 says, "Blessed are those who listen to me, watching daily at my doors, waiting at my doorway." And Psalm 119:11 says, "I have hidden your word in my heart that I might not sin against you." As Christians, our faith in God and in His word is a shield that causes us to stand. Please take the time to read all of Psalm 119 and may God bless you all!

FOCUS QUESTIONS

What is the gospel of peace?

What is a thureon shield?

How is our faith like a shield?

The Armor of God Part 5

Ephesians 6

The next piece of armor we are told to put on is the HELMET OF SALVATION. A Roman soldier's helmet was designed primarily to protect against the broadsword. The broadsword was 3 to 4 feet long with a massive handle. It was held like a baseball bat and used by a soldier on horseback to deliver a crushing blow to the skull of his opponent. Paul exhorts us to "Take the helmet of salvation…" (v.17) as part of our protection against the attempts by our enemy to strike a devastating blow to our walk with Christ.

So what is meant by the salvation aspect of the helmet? Is Paul telling us to go get saved? No, he is not. He is writing to us who have already received salvation, so what is he referring to? To help us understand the meaning of salvation let us break it down into its three aspects: past, present, and future.

The past aspect of salvation is that you and I have been SET FREE FROM THE PENALTY OF SIN. Romans 8:1-2 says, "Therefore, there is now no condemnation for those who are in Christ Jesus, because through Christ Jesus the law of the Spirit who gives life has set you free from the law of sin and death." And Galatians 2:20 says, "I have been crucified with Christ and I no longer live, but Christ lives in me. The life I now live in the body, I live by faith in the Son of God, who loved me and gave Himself for me." At the point when you and I confessed Jesus Christ and invited Him to be our Lord and Savior, we were united with Christ in His death. Our old self was put to death and our new self was born, a new self which is Christ living in us through the indwelling of the Holy Spirit. We are no longer under the condemnation of the law and we have been set free to live by faith in the Son of God. This aspect of salvation is known as JUSTIFICATION. Amen!

This leads us to the present aspect of salvation which is that you and I have been SET FREE FROM THE POWER OF SIN. Romans 6:14 says, "For sin shall no longer be your master, because you are not under the law, but under grace." Having died with Christ, we also have been resurrected with Him and have received a new life with Him. You and I as Christians have been set free from the condemnation of sin, but we should not abuse our freedom to live a life of sin. Instead, we are called to surrender our minds and bodies to God and allow His Holy Spirit to work in us and through us.

Galatians 5:16-18 says, "So I say, walk by the Spirit, and you will not gratify the desires of the flesh. For the flesh desires what is contrary to the Spirit, and the Spirit what is contrary to the flesh. They are in conflict with each other, so that you are not to do whatever you want. But if you are led by the Spirit, you are not under the law." And Ephesians 4:30 says, "And do not grieve the Holy Spirit of God, with whom you were sealed for the day of redemption." Not only are we sealed with the Spirit when we are saved, but God gives us the Spirit to provide the power we need to live for Him and overcome our fleshly desires.

This aspect of salvation is known as SANCTIFICATION, which refers to us becoming more and more like our Lord Jesus and less and less like our old selves. This is a life-long process in which believers are called to persevere and keep moving forward. We will make mistakes and when we do we are told to humbly come before God and confess our sins. 1 John 1:9 says, "If we confess our sins, He is faithful and just and will forgive us our sins and purify us from all unrighteousness." You and I must struggle with our flesh and daily make the choice to deny ourselves and choose to obey God. Our God is gracious and is faithful to forgive our mistakes and purify us from all unrighteousness. What amazing grace our God has for us!

Yet, our enemy does not want you and me to experience the victory we have in Christ. He attacks us with his broadsword attempting to strike us with blows of discouragement, doubt, guilt, and fear. He accuses us of not truly belonging to God and uses our sins as evidence to make us doubt our security in Christ. He wants us to believe that Jesus' death and resurrection were not enough. He tries to mislead us into thinking that we must do more to earn our salvation, after all, how could God's grace cover us completely. What a lie! No one can and ever has lived a sinless life except Jesus Christ! If we accept this lie then we will never be without doubt and fear and Satan knows this! Fellow Christian, our helmet of salvation is meant to protect us from such attacks.

This leads us to the future aspect of salvation which is you and I have been set FREE FROM THE PRESENCE OF SIN. Revelation 21:4 says, "He will wipe every tear from their eyes. There will be no more death, or mourning or crying or pain, for the old order of things has passed away." And 1 John 3:2 says, "Dear friends, now we are children of God, and what we will be has not yet been made known. But we know that when Christ appears, we shall be like Him, for we shall see Him as He is."

Dear brothers and sisters in Christ, we look forward to the day when we will finally meet our Lord and King face to face. At that time the fullness of our salvation shall be complete because we will no longer have to struggle with sin, the flesh, the devil and his demons. Our Lord will give us new bodies like His, perfect and flawless in every way, and we shall be with Him forever. This future aspect of salvation is called GLORIFICATION.

1 Peter 1:3-6 says, "Praise be to the God and Father of our Lord Jesus Christ! In His great mercy He has given us new birth into a living hope through the resurrection of Jesus Christ from the dead, and into an inheritance that can never perish, spoil or fade. This inheritance is kept in heaven for you, who through faith are shielded by God's power until the coming of the

salvation that is ready to be revealed in the last time. In all this you greatly rejoice, though now for a little while you may have had to suffer grief in all kinds of trials."

Taking the HELMET OF SALVATION is you and I holding on to the living hope we have in Christ our Lord. We can endure any attacks by our adversary; we can get through any trial and tribulation in this life because our future is secure. We are children of God with an inheritance kept in heaven for us. Knowing this will deflect blows of doubt, discouragement, guilt, and fear. We belong to God and nothing can change that! Hallelujah!! Praise God!! I can stand firm and hold my ground against my accuser! May this living hope give you the encouragement you need today! May God bless you all!

FOCUS QUESTIONS

What is the past aspect of salvation?

What is the current aspect of salvation?

What is the future aspect of salvation?

The Armor of God Part 6

Ephesians 6

The last piece of armor we are called to utilize is the SWORD OF THE SPIRIT, which is the word of God. (v.17) The Greek word used here for sword is machaira. The term machaira refers to the normal sword carried by a soldier. It could be anything from a six-inch long dagger to an eighteen inch sword. It was put into a sheath or scabbard by the side of the soldier and was used in hand to hand combat. It was a weapon which had to be used in a precise manner in order to be effective in close fighting.

When you and I accepted Christ as our Savior we became children of God and were sealed by the Holy Spirit. (1 John 3:2, Ephesians 4:30) As Christians, it is the Holy Spirit which gives us the ability to wield the sword of the Spirit. 1 Corinthians 2:12 says, "What we have received is not the spirit of the world, but the Spirit who is from God, so that we may understand what God has freely given us." And Jesus said, "But the Advocate, the Holy Spirit, whom the Father will send in my name, will teach you all things and will remind you of everything I have said to you." (John 14:26)

Since we have been given the Holy Spirit, we also have been given the ability to understand the word of God. Unbelievers do not possess this ability because they do not possess the Holy Spirit. 1 Corinthians 2:14 says, "The person without the Spirit does not accept the things that come from the Spirit of God but considers them foolishness, and cannot understand them because they are discerned only through the Spirit." This is the reason a non-Christian can own a bible and know what it says, yet still walk in darkness not understanding the truth. On the other hand, if Christians do not read and know their bibles, then the ability to understand it does us no good. Our swords will never leave their scabbards. Therefore it is crucial for us to read and know what the bible says so that we may utilize this powerful weapon.

The sword is a powerful offensive weapon in the hand of a righteous saint who knows how to use it. Romans 1:16 says, "For I am not ashamed of the gospel, because it is the power of God that brings salvation to everyone who believes: first to the Jew, then to the Gentile." And Hebrews 4:12 says, "For the word of God is alive and active. Sharper than any double-edged sword, it penetrates even to dividing soul and spirit, joints and marrow; it judges the thoughts and attitudes of the heart." The word of God has the power to slice through the hardest human heart. It has the authority to judge a person's motives and to sift and weigh the reality of a person's life, presenting to them the stark truth of their sinfulness. Thus, the sword of God's word has the power to rescue a person from death by bringing them to salvation found in our Lord Jesus Christ.

The sword is also an effective defensive weapon, giving us the power to parry the blows of our enemy. Matthew 4:1-11 gives the account of when Satan tried to attack Jesus with temptation in the desert. Our Lord dealt with Satan by using the sword of God's word. He used the sword with precision by quoting specific scripture related to each attack by the enemy. For example, the first attack went like this: "The tempter came to him and said, "If you are the Son of God, tell these stones to become bread."Jesus answered, "It is written: 'Man shall not live on bread alone, but on every word that comes from the mouth of God.' (v.3-4)

Satan knows our weaknesses and rest assured he will target them. But our God has not left us defenseless. He has given us everything we need to stand firm in our faith and not fall victim the attacks from our enemy. 2 Corinthians 10:4-5 says, "The weapons we fight with are not the weapons of the world. On the contrary, they have divine power to demolish strongholds. We demolish arguments and every pretension that sets itself up against the knowledge of God, and we take captive every thought to make it obedient to Christ."

The weapons of this world are scientific knowledge, personal influence, wealth, impressive credentials, and political power. The god of this age (Satan) uses these to blind the minds of unbelievers so that they will not accept the truth of the gospel message. (2 Cor. 4:4) Satan also uses false teachers who masquerade as servants of righteousness who distort the gospel by adding or taking away from it in order to mislead people. (2 Cor. 11:15) Paul reminds us that our weapons, although they may seem weak by worldly standards, have the power to "demolish strongholds, arguments, and pretensions". This is because our weapons are from the one true living God who has authority over all things! 1 Corinthians 3:19-20 says, "For the wisdom of this world is foolishness in God's sight. As it is written: "He catches the wise in their craftiness" and again, "The Lord knows that the thoughts of the wise are futile."

Let's briefly review our arsenal of God's armor:

The BELT OF TRUTH is our readiness and commitment to the truth of the gospel.

The BREASTPLATE OF RIGHTEOUSNESS is us living holy lives for God, which protects our thoughts and emotions.

The shoes of the GOSPEL OF PEACE refers to our right relationship with God through the goThe "good news" is we are at peace with God and are no longer His enemies.

The SHIELD OF FAITH is our trusting in God's word which deflects Satan's arrows of doubt and discouragement.

The HELMET OF SALVATION is knowing the three aspects of our salvation: past, present, and future. The past is that we have been forgiven for our sins (JUSTIFICATION); the present is our old self has been put to death and we now have the power to live for God (SANCTIFICATION); and the future is our living hope that one day we will be free from the presence of sin when we meet our Lord face to face and He gives us perfect bodies like His (GLORIFICATION).

Finally, we have the SWORD OF THE SPIRIT which is the word of God. It is a powerful offensive weapon for bringing salvation to the lost and a defensive weapon to parry the attacks of temptation by our enemy.

Lastly, we must pray! Paul writes, "And pray in the Spirit on all occasions with all kinds of prayers and requests. With this in mind, be alert and always keep on praying for all the Lord's people." (v.18)

This concludes our series on the armor of God. I pray you have been encouraged in your walk with God and may He richly bless you all!

FOCUS QUESTIONS

How is the sword of the spirit used offensively and defensively?

Briefly review each piece of God's armor and its meaning.

A Message of Thanksgiving

We who live in America have so much to be thankful for. It sounds cliché but it really is true. Regardless of who you are or where you live, each citizen enjoys rights and freedoms which simply do not exist in most countries on earth. Even non-citizens in our great country are afforded many of these rights. And though some of us have more or less of the material things to be earned, the poor among us are rich when compared to most people in the world.

Nevertheless, many Americans are guilty of not being thankful, because they are not happy with their circumstances. This is because people have a tendency to focus on what they don't have, rather than on what they do have. Christians are no different. It is human nature to covet the things we do not have and even Christians, although we have been born again by the Holy Spirit, still have the sin nature we were given at birth. That is why Jesus died on the cross, to save us from our sin and from death, and to give us an eternal hope, an everlasting life with Him in the Kingdom of heaven. Praise be to God for this!

Thus, as an American, I am most thankful for the freedom I have to pursue the life that I choose, especially the freedom to openly be a Christian and worship the living God in the name of Jesus Christ. And as a Christian, I have much more to be thankful for than the temporary things this world has to offer, and so do you if you also call on the name of the Lord Jesus Christ. In this essay we will list several blessings you and I can be thankful for because we are Christians. There are many so we will focus on a few major ones.

Before we begin, let us note the difference between thankfulness and thanksgiving. Thankfulness is an internal disposition, it is what we know and feel about what we have received. Thanksgiving is an outward disposition; it is what we do to express our thankfulness. Simply put, thankfulness is a feeling and thanksgiving is an action. So what have you, and I, and all Christians received that should make us feel thankfulness?

We have received freedom from sin and death.

Romans 8:1-2 says, "Therefore, there is now no condemnation for those who are in Christ Jesus, because through Christ Jesus the law of the Spirit who gives life has set you free from the law of sin and death." And 1 Peter 2:24 says, "He Himself(Jesus) bore our sins in His body on the cross, so that we might die to sins and live for righteousness; by His wounds you have been healed."

Even though I am a sinner and deserving death, Christ has set me free. Praise God for this! Jesus loved me so much that He left heaven and came to earth to save me! Why? Because I could not save myself! I was helpless and without hope. He lived the life I was unable to live because of my sin nature and then He willingly offered it up on the cross, to take my punishment upon Himself! My punishment! Your punishment! And now we can be set free! What amazing grace! Hallelujah!

We have received eternal life.

"For God so loved the world that he gave his one and only Son, that whoever believes in him shall not perish but have eternal life." John 3:16

We have received mercy from God.

"He saved us, not because of righteous things we have done, but because of His mercy. He saved us through the washing of rebirth and renewal by the Holy Spirit, whom He poured out on us generously through Jesus Christ our Savior." Titus 3:5-6

We have received grace from God.

"For it is by grace you have been saved, through faith—and this is not from yourselves, it is the gift of God—not by works, so that no one can boast." Ephesians 2:8-9

We have become God's children.

John 1:12-13 says, "Yet, to all who did receive Him, to those who believed in His name, He gave the right to become children of God—children born not of natural descent, nor of human decision or a husband's will, but born of God." By placing out trust in Jesus as our Savior we become part of God's family. We become sons and daughters of God, Jesus being the firstborn among many. (Romans 8:29)

We are heirs of God's kingdom.

Galatians 4:6-7 says, "Because you are his sons, God sent the Spirit of his Son into our hearts, the Spirit who calls out, *"Abba*, Father." So you are no longer a slave, but God's child; and since you are his child, God has made you also an heir." And Colossians 1:12 says, "...giving joyful thanks to the Father, who has qualified you to share in the inheritance of his holy people in the kingdom of light."

As sons and daughters of God, you and I have an inheritance in the kingdom of God. This cannot be lost or stolen because we did not earn it. (Ephesians 2:8-9) It is a gift to us from God by His amazing grace, rich mercy, and great love.

So fellow Christian, how do these blessings from God make you feel? How will knowing these blessings affect how you and I act and how we show our thanksgiving? Here are some passages to help guide us:

"Rejoice always, pray continually, give thanks in all circumstances; for this is God's will for you in Christ Jesus." 1 Thessalonians 5:16-18

"Let the peace of Christ rule in your hearts, since as members of one body you were called to peace. And be thankful." Colossians 3:15

"Do not be anxious about anything, but in every situation, by prayer and petition, with thanksgiving, present your requests to God. And the peace of God, which transcends all understanding, will guard your hearts and your minds in Christ Jesus." Philippians 4:6-7

"Nor should there be obscenity, foolish talk or coarse joking, which are out of place, but rather thanksgiving." Ephesians 5:4

"So then, just as you received Christ Jesus as Lord, continue to live your lives in him, rooted and built up in him, strengthened in the faith as you were taught, and overflowing with thankfulness." Colossians 2:6-7

The blessings you and I receive as Christians are everlasting. They are not subject to decay and will never go away. Hallelujah! Thank you God! Praise be to You and You alone! Doesn't this make you want to worship the Lord and praise His wonderful name? Of course it does! No matter what my circumstances, no matter what trial or pain I may be experiencing right now I can praise God and be thankful!

His Spirit is in me and I can experience joy, I can have peace knowing He loves me and has all these wonderful blessings for me. That is what the Apostle Paul and countless other Christians throughout history have held onto, the hope and assurance that God is real, God is dependable, and God will always love us and remain with us, providing everything we need. And what we need is Him! He is all that any person needs! And He promises to give all of Himself to us when we open our hearts and allow Him in.

So as a Christian, today and every day, I will give thanksgiving because I am truly blessed!

FOCUS QUESTIONS

What are you thankful for?

How will you show your thanksgiving?

Forgiveness

Have you ever been wronged by someone else? This is a dumb question isn't it? Of course you have! We all have been on the receiving end of someone else's selfish and/or thoughtless actions which have violated our rights in some way, shape, or form. If we know these acts were unintentional, we may be more likely to forgive them, but we still do not justify them as being okay because we were wronged. And if we know they were intentional, this serves to magnify our feelings of hurt and anger, making us much less likely to forgive, and worse yet, to sometimes seek revenge on the person(s) responsible.

Forgiveness is a difficult issue for all people, Christians included, and it is a topic that can't be adequately addressed in a single essay. However, there are truths from the word of God that can help us as Christians to deal with the people in our lives that are in need of our forgiveness. Let us begin with a harsh fact about you and me and all people. We are all sinners. <u>We have all committed wrongful acts against the Holy God who created us in His image and gave us the precious gift of life.</u>

Ecclesiastes 7:20 says, "Indeed, there is no one on earth who is righteous, no one who does what is right and never sins." And Romans 3:23 says, "for all have sinned and fall short of the glory of God". If you have done any self-reflection, then you know this is true. In fact, before you and I became Christians we needed to come to the realization that we were sinners in desperate need of God's forgiveness. We needed to humble ourselves before God and have an attitude of repentance, which is the desire to turn from our sins and start living in obedience to God. Then we needed to accept God's offer of salvation through Jesus Christ our Lord and Savior and invite Him to be Lord of our lives.

You and I must remember who we used to be before we met Jesus Christ and were spiritually reborn. Ephesians 2:1-5 says, "As for you, you were dead in your transgressions and sins, in which you used to live when you followed the ways of this world and of the ruler of the kingdom of the air, the spirit who is now at work in those who are disobedient. All of us also lived among them at one time, gratifying the cravings of our flesh and following its desires and thoughts. Like the rest, we were by nature deserving of wrath. But because of His great love for us, God, who is rich in mercy, made us alive with Christ even when we were dead in transgressions—it is by grace you have been saved."

You and I were deserving of God's wrath, but because of His rich mercy, because of His rich grace, you and I have been declared righteous through faith in Christ. Jesus Christ took our punishment for us by offering Himself on the cross, as the spotless, unblemished Lamb of God. His precious blood was poured out on Calvary so that you and I may have forgiveness for our sins and the hope of eternal life. What amazing grace we have received! We did nothing to earn it and God demonstrated His unconditional love for you, me, and all people by making Christ the object of His wrath. 1 Peter 2:24 says, "He (Jesus) Himself bore our sins" in his body on the cross, so that we might die to sins and live for righteousness; "by His wounds you have been healed."

Consider the suffering Jesus endured for us! No one has suffered as much as Him. He left His place in heaven and humbly took the form of a servant, so that we might live! Therefore, THE ROAD TO FORGIVENESS FOR OTHERS BEGINS WITH RECOGNIZING THAT WE OURSELVES HAVE ALREADY RECEIVED FORGIVENESS.

This does not excuse the actions of others, nor does it trivialize the pain and hurt that we suffer. <u>What it does is help us to put our pain and hurt into proper perspective.</u> Fellow Christian, we are called to live in a manner worthy of God's people. Colossians 3:12-13 says, "Therefore, as God's chosen people, holy and dearly loved, clothe yourselves with compassion, kindness, humility, gentleness and patience. Bear with each other and forgive one another if any of you has a grievance against someone. Forgive as the Lord forgave you."

So how often should we forgive others? Peter asked Jesus this very question. Matthew 18:21-22 says, "Then Peter came and said to Him, "Lord, how often shall my brother sin against me and I forgive him? Up to seven times?" Jesus said to him, "I do not say to you, up to seven times, but up to seventy times seven."

The Jewish rabbis at the time of Jesus taught that forgiving someone more than three times was unnecessary. Peter, perhaps wishing to appear especially forgiving and benevolent, asked Jesus if forgiveness was to be offered seven times. By offering forgiveness more than double that of the Old Testament example, Peter perhaps expected extra commendation from the Lord. When Jesus responded that forgiveness should be offered four hundred and ninety times, far beyond that which Peter was proposing, it must have stunned the disciples who were listening. Although they had been with Jesus for some time, they were still thinking in the limited terms of the law, rather than in the UNLIMITED TERMS OF GRACE.

Jesus was not saying to extend forgiveness literally 490 times. He is telling us we must have forgiving hearts that do not limit the number of times we forgive and continue to forgive with as much grace the thousandth time as we do the first time. Sounds impossible? It is impossible for men and women, but with God nothing is impossible. Christians are only capable of this type of forgiving spirit because the SPIRIT OF GOD LIVES WITHIN US and it is the Holy Spirit who provides the ability to offer forgiveness over and over, just as God forgives us over and over.

Fellow Christian, our Lord calls us to daily surrender ourselves to the leading of the Holy Spirit. The Holy Spirit is the source of the power we need to live our lives for God. 2 Timothy 1:7 says,

"For the Spirit God gave us does not make us timid, but gives us power, love and self-discipline." And Galatians 5:16-17 says, "So I say, walk by the Spirit, and you will not gratify the desires of the flesh. For the flesh desires what is contrary to the Spirit and the Spirit what is contrary to the flesh. They are in conflict with each other, so that you are not to do whatever you want."

Our fleshly nature wants to strike back against those who wrong us. Our fleshly nature does not want to forgive others who violate our rights. But we are not to live by the flesh; we are to live in surrender to the Holy Spirit of God. To walk by the Spirit is to put to death our selfish desires and allow His power to reign supreme in our hearts. This is what the Apostle Paul meant when he wrote in Romans 12:1 "Therefore, I urge you, brothers and sisters, in view of God's mercy, to offer your bodies as a living sacrifice, holy and pleasing to God--this is your true and proper worship."

Let us live each day with this attitude of self-sacrifice and cast all our cares on our Lord in prayer. This is how you and I can find the strength to forgive and to live our lives with peace. May God bless you all!

FOCUS QUESTIONS

What was our condition before we became Christians?

How often should we forgive others?

What is the source of our power to forgive and to live for God?

A Prayer for This Day

"The Lord is close to the brokenhearted and saves those who are crushed in spirit." Psalm 34:18

Dear Lord,

I come to you this day seeking your face, seeking your strength. I am weighed down with feelings of loneliness and emptiness, because I feel distant from you. Please come to my rescue and fill me with your presence. Make your unfailing love my food that sustains me. Remind me of your words which you have spoken to me and help me to walk in obedience to them. My mind rejoices in the truth of your words, yet my body and soul grow weary.

Restore the joy to my heart that I once knew. Help me to yield my mind to your Holy Spirit and allow you to guide my steps today. I am reminded that my hope rests in your strength, not my own. For my feelings cannot be trusted. They betray me and lead me many directions. But your love is steadfast. You are unchanging. My hope is in you and your promises, not in my own abilities. Forgive me of for my transgressions and take away my shame. I claim the promise of your words written by the apostle John, "If you confess your sins He is faithful and just and will purify you from all unrighteousness." (1 John 1:9)

The more I grow in my knowledge of you, the more I desire to be with you. The things this world has to offer mean less and less to me. Living for you is my purpose and I want to experience your joy each day. But my flesh is weak and it gets in the way of my experiencing your peace. So I come to you this day claiming the promises of Philippians 4:6-7 which says, "Do not be anxious about anything, but in every situation, by prayer and petition, with thanksgiving, present your requests to God. And the peace of God, which transcends all understanding, will guard your hearts and minds in Christ Jesus."

Today, regardless of my feelings and emotions, I will trust in the Lord. I will choose this day to give honor and praise to my God, in the name of Jesus Christ, by the power of the Holy Spirit who dwells within me. I will choose this day to get out of the way and allow you to live through me. Galatians 2:20 says, "I have been crucified with Christ and I no longer live, but Christ lives in me. The life I now live in the body, I live by faith in the Son of God, who loved me and gave himself for me." I will deny myself and pickup my cross and follow you O Lord Jesus. You are my life.

Amen.

Chapter 7

Christian Doctrine

"One act of obedience is better than one hundred sermons." – **Dietrich Bonhoeffer**

Who Is Jesus?

People offer many answers to this question. Some say he was a good man. Some say he was a teacher, others that he was a prophet. There are groups that teach that Jesus was merely a man, or an angel, or one of many gods that exist. Jesus asked Simon Peter this same question, "But what about you?" he asked. "Who do you say I am?" Simon Peter answered, "You are the Messiah, the Son of the living God." (Matthew 16:15-16)

In this essay we will examine what the infallible truth of God's word says about Jesus. My prayer for us who already believe is that these truths will strengthen our faith and knowledge about who Jesus is. My prayer for those who have yet to believe is that these truths will draw you to Jesus and to the salvation that awaits all who call upon the name of the Lord.

Let's begin by examining two Old Testament prophecies concerning the birth of the Messiah. Isaiah 7:14 says, "Therefore the Lord himself will give you a sign: The virgin will be with child and will give birth to a son, and will call him Immanuel." The word Immanuel is translated "God with us". And Isaiah 9:6 says, "For to us a child is born, to us a son is given, and the government will be on his shoulders. And he will be called Wonderful Counselor, Mighty God, Everlasting Father, Prince of Peace." Notice Isaiah writes "Mighty God", meaning that the Messiah is God Himself, and that He is the timeless God our Father. These prophecies make it very clear that the Messiah is God Himself, and these were fulfilled nearly 700 years later with the birth of Jesus (Matthew 1:23).

Now let's examine New Testament passages which confirm Jesus as being God himself. Colossians 1:16-17 says, "For in Him (Jesus) all things were created: things in heaven and on earth, visible and invisible, whether thrones or powers or rulers or authorities; all things have been created through Him and for Him. He is before all things, and in Him all things hold together." And John 1:3 says, "Through Him all things were made; without Him nothing was made that has been made." Only God has the power to create all things and the Bible says that He alone created everything (Isaiah 44:24). The Bible credits Jesus with having created all things; therefore scriptures declare that Jesus is God.

In Mark 2:1-12, there is an account of a paralytic man who was lowered by his friends through the roof of a house in order to be healed by Jesus. When Jesus saw their faith, he said to the paralyzed man, "Son, your sins are forgiven." Now some teachers of the law were sitting there, thinking to themselves, "Why does this fellow talk like that? He's blaspheming! Who can forgive sins but God alone?"(v.5-7) These scribes were correct in their statement that only God can forgive sins. Jesus words were demonstrating to them and to us that He indeed is God who has the power to forgive sins.

Jesus said, "But I want you to know that the Son of Man has authority on earth to forgive sins." So He said to the man, "I tell you, get up, take your mat and go home." He got up, took his mat and walked out in full view of them all. This amazed everyone and they praised God, saying, "We have never seen anything like this!" (v.10-12) In this account, Jesus healed what the people could see, a man stricken with palsy, in order to provide visible proof of His power to heal what they could not see, the man's sins. Again, this confirms to us that Jesus is God.

The Jewish religious leaders perfectly understood that Jesus was claiming to be God, and it was one of the chief reasons they had Him crucified. John 8:58-59 says, "Very truly I tell you," Jesus answered, "before Abraham was born, I AM!" At this, they picked up stones to stone him, but Jesus hid himself, slipping away from the temple grounds." This violent response of the Jews to Jesus' "I AM" statement indicates they clearly understood what He was declaring—that He was equating himself with the "I AM" title God gave Himself in Exodus 3:14. Thus, Jesus was saying that He is the eternal God in human flesh.

Jesus used the same phrase "I AM" in seven other declarations about Himself. In all seven, He combines I AM with tremendous metaphors which express His saving relationship toward the world. All these appear in the book of John. They are: I AM the bread of life (John 6:35,41,48,51); I AM the light of the world (John 8:12); I AM the door of the sheep (John 10:7,9); I AM the good shepherd (John 10:11,14); I AM the resurrection and the life (John 11:25); I AM the way, the truth and the life (John 14:6); and I AM the true vine (John 15: 1,5).

Like God, Jesus received worship by men. Matthew 14:33 says, "Then those who were in the boat worshiped him, saying, "Truly you are the Son of God." Like God, Jesus receives worship from angels. Hebrews 1:6 says, "And again, when God brings his firstborn (Jesus) into the world, he says, "Let all God's angels worship him." Like God, Jesus will one day receive worship from everyone. Revelation 5:13 says, "Then I heard every creature in heaven and on earth and under the earth and on the sea, and all that is in them, saying: "To him who sits on the throne and to the Lamb be praise and honor and glory and power, for ever and ever!" It is important to note that Jesus never rebuked any of His followers for worshiping Him, and yet, worship of anything or anyone other than God is absolutely forbidden in the Bible.

Jesus said, "Why do you call me good? No one is good except God alone." (Mark 10:18) Yet, Jesus called Himself good. Jesus said, "I am the good shepherd. The good shepherd lays down his life for the sheep." (John 10:11) Furthermore, Thomas called Jesus God (John 20:28), Peter called Jesus God (2 Peter 1:1), Paul called Jesus God (Titus 2:13), and John called Jesus God (John 1:1-3, 14). In Isaiah 43:10-11 God says, "Before me no god was formed, nor will there be one after me. I, even I, am the Lord, and apart from me there is no savior." Yet, in the New Testament, we read that we are told to: "...wait for the blessed hope—the appearing of the glory of our great God and Savior, Jesus Christ." (Titus 2:13)

Like God, Jesus gives eternal life. Jesus said, "My sheep listen to my voice; I know them, and they follow me. I give them eternal life, and they shall never perish; no one will snatch them out of my hand. My Father, who has given them to me, is greater than all; no one can snatch them out of my Father's hand." (John 10:27-29) Wait a minute! Jesus said the Father is greater than all, and Jesus is the Son of God, so how can Jesus be God Himself? Let's keep reading, in verse 30 Jesus said, "I and the Father are one."

There are many verses in the Bible that clearly teach there is only one God. And we have seen that the bible also clearly teaches that Jesus is God. Yet, the bible calls Jesus the Son of God, and tells us Jesus prayed many times to His Father. Jesus said "My food is to do the will of him who sent me and to finish his work." (John 4:34) How can this be? How can there be only one God but more than one person who is God?

Some will use verses out of the context of the whole Bible to support their beliefs in more than one God, but again, this is not what the bible teaches. This is an aspect of God that is beyond our human understanding. This is something that we as Christians accept by faith because God's word clearly teaches this to us. Please watch for a future post in which we will explore this biblical doctrine of the TRINITY. May God bless you all!

FOCUS QUESTIONS

How do some non-Christians answer the question "Who is Jesus?"

List at least three attributes of Jesus that support Him being God.

Upon This Hill I Will Stand!

There are so many proclaimed paths of truth. And I'm not just talking about the false religions of this world which have their origin in the "god of this world", Satan. I'm talking about Christianity and the many denominations which all claim to follow Jesus Christ. There are so many of them! Among the largest denominations in the U.S are Catholic, Baptist, Non-denominational, Methodist, Lutheran, Presbyterian, Pentecostal, Episcopalian, Evangelical, Church of Christ, Church of God, Assembly of God, Seventh-Day Adventist, Orthodox, Church of the Nazarene, Christian Reform, and so on and so on. Who is right? Who has the truth? Which way shall I go? Whom can I trust with my eternal soul? My conclusion is not one of them!

Does my answer mean that all of them are wrong? No, it does not. I believe most of them teach the truth to a certain degree, some more than others. They all possess differences in interpretations of scripture, which lead to doctrines which do not completely agree with each other. So in a sense, not one of them is 100% correct. I know this because all of them are led by people, and no person, no matter how sincere and devout, can be completely trusted with truth. All people are sinners and all are prone to error. So what am I to do?

I will give my allegiance to the only One that I know I can fully trust. Today and every day I will come to Him in humble submission, prayerfully seeking His truth. Perhaps you have heard of His name? He has many of them. These are not all of His names but it is a good start. He is called Almighty God, Alpha and Omega, Ancient of Days, Anointed One, Blessed of God, Bread of Life, Bridegroom, Bright and Morning Star, Chief Cornerstone, Chosen of God, Christ the Lamb, Comforter, Creator, Emmanuel, Eternal God, Everlasting Father, Faithful and True, Firstborn, God of Abraham, God of Isaac, God of Israel, God of Jacob, God of Whole Earth, Good Shepherd, Great I AM, Head of the Church, Healer, Heir of All Things, Holy Messiah, Holy One of Israel, Jehovah, King of Israel, King of Kings, King of the Jews, Lamb of God, Light of the World, Lion of Judah, Living Bread, Lord, Lord of All, Mediator, Prince of Peace, Redeemer of the World, Resurrection and the Life, Righteous Judge, The Rock, The Sacrifice, Savior of the World, Shepherd, Son of God, Son of Man, Son of the Living God, True Vine, The Truth, Unchangeable One, The Way, Wonderful, Word of Life, The Word.

HE IS JESUS CHRIST! HE IS EVERYTHING! I WILL PLACE ALL OF MY TRUST IN HIM ALONE! ON THIS HILL OF TRUTH I WILL CHOOSE TO STAND AND IF NECESSARY TO DIE, BECAUSE HE IS ALL THAT MATTERS!

Please join me in following the One True Living God! We are not religious. We have a relationship with the One and Only God. We are followers of Jesus and we believe in His name and His name only! The words of this beautiful communion song remind us of all that really matters about the gospel.

BEHOLD THE LAMB

Behold the Lamb who bears our sins away

Slain for us; and we remember the promise made

that all who come in faith find forgiveness at the cross

So we share in this bread of life

And we drink of His sacrifice

As a sign of our bonds of peace

Around the table of the King

The body of our Savior Jesus Christ torn for you

Eat and remember the wounds that heal

The death that brings us life paid the price to make us one

The blood that cleanses ev'ry stain of sin

Shed for you drink and remember

He drained death's cup that all may enter in

To receive the life of God

And so with thankfulness and faith we rise

To respond and to remember

Our call to follow in the steps of Christ

As his body here on earth.

The gospel message is simple. You must start by admitting who you are before God, a sinner in desperate need of forgiveness. Repent and turn from your sin. Believe in the death and resurrection of Jesus Christ, who shed His precious blood on the cross to redeem all of us from death and condemnation. Accept God's free gift for the salvation of your soul by placing your trust in Jesus as Lord of your life. In doing so, you will receive the gift of the Holy Spirit and pass from death unto life. Then start living this new life you have freely received by following in the footsteps of our King!

This is the true church: The body of believers from all nations and ethnicities who have made this profession of faith. Wherever you choose to worship God should depend upon the teaching of the sufficiency of Jesus Christ for your salvation, not the name on the door. May our God richly bless you all!

FOCUS QUESTION

What is the true church?

The Trinity Part 1

The most difficult thing about the Christian doctrine of the Trinity is that it is a concept that is impossible for any human being to fully understand, let alone explain. God is infinitely greater than we are; therefore, we should not expect to fully understand Him. The Bible teaches that the Father is God, that Jesus is God, and that the Holy Spirit is God. The Bible also teaches that there is only one God. Though we can understand some facts about the relationship of the different Persons of the Trinity to one another, ultimately, it is incomprehensible to our human minds.

The Trinity is one God existing in three Persons. Understand that this is not in any way suggesting three Gods. This is a term that is used to attempt to describe the triune God—three coexistent, co-eternal Persons who make up God. Some people who reject the Trinity doctrine often claim that the word "Trinity" is not found in Scripture. Of course, there is no verse that says "God is three Persons" or "God is a Trinity." However, this does not mean the Trinity is not true or that it is not based on the teachings of the Bible. There are many words and phrases that Christians use, which are not found in scripture. For example, the word "Bible" is not found in the Bible. Of real importance is that the concept represented by the word "Trinity" does exist in Scripture.

Let's start by recognizing the Bible clearly teaches there is only one God. Deuteronomy 6:4 says, "Hear, O Israel: The Lord our God, the Lord is one." And Isaiah 44:6 says, "This is what the Lord says— Israel's King and Redeemer, the Lord Almighty: I am the first and I am the last; apart from me there is no God." There are many other references that teach there is only one God, including Isaiah 43:10, 1 Corinthians 8:4, Galatians 3:20, 1 Timothy 2:5 and James 2:19.

Christians believe that this one God is the Creator of all things. Genesis 1:1 says, "In the beginning God created the heavens and the earth." In this verse, the Hebrew plural noun "Elohim" is used. Later we read in Genesis 1:26, "Then God said, "Let us make mankind in our image, in our likeness…" Here the plural pronoun for "us" is used. It is also used in Genesis 3:22, 11:7 and in Isaiah 6:8. The words "Elohim" and "us" are plural forms, definitely referring in the Hebrew language to more than two. So who are these words referring to?

Isaiah 64:8 says, "Yet you, Lord, are our Father. We are the clay, you are the potter; we are all the work of your hand." And Revelation 4:11 says, "You are worthy, our Lord and God, to receive glory and honor and power, for you created all things, and by your will they were created and have their being." These verses teach us that God the Father created all things as a result of His will. Now let's go to the Gospel of John and read about Jesus.

John 1:1-3 says, "In the beginning was the Word, and the Word was with God, and the Word was God. He was with God in the beginning. Through Him all things were made; without Him nothing was made that has been made." And John 1:14 says, "The Word became flesh and made His dwelling among us. We have seen His glory, the glory of the one and only Son, who came from the Father, full of grace and truth." Here we read that the "Word" is Jesus Christ the Son of God, and that Jesus was there in the beginning, in Genesis 1:1 when all things were created! "Through Him (Jesus), all things were made..." This is an astounding statement! The God who created all things and has always existed includes Jesus Christ, the Son who came from the Father!

Furthermore, the Apostle Paul wrote in Colossians 1:15-17, "The Son is the image of the invisible God, the firstborn over all creation. For in Him all things were created: things in heaven and on earth, visible and invisible, whether thrones or powers or rulers or authorities; all things have been created through Him and for Him. He is before all things, and in Him all things hold together."

Now let's consider the role of the Holy Spirit. Job 26:13 says, "By His breath the skies became fair; His hand pierced the gliding serpent." We know from other passages that God's breath refers to the Holy Spirit of God. 2 Timothy 3:16 reminds us that "All Scripture is God-breathed..." and 2 Peter 1:21 says, "For prophecy never had its origin in the human will, but prophets, though human, spoke from God as they were carried along by the Holy Spirit." Thus, the scriptures of the bible were written by men under the inspiration of the Holy Spirit. Furthermore, the Holy Spirit is also given credit for being active in creation.

Job 33:4 says, "The Spirit of God has made me; the breath of the Almighty gives me life." And Genesis 1:2 says; "Now the earth was formless and empty, darkness was over the surface of the deep, and the Spirit of God was hovering over the waters." We have already seen scripture that places the Father and the Son Jesus Christ at the beginning of creation, and here we read the Holy Spirit was also there. Remember, we pointed out that the word for God in Genesis 1:1 is the plural noun "Elohim" which means more than two. Thus, taking into account all of these scriptures shows us all three persons of God were there at the beginning when all things were made.

As stated before, this is very difficult concept for us to understand. The bible tells us there is only one God, yet it teaches us there are three persons who make up the one God. All three work together and are unified as one, yet each one possesses full deity as God. Fellow Christian, you and I can't explain this because it is beyond our reason. But it is something we can accept on the basis of faith. After all, is it any easier to understand that the God of the bible has always existed and created the entire universe from nothing? We can believe it because God has shown us enough of Himself for us to know it is true. He has revealed Himself to us in Jesus Christ, who is the "image of the invisible God". John 1:18 says, "No one has ever seen God, but the one and only Son, who is Himself God and is in closest relationship with the Father, has made Him known."

There are many more scriptures which describe the three persons of God, but that is all for now. May God richly bless you all!

FOCUS QUESTIONS

Name at least two verses which say there is only one God.

Who was present in the beginning when all things were made?

The Trinity Part 2

In part one we introduced the biblical teaching known as the trinity. The Bible teaches that the Father is God, that Jesus is God, and that the Holy Spirit is God. The Bible also teaches that there is only one God. Though we can understand some facts about the relationship of the different Persons of the Trinity to one another, ultimately, it is beyond the limits of human logic and reason. Today we will examine more passages which teach us about this incomprehensible truth.

Let's begin with the account of Jesus' baptism. Matthew 3:16-17 says, "As soon as Jesus was baptized, He went up out of the water. At that moment heaven was opened, and He saw the Spirit of God descending like a dove and alighting on Him. And a voice from heaven said, "This is my Son, whom I love; with Him I am well pleased." Here we have a clear distinction of the three Persons of the trinity. Jesus the Son, God in the flesh, has the Holy Spirit descend on Him as the Father voices His pleasure and love for the Son.

After His resurrection, Jesus Himself made the distinction between the three Persons of God when He commissioned His disciples to preach the gospel. Jesus said, "Therefore go and make disciples of all nations, baptizing them in the name of the Father and of the Son and of the Holy Spirit" (Matthew 28:19). The apostle Paul also made this distinction in his letters to the churches. For example, 2 Corinthians 13:14 says, "May the grace of the Lord Jesus Christ, and the love of God, and the fellowship of the Holy Spirit be with you all."

Our finite perspective leads some to think that because the Father, Son, and Holy Spirit are distinct Persons, then the Father alone must be God, and Son and the Holy Spirit are not themselves God. Perhaps they were created by God the Father, or they are manifestations of God that do His will on earth. Watch out! This is not what the bible teaches! The bible shows us in many passages that EACH PERSON OF THE TRINITY IS FULLY GOD based on the attributes shared by each one. We will look at just 3 of these attributes, but there are many more.

Isaiah 45:18 says, "For this is what the Lord says—He who created the heavens, He is God; He who fashioned and made the earth, He founded it; He did not create it to be empty, but formed it to be inhabited—He says: "I am the Lord, and there is no other." The one and only God created the heavens and the earth. In our last post, we examined several scriptures which describe the creation of all things as an attribute of each Person of the trinity. (See Isaiah 64:8, Revelation 4:11, John 1:1-3, Job 33:4)

Another attribute of the one and only God is omniscience (knowing all things). The bible credits each Person of the trinity with this attribute. The Father knows all things: 1 John 3:20 says, "If our hearts condemn us, we know that God (Father) is greater than our hearts, and He knows everything." The Son knows all things: John 16:30 says, "Now we can see that you know all things and that you do not even need to have anyone ask you questions. This makes us believe that you came from God." The Holy Spirit knows all things: 1 Corinthians 2:10-11 says, "…The Spirit searches all things, even the deep things of God. For who knows a person's thoughts except their own spirit within them? In the same way no one knows the thoughts of God except the Spirit of God."

A third attribute of the one and only God of the bible is He is the author and giver of life. Genesis 2:7 says, "Then the Lord God formed a man from the dust of the ground and breathed into his nostrils the breath of life, and the man became a living being." There is nothing fancy about the chemicals which make up a person. We are simply dust. Our bodies are a lifeless shell until God brings it to life with his "breath of life". We noted in part one that the breath of God refers to the Holy Spirit.

2 Corinthians 3:4-6 says, "Such confidence we have through Christ before God. Not that we are competent in ourselves to claim anything for ourselves, but our competence comes from God. He has made us competent as ministers of a new covenant—not of the letter but of the Spirit; for the letter kills, but the Spirit gives life." Our life and worth comes from God's Spirit, and when God removes His life-giving breath, our bodies once again return to dust.

Jesus is also given this same life-giving attribute. John 5:21 says, "For just as the Father raises the dead and gives them life, even so the Son gives life to whom He is pleased to give it." And John 10:27-30 says, "My sheep listen to my voice; I know them, and they follow me. I give them eternal life, and they shall never perish; no one will snatch them out of my hand. My Father, who has given them to me, is greater than all; no one can snatch them out of my Father's hand. I and the Father are one."

Here we read a remarkable passage in which Jesus acknowledges that the Father gives life, and then He claims that He Himself gives life. He asserts that no one can snatch His sheep from His hand, and then He says no one can snatch them from His Father's hand. Jesus finishes this incredible statement with an unmistakable claim of deity and equality with the one and only God by saying "I and the Father are one". In the Old Testament, the prophet Isaiah wrote the following about the promised Messiah. "For to us a child is born, to us a son is given, and the government will be on his shoulders. And he will be called Wonderful Counselor, Mighty God, Everlasting Father, Prince of Peace." (Isaiah 9:6) This message of hope was fulfilled in the birth of Jesus Christ.

The Father, Son, and Holy Spirit are connected in a marvelous and mysterious way. Each is referred to separately, yet each is one and the same in unity, purpose, and deity. If someone claims they understand God and that it is simple thing to distinguish the workings of God, then beware the message which that person brings! God is far beyond our finite understanding, but He has revealed enough of Himself to us to know the way of salvation.

That message is very simple and clear. The way of salvation is found in Jesus Christ. He is the way, and the truth, and the life (John 14:6). Jesus is the King of kings and Lord of lords. "Salvation is found in no one else, for there is no other name under heaven given to mankind by which we must be saved." (Acts 4:12) Let us remain fixed on this simple truth and live for Him each and every day. May God bless you all!

FOCUS QUESTIONS

Name 3 characteristics of God that are possessed by the Father, the Son, and the Holy Spirit.

What is the way of salvation?

Free Will Part 1

There are some teachings found in God's word we simply can't understand until we get to heaven. Take for example the doctrine of the Trinity. Scripture clearly teaches that God is three Persons in One God. This doesn't make sense to our human reason, but that does not make it false. And because scripture teaches this and other doctrines that are difficult to comprehend, we accept them as truth because of God's character. They are true because God said them (2 Timothy 3:16-17) and we also can trust He has good reasons for saying them. Therefore, we must recognize that the truth of these doctrines is not dependent upon our ability to fully grasp them with our human reason.

One such topic that many Christians and non-Christians alike have struggled with is the concept of free will. Do people have the choice to choose or reject God, or does God do the choosing? The answer is YES TO BOTH! I'm sorry if this doesn't make it easier for you but it is the same answer to the question of the Trinity. Is God One God or three Persons? The answer is YES TO BOTH!

In this essay we will examine scripture about this topic and my prayer is you will find peace through the Holy Spirit and understand that in the end God is in control. Furthermore, our salvation is not dependent on our ability to understand this topic. We are saved by God's grace through faith in Jesus Christ and nothing else! Please take pleasure in knowing this unchangeable truth regardless of your agreement with the conclusions of this essay. Okay, let's start with this question: Did Adam and Eve have free will?

Genesis 2:16-17 says, "And the Lord God commanded the man, "You are free to eat from any tree in the garden; but you must not eat from the tree of the knowledge of good and evil, for when you eat from it you will certainly die." This verse is very clear that God gave Adam freedom to choose for himself. God's love for Adam required that He give Adam free will. In the same way God gives you and I free will because He loves us and He wants us to love Him in return. So how do we demonstrate our love for God? 1 John 5:3 says, "For this is the love of God, that we keep His commandments; and His commandments are not burdensome."

Therefore, God gave Adam free will to choose to obey Him because without choice Adam's love for God would not be genuine. The tree was planted in the garden and the law was established by God so that Adam and Eve would have the **choice** to obey or disobey Him. Without choice, there can be no true obedience or true love, only mindless followers with no will of their own. In the same way our love for God would not be real if it were forced. We'd be little better than robots programmed to behave a certain way. What person does not want to have freedom? God values freedom and so does every person who is truly honest about their desires.

Did God want Adam and Eve to disobey His command by eating the fruit? Of course not, but He knew that they would. He knows all of history; past, present, and future. And God had already established His plan to rescue all of mankind from the evil and death He knew would result from man's free will. 1 Peter 1:18-20 says, "For you know that it was not with perishable things such as silver or gold that you were redeemed from the empty way of life handed down to you from your ancestors, but with the precious blood of Christ, a lamb without blemish or defect. He was chosen before the creation of the world, but was revealed in these last times for your sake." God in His wisdom and love for mankind had predetermined that He would take the form of a man, Jesus Christ, and suffer the punishment of our disobedience. Wow! God not only says He loves us, He proved it by nailing every one of our sins to that cross!

Some say if God is so good then why didn't He create a perfect world with no evil. The answer is He did just that! Genesis 1:31 says, "And God saw every thing that He had made, and, behold, it was very good..." The world Adam and Eve enjoyed before they rebelled was perfect! They lived in harmony with all of creation and most of all knew God personally. Genesis tells us of God being present, walking among Adam and Eve in the garden (Genesis 3:8).

Others say if God is all-powerful then why couldn't He create beings with free will who He knew would not make wrong choices? But this objection is completely nonsensical and illogical. To say God should be able to give people free will without the possibility of making a wrong choice is contradictory! It would be like asking God to make a square-shaped circle. Such a thing has no objective reality!

The reality is in order for free will to exist, there must exist the possibility for wrong choices to be made. And in order for a choice to be wrong there must exist a standard in which to compare them to. God is that standard. This is the basis for the moral argument for the existence of God which we will not explain in this essay, but it provides us with a starting point to grapple with the idea that God found it necessary to create man with the freedom to obey Him or not. And the consequence of that freedom would inevitably be evil and suffering which we now experience in the world.

Some may ask why God would create people if He knew they would rebel against Him. But I would assert that I am thankful God created me! He has given you, me, and all people the precious gift of life! Even with the pain and suffering that comes with being born into this world, life is a gift from God. Furthermore, God offers us the opportunity to experience eternal life with Him as it was meant to be from the beginning. Once again, God has provided the remedy to the problem of evil and suffering through the finished work of Jesus Christ on the cross and His resurrection from the dead!

Brothers and sisters in Christ, we can look forward to the day when God will make it all things new and there will no longer be any pain or death. This is not to trivialize the trials we face in this life, or to minimize the pain people endure. But Christians can look forward to an eternity without the pain and suffering this life offers. Revelation 21:4 says, "He (God) will wipe every tear from their eyes. There will be no more death or mourning or crying or pain, for the old order of things has passed away."

We may not understand why God does certain things, but we can be sure that He has His reasons, and I for one am thankful for the hope of eternal life!

May this blessed hope fill you will peace and joy! May God richly bless you all!

FOCUS QUESTIONS

Why would love require God to give people free will?

According to 1 John, how do we show love for God?

Why couldn't God create people with free will that He knew would not disobey Him?

Free Will Part 2

The theological question we are examining is "Do people have free will to choose or reject God, or does God do the choosing? We answered this question with YES TO BOTH. It is one of those doctrines that we won't fully understand until we get to heaven, but we accept it as true because God's word says it.

In part one we learned that God gave Adam and Eve free will to choose to obey Him or not, and that He gives you and me the same freedom. We learned that God loves us and His desire is for us to love Him in return by obeying His commands. Therefore, God's love for us required that He give us free will. We also learned that the reality of free will demands that there be the possibility of wrong choices to be made, otherwise free will could not exist.

Finally, we learned Adam's choice to violate God's law brought sin and death into the world, but God had a plan of salvation to rescue mankind. Now let's examine that plan. We will begin with the question "Are all people totally sinful?"

Romans 3:10-12 says, "As it is written: "There is no one righteous, not even one; there is no one who understands; there is no one who seeks God. All have turned away; they have together become worthless; there is no one who does good, not even one." And Romans 3:23 says, "for all have sinned and fall short of the glory of God." God's word is very clear that no one is good. No one is righteous in God's sight. Jesus said, "Therefore you are to be perfect, as your heavenly Father is perfect." (Matthew 5:48) Jesus meant in order to be found righteous by God's standard a person must be morally perfect. But no one is perfect!

If anyone thinks they are good, then they only need examine themselves under the light of God's law, the Ten Commandments. There is no one who can say that they have never lied, taken God's name in vain, disobeyed their parents, or lusted in their heart for another person. In addition, every person, including atheists, worships a god of some kind, whether it is money, selfish pride, the desire for power, etc… God is the standard of moral perfection and as such He requires that anyone who is to enter into His kingdom must be morally perfect in thought, word, and deed.

Some people try to earn forgiveness for their sins through good works, but the bible is very clear that good works cannot save us. Ephesians 2:8-9 says, "For by grace you have been saved through faith. And this is not your own doing; it is the gift of God, not a result of works, so that no one may boast." And Isaiah 64:6 says, "…all our righteous acts are like filthy rags". A person trying to earn salvation by good works is like a serial killer trying to earn forgiveness by doing a few hours of community service.

The moral perfection God requires was realized for us through the person of Jesus Christ and it is only through Him that we can be found morally perfect by God. A person must humble themselves before God, repent of their sin, believe and accept Jesus Christ as their Lord and Savior. When this occurs the Holy Spirit of God comes to dwell within that person and they receive credit for Jesus' righteousness. This is known as "imputed righteousness". 2 Corinthians 5:21 says, "God made him (Jesus) who had no sin to be sin for us, so that in Him we might become the righteousness of God."

Okay, we've seen that all people are sinful and no one is found righteous by their good works. But did Jesus die for everyone's sins, or only for the sins of believers?

First, there are many scriptures which say that Jesus is the Savior of the world. 1 John 2:1-2 says, "My dear children, I write this to you so that you will not sin. But if anybody does sin, we have an advocate with the Father—Jesus Christ, the Righteous One. He is the atoning sacrifice for our sins, and not only for ours but also for the sins of the whole world." And John 1:29 says, "The next day he saw Jesus coming to him, and said, 'Behold, the Lamb of God who takes away the sin of the world! (Also see John 4:42 and 1 John 4:14)

Second, there are many scriptures which refer to Jesus as the Savior for all who believe. Romans 1:16 says, "For I am not ashamed of the gospel, because it is the power of God that brings salvation to everyone who believes: first to the Jew, then to the Gentile." And Romans 3:21 says, "But now apart from the law the righteousness of God has been made known, to which the law and the prophets testify. This righteousness is given through faith in Jesus Christ to all who believe." Also 1 Timothy 4:10 says, "For it is for this we labor and strive, because we have fixed our hope on the living God, who is the Savior of all men, especially of believers."

One may argue that these scriptures refer to Jesus being the Savior for only those who believe. That is true. God will not credit the righteousness of Jesus to those who reject Him. But the question we are examining is "Do people have free will to choose or reject God, or does God do the choosing?" So we are trying to get at the heart of this issue which is do people have the free will to accept Jesus or not? We have already seen very strong evidence that God has endowed men with free will. This free will includes the ability to make wrong choices, so why would it not include the ability to make right choices? And what could be more right then humbling oneself before God, repenting of your sin, and accepting Jesus as your Savior?

To this point we have seen that man has free will, which brought sin and death into the world. God knew this would happen and He has a plan to save mankind. God became a man, Jesus Christ, who died on the cross to pay for the sin of the whole world. And this salvation is available for all people who believe in His name.

Since each of us has free will to make right or wrong choices, we have the option to choose Christ as Savior. Revelation 3:20 says, "Here I am! I stand at the door and knock. If anyone hears my voice and opens the door, I will come in and eat with that person, and they with me." We also have the option to reject Christ, by resisting the call of the Holy Spirit. Acts 7:51 says, "You stiff-necked people! Your hearts and ears are still uncircumcised. You are just like your ancestors: You always resist the Holy Spirit!"

In summary, it seems clear that every person has free will to choose or reject God. However, the bible also tells us that God does the choosing. But that is for next time. May God truly bless you all!

FOCUS QUESTIONS

What Did Jesus say in Matthew 5:48?

How can a person become perfect in God's sight?

Free Will Part 3

In part one we introduced the question "Do people have the choice to choose or reject God, or does God do the choosing? To this point we have seen scriptures that support the concept that God has given each person free will, which includes the choice to accept or reject Jesus Christ as Lord and Savior. But the bible does teach that God calls people to Himself. There are many accounts which describe this fact.

In the Old Testament God called Abraham. Genesis 12:1 says, "The Lord said to Abram, 'Go from your country, your people and your father's household to the land I will show you." Psalm 106:23 refers to Moses as God's chosen one. There is also Jacob, Aaron, Saul, and David to name a few others. In the New Testament Jesus said to His disciples "You did not choose me, but I chose you and appointed you." (John 15:16) And referring to Saul, Acts 9:15 says, "But the Lord said to Ananias, 'Go! This man is my chosen instrument to proclaim my name to the Gentiles and their kings and to the people of Israel."

The New Testament uses words such as chosen and elect to describe those belonging to the church, all people from all nations who have placed their faith in Jesus Christ. 1 Peter 1:1-2 says, "Peter, an apostle of Jesus Christ, To God's elect, exiles scattered throughout the provinces of Pontus, Galatia, Cappadocia, Asia and Bithynia, who have been chosen according to the foreknowledge of God the Father, through the sanctifying work of the Spirit, to be obedient to Jesus Christ and sprinkled with His blood"

Going further, the bible also teaches that we who come to Christ have been predestined by God the Father to do just that. Romans 8:28-29 says, "For those God foreknew He also predestined to be conformed to the image of His Son, that they might be the firstborn among many brothers and sisters. And those He predestined, He also called; those He called, He also justified; those He justified, He also glorified." And Ephesians 1:3-5 says, "Praise be to the God and Father of our Lord Jesus Christ, who has blessed us in the heavenly realms with every spiritual blessing in Christ. For He chose us in Him before the creation of the world to be holy and blameless in His sight. In love He predestined us for adoption to sonship through Jesus Christ, in accordance with His pleasure and will."

The question arises "Since God has endowed mankind with free will, why would He need to call them?

We have already seen that all people are completely and utterly sinful and that no one is righteous. This is termed as the "total depravity" of mankind. The Wesleyan view of total depravity is that an unregenerate man can do nothing to save himself, unless he is aided and led by the Holy Spirit. It is the view that man left to himself would never seek after God and therefore never find Him on his own. God must take the initiative to call the individual sinner to repentance because he or she would not and could not call upon God.

Passages which support this view are Psalm 53:2-3 which says, "God looks down from heaven on all mankind to see if there are any who understand, any who seek God. Everyone has turned away, all have become corrupt; there is no one who does good" And Romans 3:11 says, "there is no one who understands; there is no one who seeks God." Our Lord Jesus said, "No one can come to me unless the Father who sent me draws them, and I will raise them up at the last day." (John 6:44)

Even repentance and faith are impossible without the help of God!

Acts 11:18 says, "When they heard this, they had no further objections and praised God, saying, "So then, even to Gentiles God has granted repentance that leads to life." Philippians 1:29 says, "For it has been granted to you on behalf of Christ not only to believe in him, but also to suffer for him" And Ephesians 2:8 says, "For it is by grace you have been saved, through faith—and this is not from yourselves, **it is the gift of God."** Our faith is a gift from God and there are references to all three persons of the trinity being involved in this process.

1 Corinthians 2:4-5 says, "My message and my preaching were not with wise and persuasive words, but with a demonstration of the Spirit's power, so that your faith might not rest on human wisdom, but on God's power." Ephesians 6:23 says, "Peace to the brothers and sisters, and love with faith from God the Father and the Lord Jesus Christ."

Faith also comes from hearing the gospel and from the word of God. Jesus said, "My prayer is not for them alone. I pray also for those who will believe in Me through their message" And Acts 15:7 says, "After much discussion, Peter got up and addressed them: "Brothers, you know that some time ago God made a choice among you that the Gentiles might hear from my lips the message of the gospel and believe."

In summary, the bible teaches that God calls people because man on his own does not seek God. Also, before the creation of the world God had predestined that people should be saved through faith in Jesus Christ. Furthermore, the faith an individual needs in order to believe comes from God and is a gift. It is only through the workings of the Father, the Son, the Holy Spirit and the message of the gospel that people are able to believe and be saved. Some see these teachings as contrary to free will because they see them as saying only people God chooses can be saved and the rest have no choice but to be condemned. We will discuss these next time. May God richly bless you all!

FOCUS QUESTIONS

Why does God call people?

Where does the faith to believe come from?

Free Will Part 4

We concluded part 3 by noting that the bible teaches God calls people because man on his own does not seek God. Also, before the creation of the world God had predestined that people should be saved through faith in Jesus Christ. Furthermore, the faith an individual needs in order to believe comes from God and is a gift. It is only through the workings of the Father, the Son, the Holy Spirit and the message of the gospel that people are able to believe and be saved.

Some see these teachings as contrary to free will because they see them as saying only people God chooses can be saved and the rest have no choice but to be condemned. Yet, we have explored many passages which teach that man does have free will to choose or reject God. Remember in part one we introduced this topic with the caveat that there are some teachings found in God's word we simply can't understand until we get to heaven.

Because scripture teaches this and other doctrines that are difficult to comprehend, we accept them as truth because of God's character. Therefore, we recognize that the truth of these doctrines is not dependent upon our ability to fully grasp them with our human reason. They are true because God said them (2 Timothy 3:16-17) and we also can trust He has good reasons for saying them. We will now answer three key questions to help us come to peace with this issue of free will versus God choosing.

Let us first answer the question "Does God want everyone to be saved?"

2 Peter 3:9 says, "The Lord is not slow in keeping His promise, as some understand slowness. Instead He is patient with you, **not wanting anyone to perish, but everyone to come to repentance.**" And 1 Timothy 2:1-4 says, "I urge, then, first of all, that petitions, prayers, intercession and thanksgiving be made for all people—for kings and all those in authority, that we may live peaceful and quiet lives in all godliness and holiness. **This is good, and pleases God our Savior, who wants all people to be saved and to come to a knowledge of the truth.**"

Now let us answer the question "Who can receive salvation?

Romans 10:12-13 says, "For there is no distinction between Jew and Greek; for the same Lord is Lord of all, abounding in riches for **ALL WHO CALL ON HIM**; for "**WHOEVER WILL CALL ON THE NAME OF THE LORD WILL BE SAVED.**" And Acts 10:34-35 says, "Then Peter began to speak: "I now realize how true it is that **GOD DOES NOT SHOW FAVORITISM** but accepts from every nation the one who fears Him and does what is right." Also Revelation 22:17 says, "The Spirit and the bride say, "Come!" And let the one who hears say, "Come!" Let the one who is thirsty come; and let the one who wishes take the free gift of the water of life. Also read John 3:16-17 and Romans 3:23-24.

Finally let's ask the question, "Is God Holy, Good, and Just?

God is holy. Leviticus 11:44 says, "I am the Lord, who brought you up out of Egypt to be your God; therefore be holy, because I am holy." God is good. Matthew 19:17 says, ""Why do you ask me about what is good?" Jesus replied. "There is only One who is good. If you want to enter life, keep the commandments." And God is just. Isaiah 30:18 says, "Yet the Lord longs to be gracious to you; therefore he will rise up to show you compassion. For the Lord is a God of justice. Blessed are all who wait for Him!"

It is true that we cannot understand God and our minds cannot grasp the greatness and power of God. Nor can we understand all that is involved in the fall of man or the curse of God upon the human family because of Adam's sin. Even though these are mysteries that we cannot fully understand, we are assured by the word of God that He has no respect of persons in assuring all have opportunity to be saved. God always does what is right and good toward all men.

In part 2 we firmly established that Jesus died to take away the sin of the whole world. In other words, the sin of all people has been paid for and forgiveness is available for all who will believe in Jesus Christ. Adding this to the message that God genuinely wants all people to be saved diffuses any idea that some people have no choice but to be condemned to hell. Furthermore, Romans 2:4 says, "Or do you show contempt for the riches of His kindness, forbearance and patience, not realizing that **God's kindness is intended to lead you to repentance.**" And Romans 2:11 says, "For God does not show favoritism."

Do people have the choice to choose or reject God, or does God do the choosing? The answer is YES TO BOTH! However, my prayer is you will find peace through the Holy Spirit and understand that in the end God is in control. And we can rest in the assurance that God is holy, good, and just, and wants all people to be saved.   Furthermore, our salvation is not dependent on our ability to understand this topic. We are saved by God's grace through faith in Jesus Christ and nothing else! Please take pleasure in knowing this unchangeable truth regardless of your agreement with the conclusions of this essay.

"For God so loved the world that He gave His one and only Son, that whoever believes in Him shall not perish but have eternal life. For God did not send his Son into the world to condemn the world, but to save the world through Him" John 3:16-17.

May God richly bless you all!

FOCUS QUESTIONS

Does God want all people to be saved? Explain.

Is God holy, just, and good? Explain.

Who can be saved?

Paradoxes of the Bible

The Bible is a unique and marvelous book. It is fundamentally different from any other "sacred book" of other religions because the Bible contains "God's thoughts". Among them are spiritual teachings in the form of paradoxes. A Paradox is defined as a seemingly self-contradictory declaration but is in fact true. Biblical authors (especially Jesus and Paul) frequently utilized this special form of instruction to communicate God's "backward wisdom". G. K. Chesterton defined biblical paradox as "truth standing on her head to attract attention."

Paradoxical statements arrest our attention because of their apparent contradiction—and motivate us to resolve the contradiction by learning, reflection, and rethinking our presuppositions. EXAMPLE: "In order to get big, you have to stay small." On the surface, this sounds contradictory. But since we presume rationality, this statement invites us to listen more closely to the context and explanation—that churches can only grow large by effectively utilizing small groups that build community.

To some, such biblical paradoxes seem ridiculous and yet such are the very words of God which were written for our admonition and learning. NOTE: Biblical paradox is very different from Zen Buddhist *koan* paradoxes. These statements seek to deliver a person from rationality as a precondition to spiritual enlightenment. <u>Biblical paradox presumes rationality.</u>

This essay looks at one of the great Bible paradoxes, which is: EXALTATION THROUGH HUMILITY

The Bible describes humility as meekness, lowliness and absence of self. The Greek word translated "humility" in Colossians 3:12 and elsewhere literally means "lowliness of mind," so we see that humility is a heart attitude, not merely an outward demeanor. One may put on an outward show of humility but still have a heart full of pride and arrogance. Jesus said that those who are "poor in spirit" would have the kingdom of heaven. (Matthew 5:3) Being poor in spirit means to admit an absolute bankruptcy of spiritual worth before holy God. This is necessary before a person can come to faith in Christ and inherit eternal life.

When we come to Christ, we must come in humility. We acknowledge that we are spiritual paupers and beggars who come with nothing to offer Him but our sin and our need for salvation. We recognize our lack of merit and our complete inability to save ourselves. We accept the grace and mercy that God offers to us with humble gratitude and commit our lives to Him. We "die to self" so that we can live as new creations in Christ (2 Corinthians 5:17). We never forget that He has exchanged our worthlessness for His infinite worth, our sin for His righteousness, and the life we now live, we live by faith in the Son of God who loved us and gave Himself for us (Galatians 2:20). This is true humility.

Biblical humility is not only necessary to enter the kingdom, it is also necessary to be great in the kingdom. Matthew 20:26-28 says, "Not so with you. Instead, whoever wants to become great among you must be your servant, and whoever wants to be first must be your slave—just as the Son of Man did not come to be served, but to serve, and to give His life as a ransom for many." Just as our Lord did not come to be served, but to serve, so must we commit ourselves to serving others in lowliness of mind.

Philippians 2 addresses humility in the Christian life and the outcome of having this selfless attitude. Philippians 2:3 says, "Do nothing out of selfish ambition or vain conceit. Rather, in humility value others above yourselves, not looking to your own interests but each of you to the interests of the others." This attitude precludes selfish ambition, conceit, and the strife that comes with when a person is full of pride. When we are truly humble we do not need to defend ourselves when falsely accused or unjustly treated. We defend and stand for the truth of the gospel, not our own ego or reputation. Our sufficiency is found in Christ and the example He gives us to follow.

Philippians 2:5-8 says, "In your relationships with one another, have the same mindset as Christ Jesus: Who, being in very nature God, did not consider equality with God something to be used to His own advantage; rather, He made Himself nothing by taking the very nature of a servant, being made in human likeness. And being found in appearance as a man, He humbled Himself by becoming obedient to death— even death on a cross!" Jesus was not ashamed to humble Himself as a servant, even to a humiliating and agonizing death on the cross. In His humility, He was always obedient to the Father. We too should be humble Christians willing to put aside all selfishness and submit in obedience to God and to His Word.

The conventional wisdom of this world says in order to be exalted and rise to the top a person cannot put others first. People must look out for themselves to be successful. Remember the phrase "Looking out for #1"? Thus, the idea that a person gets exalted by being humble and putting the needs of others first contradicts this philosophy. On its surface, this appears to be a paradox because it challenges the presuppositions of success according to this world. But the wisdom of God does not conform to this world and as Christians neither should we. Again, we must look at the model our Lord Jesus gave us to follow. What was the result of Jesus' humility and servitude?

Philippians 2:9-11 says, "Therefore God exalted Him to the highest place and gave Him the name that is above every name, that at the name of Jesus every knee should bow, in heaven and on earth and under the earth, and every tongue acknowledge that Jesus Christ is Lord, to the glory of God the Father." By humbling Himself more than we can imagine, our Lord Jesus Christ saved us by conquering sin and death once and for all and established His position as the most exalted name in all the heavens and the earth! Jesus is the King of Kings and the Lord of

Lords and the day is coming when every knee will bow and every tongue confess this awesome truth! Amen!

God has also promised to exalt those who are humble and to humble those who are proud. Luke 14:11 says, "For all those who exalt themselves will be humbled, and those who humble themselves will be exalted." And James 4:10 says, "Humble yourselves before the Lord, and He will lift you up." God has never been pleased with the proud, boastful and over-confident. We know that Lucifer in his prideful madness was cast out of heaven and became Satan because he tried to exalt himself to be like God. The Most High God sees to it that all who attempt to be exalted by their own effort will fall.

The truly humble glory in the grace of God and in the cross, not in self-righteousness. As stated earlier, this humble recognition of our sinfulness and lack of merit before God brings about a heart ready to receive God's grace. 2 Corinthians 7:10 says, "Godly sorrow brings repentance that leads to salvation and leaves no regret, but worldly sorrow brings death." Fellow Christian, we look forward to spending eternity with God and He has given us the Holy Spirit as a deposit, a guarantee that we belong to Him.

Romans 8:16-17 says, "The Spirit himself testifies with our spirit that we are God's children. Now if we are children, then we are heirs—heirs of God and co-heirs with Christ, if indeed we share in His sufferings in order that we may also share in His glory." What greater exaltation could we ask for than to be forgiven for our trespasses and receive salvation by grace through faith? What greater exaltation could we receive than to be co-heirs with Christ and be a part of His eternal kingdom? May God fill you with joy as you ponder these wonderful truths! May God bless you all!

FOCUS QUESTIONS

What is a paradox?

What does humility mean in the Bible? Give examples.

How does God exalt the humble?

Once Saved Always Saved? Part 1

I have heard the gospel message and believed. I have admitted that I am a sinner in need of forgiveness. I have humbly come to God with a repentant attitude, sincerely sorry for my sins and eager to change my life. I have prayed to God in the name of Jesus Christ, verbally confessing that I believe Jesus is the Son of God and that He died for my sins and rose again from the dead. I have accepted what Christ has done for me on the cross. I have asked Him into my heart to be Lord of my life and expressed my desire to live for him.

Am I now saved from death and eternal punishment in hell? Am I now a child of God with the inheritance of heaven awaiting me? What must I still do to keep my salvation? Am I free to live however I want? How can I be sure of my salvation? If I commit a sin am I in danger of losing my salvation? Now that I am saved does God expect me to never sin again? These are questions that I and many other Christians ask themselves, and rightfully so. We all want to know that we have made the right decision and done what is required of us. In this series of posts we will look at scripture and answer these questions concerning our salvation. Today in part one we will answer the first three questions.

Let's begin by pointing out that a person is not born into this world as a Christian. In other words, it is not passed on to us from our parents. Neither does a person become a Christian by joining a church or completing a course of study. Many people believe water baptism makes a person a Christian, but this is not so. Baptism is a command Jesus gave to His followers to do as a public witness that they have committed to living for Him. Therefore, it is an important ceremony to complete out of obedience to our Lord Jesus, but it is not the source of our salvation.

Becoming a Christian is an individual decision a person makes for themselves. It is the choice to accept the gospel message of Jesus Christ as described in the opening paragraph. A person must hear the gospel message and believe it. They must humble themselves and admit they are sinners who have broken God's law and are in need of forgiveness. They must have a repentant attitude, which means having a genuine sorrow for their sins and a desire to change their life. They must believe Jesus is who he claimed to be, the Son of God who died to pay for their sin and rose again from the dead. Finally, they must invite Christ into their heart to be Lord of their lives.

When a person takes these steps many remarkable things happen! Let's look at a few passages which describe to us the benefits of our placing our trust in Jesus Christ. Romans 10:9-10 says, "If you confess with your mouth Jesus is Lord and believe in your heart that God raised Him from the dead, you will be saved. For it is with your heart that you believe and are justified, and it is with your mouth that you profess your faith and are saved." And Romans 8:1-2 says, "Therefore, there is now no condemnation for those who are in Christ Jesus, because through Christ Jesus the law of the Spirit who gives life has set you free from the law of sin and death." Also, John 3:16 says, "For God so loved the world that he gave his one and only Son, that whoever believes in him shall not perish but have eternal life."

These passages tell us that those who believe and take the step of accepting Christ as their Lord are saved! They are set free from the law of sin and death. They will not perish, which is referring to spiritual death apart from God, instead they will receive eternal life! They have received salvation and no longer under condemnation, which means they are not destined to be separated from God for all eternity in that terrible place called hell. Therefore, if I have also taken these steps of faith, am I now saved from death and eternal punishment in hell? My answer to this, our first question, is YES! Praise God for this! This is good news!

Let's continue with more scripture.

John 1:12 says, "Yet, to all who did receive Him, to those who believed in His name, He gave the right to become children of God." And Galatians 4:6-7 says, "Because you are his sons, God sent the Spirit of his Son into our hearts, the Spirit who calls out, 'Abba, Father.' So you are no longer a slave, but God's child; and since you are his child, God has made you also an heir." Also, Colossians 1:13-14 says, "For He has rescued us from the kingdom of darkness and brought us into the kingdom of the Son He loves, in whom we have redemption, the forgiveness of sins."

Another benefit of receiving Christ as my Savior is I am now a child of God. Jesus redeemed me, that is to say He bought me back, paying the price for me with His precious blood on the cross! I have been rescued from the kingdom of darkness and I now have an inheritance awaiting me, a place in the kingdom of my Lord Jesus Christ! Therefore, regarding the second question "Am I now a child of God with the inheritance of heaven awaiting me?" The answer is YES!

Wow! That is something to celebrate and to look forward to! The Apostle Paul wrote "I consider that our present sufferings are not worth comparing with the glory that will be revealed in us." (Romans 8:18) No matter what trials or troubles I must endure now, I know that my destiny is to be with my Lord in His kingdom, a place of awesome wonder beyond my ability to imagine!

Now let us answer the third question, which is "What must I still do to keep my salvation?

Ephesians 1:13-14 says, "And you also were included in Christ when you heard the message of truth, the gospel of your salvation. When you believed, you were marked in Him with a seal, the promised Holy Spirit, who is a deposit guaranteeing our inheritance until the redemption of those who are God's possession—to the praise of His glory." And 1 Peter 1:3-5 says, "Praise be to the God and Father of our Lord Jesus Christ! In His great mercy He has given us new birth into a living hope through the resurrection of Jesus Christ from the dead, and into an inheritance that can never perish, spoil or fade. This inheritance is kept in heaven for you, who through faith are shielded by God's power until the coming of the salvation that is ready to be revealed in the last time."

When I believed and placed my faith in Jesus Christ, not only did I become a child of God, I also received the Holy Spirit as a deposit, a guarantee that I belong to God! My inheritance in heaven is assured by God Himself! In fact, it is kept in heaven for me, protected and safe from perishing, spoiling or fading away! Can you think of a safer place to keep your inheritance than in heaven with God? Can you think of a more reliable guarantee than one issued by God Himself? I can't! And there are several other scriptures which reference the protection of our salvation, such as John 6:37-40, Romans 8:38-39, and John 10:27-29. Therefore, in regards to the question "What must I do to keep my salvation?" my answer is nothing! It is not up to me to protect it! Thank God for this! If it was up to you and me to watch over and keep our salvation, we would be in big trouble! Hallelujah and praise God for His rich grace and mercy!

Does this mean I am free to live however I want? In our next post we will answer this question and the remaining questions: How can I be sure of my salvation? If I commit a sin am I in danger of losing my salvation? Now that I am saved does God expect me to never sin again? Thank you for reading this and may God bless you all!

FOCUS QUESTIONS

How does a person become a Christian?

What are benefits we receive when we become a Christian?

Where is my salvation kept and who protects it?

Once Saved Always Saved? Part 2

In part one we learned that when you and I became a Christian, we were saved from death and eternal punishment in hell. We have been rescued from the kingdom of darkness and now have an inheritance awaiting us in the kingdom of our Lord Jesus Christ. Not only did we become children of God, we also received the Holy Spirit as a deposit, a guarantee that we belong to God. And our inheritance in heaven is assured by God Himself. In fact, it is kept in heaven for us, protected and safe from perishing, spoiling or fading away.

There are four more questions I would like to address regarding our salvation. As a Christian am I free to live however I want? If I commit a sin am I in danger of losing my salvation? Now that I am saved does God expect me to never sin again? How can I be sure of my salvation? Today we will focus on the first question, "As a Christian am I free to live however I want?" Our answer to this will overlap with the answers to the other questions, but we will revisit them again and wrap up them up more completely next time.

Let's begin by again pointing out that as people you and I are habitual sinners who by our very nature are opposed to God. Each one of us sins on a daily basis. Let's be honest with ourselves, if our thoughts were broadcast on the evening news for all to see and hear, then the news would be even more disturbing than it is now! We can't help ourselves from sinning. That is the point of the gospel message. Jesus came to save us because we are incapable of saving ourselves!

The apostle Paul wrote about this in Romans 6:21-25, which says, "So I find this law at work: Although I want to do good, evil is right there with me. For in my inner being I delight in God's law; but I see another law at work in me, waging war against the law of my mind and making me a prisoner of the law of sin at work within me. What a wretched man I am! Who will rescue me from this body that is subject to death? Thanks be to God, who delivers me through Jesus Christ our Lord! So then, I myself in my mind am a slave to God's law, but in my sinful nature a slave to the law of sin."

It is difficult to imagine a more dedicated Christian who performed more works for the Kingdom of God than Paul. He started several churches all over the Mediterranean and endured incredible hardships as a missionary for Jesus Christ, including imprisonment and a martyr's death. Yet, even Paul struggled with the sin nature of his flesh. Is this to say Paul did not love the Lord? Of course not! Is this to say Paul was a hypocrite because he sinned? No way! A hypocrite is someone who pretends to be virtuous when people are watching, to receive the praise of men, but inwardly do not delight in God's law. Paul was not like this and neither are you and me who have sincerely accepted Christ as our savior.

The point Paul makes is that even though we as Christians delight in God's law, we still must grapple with our bodies, that is our flesh, which desires to sin. This is where the Holy Spirit becomes so critical for us as Christians. Not only are we sealed with the Spirit when we are saved, but God gives us the Spirit to provide the power we need to live for Him and overcome our fleshly desires. Galatians 5:16-18 says, "So I say, walk by the Spirit, and you will not gratify the desires of the flesh. For the flesh desires what is contrary to the Spirit, and the Spirit what is contrary to the flesh. They are in conflict with each other, so that you are not to do whatever we want. But if you are led by the Spirit, you are not under the law."

There is our answer! You and I ARE NOT TO DO WHATEVER WE WANT! Our flesh wants to do evil. Instead, you and I are to be led by the Spirit, not by our flesh. Does this mean we will never sin again? Of course not! That is absurd! Abraham, Isaac, Jacob, Moses, King David, King Solomon, Peter, Paul and all believers still sinned! What it means is that our lives should not be characterized by sin, and if we submit ourselves to the workings of the Holy Spirit, we can overcome the habitual sins that plague us. 2 Timothy 1:7 says, "For the Spirit God gave us does not make us timid, but gives us power, love and self-discipline." And Jesus said, ""Whoever wants to be my disciple must deny themselves and take up their cross daily and follow me." (Luke 9:23)

You and I as Christians have been set free from the condemnation of sin, but we should not abuse our freedom to live a life of sin. Instead, we are called to surrender our minds and bodies to God and allow His Holy Spirit to work in us and through us. Over time this mindset, along with prayer and reading of God's word, conforms us more and more into the image of Jesus and less and less to our old selves. And we begin to produce the fruits of the Spirit, such as love, joy, peace, patience, kindness, goodness, faithfulness, gentleness, and self-control. (Galatians 5:22-23)

There are some Christians who maintain we must do good works in order to be saved. I agree that we should do good works. We do them to bring glory to God and to share His love with others, but works are not the source of our salvation! Read the entire book of Galatians. In it Paul writes to counter the claims of the legalistic Judaizers (Jewish Christians) who were telling the Galatian believers that they must be circumcised and keep the Law of Moses in order to be saved. This teaching is heresy because it adds to the gospel message a legal requirement that is dependent upon works rather than on faith and God's grace!

Paul writes "I am astonished that you are so quickly deserting the one who called you to live in the grace of Christ and are turning to a different gospel— which is really no gospel at all. Evidently some people are throwing you into confusion and are trying to pervert the gospel of Christ." (Galatians 1:6-7) Later Paul writes "Clearly no one who relies on the law is justified before God, because "THE RIGHTEOUS WILL LIVE BY FAITH." (Galatians 3:11)

There we read what is a key principle of the gospel message. THE RIGHTEOUS WILL LIVE BY FAITH! We will continue this point in our next post. God bless you all!

FOCUS QUESTIONS

Do Christians never sin?

How can we overcome habitual sin and live our lives for God?

Once Saved Always Saved? Part 3

We finished our last post with this verse: "Clearly no one who relies on the law is justified before God, because "THE RIGHTEOUS WILL LIVE BY FAITH." (Galatians 3:11) There are many scriptures which teach us that a person must have faith in order to receive their salvation. But let us first make a distinction between having a saving type of faith and simply believing. For instance, a person may believe there is a God, but not the God who has revealed Himself to us in the bible. Or a person may accept the God who revealed himself to us in the Old Testament, but reject Jesus as the Son of God, the Messiah who has provided for our salvation. Others accept Jesus as the Son of God but then add further requirements to the gospel, mixing legalistic practices (works) in an attempt to reach a righteous standing with God.

These types of believing reject the gospel message, a message which takes away the requirements of you and me perfectly keeping the law and replaces it with the finished work of our Lord Jesus. Jesus fulfilled the law and all righteousness and became our sacrifice on the cross, and His righteousness is credited to us when we place our trust in Him as our Savior. This is the meaning of grace: God's favor towards us which is unearned and undeserved.

Let's begin by looking at scriptures which support the idea that **salvation is a GIFT from God by His GRACE, and is to be received by FAITH.**

"For in the gospel the righteousness of God is revealed—a righteousness that is by FAITH from first to last, just as it is written: "The righteous will live by FAITH." Romans 1:17

"For it is by GRACE you have been saved, through FAITH—and this is not from yourselves, it is the GIFT of God— NOT BY WORKS, so that no one can boast." Ephesians 2:8-9

"Therefore, since we have been justified through FAITH, we have peace with God through our Lord Jesus Christ, through whom we have gained access by FAITH into this GRACE in which we now stand." Romans 5:1-2

"For if, by the trespass of the one man, death reigned through that one man, how much more will those who receive God's abundant provision of GRACE and of the GIFT of righteousness reign in life through the one man, Jesus Christ!" Romans 5:17

"For the wages of sin is death, but the GIFT of God is eternal life in Christ Jesus our Lord." Romans 6:23

Clearly the bible teaches salvation is not something we can earn. So what about works? What is their value? As a Christian, should I be doing good works? Absolutely! Remember, in our previous post we learned that as a Christian, you and I are not to do whatever we want. Instead, we are called to surrender our minds and bodies to God and allow His Holy Spirit to work in us and through us. Our flesh desires to sin, but we are to deny ourselves and instead be led by the Holy Spirit. (Galatians 5:16-18) Our Lord expects us to produce fruit of the Spirit, bringing blessing to ourselves and others around us.

Now let's look at scriptures which show that works are evidence of faith, and faith without works is dead.

James 2:14-20 says, "What good is it, my brothers and sisters, if someone claims to have faith but has no deeds? Can such faith save them? Suppose a brother or a sister is without clothes and daily food. If one of you says to them, "Go in peace; keep warm and well fed," but does nothing about their physical needs, what good is it? In the same way, faith by itself, if it is not accompanied by action, is dead. But someone will say, "You have faith; I have deeds."Show me your faith without deeds, and I will show you my faith by my deeds. You believe that there is one God. Good! Even the demons believe that—and shudder. You foolish person, do you want evidence that faith without deeds is useless?"

In this passage James is not referring to a genuine saving faith that you and I have through placing our trust in Christ as our Savior. Instead, he is writing about a person having an intellectual knowledge of truth that is dead (v.17), demonic (v.19) and useless (v.20). James is also not saying that a person is saved by works and not by genuine faith. Rather, he is saying, to use Martin Luther's words, that "people are justified by faith alone, but not by a faith that is alone."

James further writes, "Was not our father Abraham considered righteous for what he did when he offered his son Isaac on the altar? You see that his faith and his actions were working together, and his faith was made complete by what he did. And the scripture was fulfilled that says, "Abraham believed God, and it was credited to him as righteousness," and he was called God's friend. You see that a person is considered righteous by what they do and not by faith alone." (James 2:21-24)

If we read the last verse without taking into account the context of the entire passage it would appear that James is contradicting Paul's writings that people are saved by faith and not by works. But James is simply reinforcing his point that righteous action is evidence of genuine faith. If we look back to Genesis 15:6 we will see that Abraham's faith was credited to him as righteousness by God BEFORE Abraham offered up his son Isaac on the altar (Genesis 22).

Now let's go back to Ephesians 2:8-9 which says, "For it is by GRACE you have been saved, through FAITH—and this is not from yourselves, it is the GIFT of God— NOT BY WORKS, so that no one can boast." The next verse says, "For we are God's workmanship, created in Christ Jesus to do good works, which God prepared in advance for us to do." (Ephesians 2:10) Again, this shows the same order James wrote about with Abraham. Salvation is by faith and by God's grace, and then it is followed (evidenced) by doing good works which God has planned we should do.

Again, the context of James' message to us believers is that faith and works go together, and you can't have one without the other, but righteousness by faith is not contradicted and made false. Remember that all scripture is God-breathed (2 Timothy 3:16), that is to say it comes from the mind of God and was communicated to the writers of the bible through the Holy Spirit. Also, we know that it is impossible for God to lie (Titus 1:2) or contradict Himself. Therefore, it is important not to read single verses or passages to support our beliefs, but to take scripture in its totality. We must consider everything God has given us and weigh it together with the whole bible message.

Thank you for reading this and may God grow your faith to stand firm in His truth. Until next time may God richly bless you!

FOCUS QUESTIONS

Is it possible to believe in God and not be saved? Explain.

What role do good works have in the Christian life?

Once Saved Always Saved? Part 4

This post is a review of the main points from parts 1-3. I encourage each of us to prayerfully read through the scripture references and allow the Holy Spirit to do His work as our Counselor.

First we outlined the steps to salvation:

A person must hear the gospel message and believe it. (Ephesians 1:13) They must humble themselves and admit they are sinners who have broken God's law and are in need of forgiveness. (Romans 3:10) (Romans 3:23) (Proverbs 22:4) They must have a repentant attitude, which means having a genuine sorrow for their sins and a desire to change their life. (Mark 1:15) (Matthew 3:2) They must believe Jesus is who He claimed to be, the Son of God who died to pay for their sin and rose again from the dead. (Romans 10:9-10)(Romans 1:16) Finally, they must invite Christ into their heart to be Lord of their lives. (John 1:12)

Then we read scripture which taught us that when we believed and placed our faith in Jesus Christ as our Savior, not only do we become children of God, we also receive the Holy Spirit as a deposit, a guarantee that we belong to God! Our inheritance in heaven is assured by God Himself! In fact, it is kept in heaven for us, protected and safe from perishing, spoiling or fading away! (Ephesians 1:13-14) and (1 Peter 1:3-5) We also referenced other scriptures which support the fact that our salvation is secure, held firmly in the hand of our heavenly Father. (John 6:37-40, Romans 8:38-39, and John 10:27-29)

Knowing our salvation is secure then raises the question "As a Christian am I free to live however I want?" The answer is NO! We read a passage in Romans in which Paul described his and our condition as wretched sinners who need rescuing from our bodies which are subject to death. It says, "So I find this law at work: Although I want to do good, evil is right there with me. For in my inner being I delight in God's law; but I see another law at work in me, waging war against the law of my mind and making me a prisoner of the law of sin at work within me. What a wretched man I am! Who will rescue me from this body that is subject to death? Thanks be to God, who delivers me through Jesus Christ our Lord! So then, I myself in my mind am a slave to God's law, but in my sinful nature a slave to the law of sin." (Romans 6:21-25)

The point Paul makes is that even though we as Christians delight in God's law, we still must grapple with our bodies, that is our flesh, which desires to sin. This is where the Holy Spirit becomes so critical for us as Christians. Not only are we sealed with the Spirit when we are saved, but God gives us the Spirit to provide the power we need to live for Him and overcome our fleshly desires. Galatians 5:16-18 says, "So I say, walk by the Spirit, and you will not gratify the desires of the flesh. For the flesh desires what is contrary to the Spirit, and the Spirit what is contrary to the flesh. They are in conflict with each other, so that <u>you are not to do whatever we want. But if you are led by the Spirit, you are not under the law." Surrendering our will to the Holy Spirit is the key to living each day for God.</u>

Next, we addressed the issue of doing good works and their role in our salvation. There are many people who maintain we must do good works in order to be saved. This is nothing new to the church. Paul had to address the same issue with the Galatian Christians. Paul wrote "I am astonished that you are so quickly deserting the one who called you to live in the grace of Christ and are turning to a different gospel— which is really no gospel at all. Evidently some people are throwing you into confusion and are trying to pervert the gospel of Christ." (Galatians 1:6-7) Paul also wrote "Clearly no one who relies on the law is justified before God, because "THE RIGHTEOUS WILL LIVE BY FAITH." (Galatians 3:11)

The central theme of the entire book of Galatians is Paul correcting the heretical teachings of the Judaizers (Jewish Christians) who were telling the Galatian believers they must be circumcised and keep the Law of Moses in order to be saved. This teaching is heresy because it adds to the gospel message a legal requirement that is dependent upon works rather than on faith and God's grace! We can agree that Christians should do good works, in order to bring glory to God and to share His love with others, but God's word tells us works are not the source of our salvation!

This led us to read scriptures which support the idea that **salvation is a GIFT from God by His GRACE, and is to be received by FAITH.** There are many passages which teach us these truths but we only had time to look at Romans 1:17, Ephesians 2:8-9, Romans 5:1-2, Romans 5:17, and Romans 6:23.

Next, we read James 2:14-24. We learned in this passage James is not referring to a genuine saving faith that you and I have through placing our trust in Christ as our Savior. Instead, he is writing about a person having an intellectual knowledge of truth that is dead (v.17), demonic (v.19) and useless (v.20). In verse 24 we read "You see that a person is considered righteous by what they do and not by faith alone." If we read this verse without taking into account the context of the entire passage it would appear that James is contradicting Paul's writings that people are saved by faith and not by works. He is not, rather he is saying, to use Martin Luther's words, that "people are justified by faith alone, but not by a faith that is alone."

The main idea of this passage is <u>righteous action is evidence of genuine faith.</u> If we look back to Genesis 15:6 we will see that Abraham's faith was credited to him as righteousness by God BEFORE Abraham offered up his son Isaac on the altar. (Genesis 22) The context of James' message to believers is that faith and works go together, but righteousness by faith is not contradicted and made false. Works should naturally follow our salvation by faith, just as Abraham's faith led to his actions of obeying God.

We must remember that all scripture is God-breathed (2 Timothy 3:16), that is to say it comes from the mind of God and was communicated to the writers of the bible through the Holy Spirit. Also, we know that it is impossible for God to lie (Titus 1:2) or contradict Himself. Therefore, it is important not to read single verses or passages to support our beliefs, but to take scripture in its totality. <u>We must consider everything God has given us and weigh it together with the whole bible message.</u> Thank you for reading this and may God bless you all!

FOCUS QUESTIONS

Where is our salvation kept and who protects it?

What is the key for living our lives for God?

What role do good works have in the Christian life?

Once Saved Always Saved? Part 5

In this our final post we will finish by addressing the following questions: If I commit a sin am I in danger of losing my salvation? Now that I am saved does God expect me to never sin again? How can I be sure of my salvation? We will begin with a passage written by the apostle John.

"If we claim to be without sin, we deceive ourselves and the truth is not in us. If we confess our sins, he is faithful and just and will forgive us our sins and purify us from all unrighteousness. If we claim we have not sinned, we make him out to be a liar and his word is not in us." (1 John 1:8-10) Also, 1 John 2:1-2 says, "My dear children, I write this to you so that you will not sin. But if anybody does sin, we have an advocate with the Father—Jesus Christ, the Righteous One. He is the atoning sacrifice for our sins, and not only for ours but also for the sins of the whole world."

When John wrote his letter Christianity had been around about 50 years. The main problem confronting the church at this time was declining commitment: many believers were conforming to the world's standards, failing to stand up for Christ and compromising their faith. False teachers were plentiful and they were accelerating the church's downward slide away from the Christian faith.

John wrote his letter to put believers back on track, to show the difference between light and darkness (truth and error), and to encourage the church to grow in genuine love for God and for one another. He also wrote to assure true believers that they possessed eternal life and to help them know their faith was genuine, so that they could enjoy the benefits of being God's children. This doesn't sound much different than today's church does it?

Jesus' sacrifice paid the penalty for ALL SIN, therefore when you and I are born again all our sins are forgiven, PAST, PRESENT, and FUTURE. He gives us the Holy Spirit to help us live for Him, to combat the fleshly desires that remain in our earthly bodies. We are no longer under the curse of the law but we are now under His grace. As we have seen already, this does not give us license to sin! Rather, it frees us to live for God by producing the fruits of the Holy Spirit. (Galatians 5:22-23) Thus, as Christians, our lifestyles should be characterized by these fruits, especially love, and not by habitual sin.

However, not one of us are perfect, we will make mistakes and commit sin. When we do we must be humble enough to admit it and come to God with remorse, confessing it and seeking His forgiveness. Our confession eases our conscience and lightens our cares, freeing us to enjoy fellowship with our Lord. Some Christians feel so guilty they do not want to approach God in confession. Others believe if they die with unconfessed sin, they will lose their salvation. This is not so! God wants to forgive your sins! He allowed His beloved Son to die so He could offer us forgiveness! And we have already seen our relationship with God through Jesus Christ is secure. (Ephesians 1:13-14) (1 Peter 1:3-5)

Dear Christian, Satan is your accuser, and he is also "the accuser of our brothers and sisters, who accuses them before our God day and night…" (Revelation 12:10) John reminds us that Christ is our advocate, He is our defense attorney who pleads our case to the Father, a case He has already had dismissed by His atoning sacrifice on the cross! Hallelujah for this! John reminds us that when we do sin we are breaking fellowship with our heavenly Father, not forfeiting our salvation. We must confess our sins to the Father in the name of our Lord Jesus Christ and when we do the Father forgives us and purifies us from all unrighteousness. We are God's children. We may wander away from our faith but He never stops loving us.

Many of us are parents. We love our children unconditionally and they never stop being our children despite their disobedience. If we who are sinners by nature love our children like this, how much more will our heavenly Father continue to love us and show us mercy, even when we make poor choices and are disobedient. We discipline our children for their disobedience because we love them and want only the best for them. Our heavenly Father disciplines us too and our disobedience has consequences, but we can never undo His love and endless grace which is beyond all comprehension! Amen to this!

"Here is a trustworthy saying that deserves full acceptance: Christ Jesus came into the world to save sinners—of whom I am the worst. But for that very reason I was shown mercy so that in me, the worst of sinners, Christ Jesus might display His immense patience as an example for those who would believe in Him and receive eternal life." (1 Timothy 1:15-16)

These words were written by Paul under the inspiration of the Holy Spirit. We read that Paul considers himself the worst of sinners, yet God's mercy and immense patience triumphs over all! And Paul is not just referring to the sins he committed before he came to know Jesus Christ. He also writes about the struggles he (and us) face each day with the flesh. Let us look at this passage in Romans one more time:

"So I find this law at work: Although I want to do good, evil is right there with me. For in my inner being I delight in God's law; but I see another law at work in me, waging war against the law of my mind and making me a prisoner of the law of sin at work within me. What a wretched man I am! Who will rescue me from this body that is subject to death? Thanks be to God, who delivers me through Jesus Christ our Lord! So then, I myself in my mind am a slave to God's law, but in my sinful nature a slave to the law of sin." (Romans 6:21-25)

After years of studying God's word, serving and following after my Lord and Savior Jesus Christ, the more I realize how spiritually bankrupt I am. I am a sinner! Nothing good dwells within me!

The process of sanctification, becoming more and more like Jesus and less and less like my old self, teaches me this. I have grown to understand that I must get up each and every day and submit myself to the leading of the Holy Spirit, because I am incapable of keeping God's law on my own. That is why a dedicated missionary like Paul, who accomplished so much for God's kingdom, can write about his struggles with sin.

If you have done any self-reflection in your own life then you know this is true. When someone tells me that if I commit a sin I am in danger of losing my salvation, then I say not one of us is secure! God despises all sin, no matter how insignificant it may seem to us. He considers hateful feelings the same as murder and lust the same as adultery. He requires perfection and not one of us can live up to that! Only Christ could and did! Hallelujah!

But therein lies the key to answer these questions: **none of it depends on us!** **ALL OF IT DEPENDS ON GOD AND HIS PROMISES. SALVATION IS A GIFT FROM GOD AND WE CANNOT DO ANYTHING TO EARN IT. JESUS CHRIST DID IT ALL!**

Therefore, if I commit a sin am I in danger of losing my salvation? No. Jesus Christ is the author of my salvation and He keeps it for me. Now that I am saved does God expect me to never sin again? Yes. But when I do, I do not lose my salvation. My fellowship with Him is disrupted and once I confess my sin He is faithful to forgive me and purify me from all unrighteousness. How can I be sure of my salvation? I can be sure because my salvation is not dependent upon me, it is dependent on Jesus. He is my Redeemer! He is my King! He is my God! He is everything! Amen!

FOCUS QUESTIONS

What does it mean that Jesus is our Advocate?

How is the parent/child relationship a picture of our relationship with God?

Imputed Righteousness

In His Sermon on the Mount, Jesus uttered these words: "You therefore must be perfect, as your heavenly Father is perfect" (Matthew 5:48). This comes at the end of the section of the sermon where Jesus corrects His listeners' misunderstanding of the Law.

In Matthew 5:20, Jesus says that, if His hearers want to enter into the kingdom of heaven, their righteousness must exceed that of the Pharisees, who were the experts in the Law. Then, in Matthew 5:21–48, Jesus proceeds to radically redefine the law from mere outward conformity, which characterized the "righteousness" of the Pharisees, to an obedience of both outward and inward conformity. Jesus would say, "You have heard it said, but I say unto you" in order to differentiate between the way people had heard the law taught by the religious elite to the way He was teaching it.

Jesus taught that obeying the law is more than simply abstaining from killing, committing adultery, and breaking oaths. It's also not getting angry with your brother, which God considers the same as murder (v.22). It is not lusting in your heart, which God considers the same as adultery (v.28). At the end of all this, we learn that God's standard for righteousness is perfection, in both our actions and our thoughts!
Our natural response to this expectation is "But I can't be perfect!", which is absolutely true.

Later in Matthew's Gospel, Jesus summarizes the Law of God with two commandments: Love the Lord your God with all your heart, soul, mind, and strength and love your neighbor as yourself (Matthew 22:37–40). This is certainly an admirable goal, but has anyone ever loved the Lord with all their heart, soul, mind, and strength and their neighbor as themselves? Everything we do, say, and think has to be done, said, and thought from love for God and love for neighbor. If we are completely honest with ourselves, we have to admit that we have never achieved this level of spirituality. No one can.

The truth of the matter is that, on our own and by our own efforts, we can't possibly be perfect as our heavenly Father is perfect. We can't love God with all our heart, soul, mind, and strength. We can't love our neighbors as ourselves. You see, we have a problem and it's called sin. We are born with it and we cannot overcome it on our own. Sin radically affects us to our core. Sin affects what we do, say, and think. In other words, it taints everything about us. Therefore, no matter how good we try to be, we can never meet God's standard of perfection. This is where many religions fall short by teaching people to do works in order to get right with God. The bible says that "...all our righteous acts are like filthy rags" (Isaiah 64:6).

So what are we to do? If we can't live up to God's standard for righteousness, then how can anyone make it to heaven? The answer: It is only through Jesus. (John 14:6) Jesus' mission was not only to pay the penalty for our sin by dying on the cross. It was also to live a life of perfect righteousness in full obedience to the law of God in thought, word, and deed. Thus, Jesus lived the perfect life you and I are not able to live.

Theologians refer to this as the "active and passive obedience of Christ." Active obedience refers to Christ's life of sinless perfection. Passive obedience refers to Christ's submission to the crucifixion. He went willingly to the cross and allowed Himself to be crucified without resisting (Isaiah 53:7). His passive obedience pays our sin debt before God, but it is the active obedience that gives us the perfection God requires.

The apostle Paul wrote, "But now the righteousness of God has been manifested apart from the law, although the Law and the Prophets bear witness to it—the righteousness of God through faith in Jesus Christ for all who believe." (Romans 3:21–22) Through our faith in Christ, the righteousness of God is given to us. This is called "imputed" righteousness.

To impute something is to ascribe or attribute something to someone. When we place our faith in Christ, God ascribes the perfect righteousness of Christ to our account so that we become perfect in His sight. "For our sake He made him [Jesus] to be sin who knew no sin, so that in Him we might become the righteousness of God." (2 Corinthians 5:21)

Not only is Christ's righteousness imputed to us through faith, but our sin is imputed to Christ. That is how Christ paid our sin debt to God. He had no sin in Himself, but our sin is imputed to Him so, as He suffered on the cross, He suffered the just penalty that our sin deserves. That is why Paul can say, "I have been crucified with Christ. It is no longer I who live, but Christ who lives in me. And the life I now live in the flesh I live by faith in the Son of God, who loved me and gave Himself for me." (Galatians 2:20)

By having the righteousness of Christ imputed to us, we can be seen as sinless, as Jesus is sinless. It is not, therefore, our perfection, but His. This is known as justification. Fellow Christian, when God looks at us, He sees the holiness, perfection, and righteousness of Christ. Therefore, we can say with confidence, "I am sinless, as Jesus is sinless." Does this mean once we accept Christ as our Lord and Savior that you and I will never sin again? Unfortunately not.

When we are born again we receive the gift of the Holy Spirit, as a deposit and guarantee that we belong to God. (2 Corinthians 1:22, Ephesians 1:13-14) However, we still have the sin nature that we were born with. Colossians 3:5 says, "So put to death the sinful, earthly things lurking within you. Have nothing to do with sexual immorality, impurity, lust, and evil desires. Don't be greedy, for a greedy person is an idolater, worshiping the things of this world." We have both our sin nature and the nature of God living in us. This is why we are called to put to death the deeds of the flesh and surrender our bodies and minds to Christ, through the power of the Holy Spirit.

The Christian life is a daily struggle to die to ourselves. In other words, to live more and more like Jesus and less and less like our old ways, before we came to faith in Christ. This process is called sanctification and it is a life-long pursuit. Dear Christian, know that when we fail and we commit sin, we must confess our sin to the Father and He promises to forgive us and purify us from all unrighteousness. (1 John 1:9) We put it behind us and move forward, striving to grow in our faith and love. May God bless you all!

FOCUS QUESTIONS

How does Jesus' teaching of the law differ from the religious elite (Pharisees)?

Why are works not enough to earn righteousness for ourselves?

How does a person get the righteousness that God requires to enter heaven?

Is Hell for Real?

Fellow Christian, please be aware that the answer to this question is foundational to the accuracy, authenticity, and truth of the Bible. It is every bit as important as the truth that Jesus is the Messiah, that there is a heaven, and that there is a holy, righteous God who has made all things. For if hell is not real, then the bible cannot be trusted for being truthful about these or any other teachings. If we cannot say hell is real, then neither can we say God is real, heaven is real and that Jesus' death on the cross really saves!

For if hell is not real, then what did Jesus come to save us from? An everlasting non-existence? An eternal sleep with no pain, no punishment, no conscious regret for having lived an evil life in rebellion against a holy God? The idea that hell is not real is a lie and deception which emanates from the father of lies, Satan, in an attempt to make people comfortable with their sin and unmotivated to change their attitudes towards God. Why repent and come to God if there is no judgment for not doing so?

Many will say that to mention hell brings fear, and fear is wrong and should not be taught! Really? Should a child not be taught to fear walking into the middle of a busy street? Should a person be taught not to fear falling from high places? Fear is akin to respect. Should a person be taught not to fear (respect) God? Of course not! The bible clearly teaches from cover to cover that people are to fear God. Proverbs 1:7 says, "The fear of the Lord is the beginning of knowledge, but fools despise wisdom and instruction."

Only a fool would not fear walking into a busy street or falling from high places. Likewise, fools are not interested in being taught to fear God because they are not interested in being changed. They love their sin and they don't want to listen to any message of judgment for their actions. They do not fear (respect) God, nor His promise to judge sin! They have no internal motivation to alter their behavior according to what wisdom would dictate. Fools love foolishness, whereas the wise love being instructed in wisdom.

According to the Bible, hell is just as real as heaven. The Bible clearly and explicitly teaches that hell is a real place to which the wicked/unbelieving are sent after death. All people have sinned against God (Romans 3:23), and the just punishment for that sin is death (Romans 6:23). Since all of our sin is ultimately against God (Psalm 51:4) and God is an infinite and eternal being, the punishment for sin must also be infinite and eternal. Make no mistake, hell is the infinite and eternal death which we have earned because of our sin!

Our Lord and Savior warned of this coming judgment in Matthew 25:31-46, the parable of the sheep and goats. Remember, Jesus used parables to teach us about ACTUAL TRUTH. In this parable the sheep represent those who have placed their faith in Christ and the goats are those who have not. The Son of Man is Jesus Himself. In this story, Jesus is telling us of an ACTUAL JUDGMENT that will take place in the future, after the end of the seven-year tribulation. (Revelation 20:1-6)

The true believers, "sheep", have demonstrated their belief by producing good fruit, which naturally follows being saved by God's grace through faith. (Ephesians 2:8-10)(Matthew 7:16) The unbelievers, "goats", have not. While unbelievers can indeed perform acts of kindness and charity, their hearts are not right with God, and their actions are not for the right purpose – to honor and worship God.

The end result of our Lord's righteous judgment will be as follows: "Then He will say to those on his left, 'Depart from me, you who are cursed, into the eternal fire prepared for the devil and his angels." (Matthew 25:41) And verse 46 says, "Then they (goats) will go away into eternal punishment, but the righteous (sheep) into eternal life." Here we have Jesus in His own words warning us that punishment of the wicked in hell is just as everlasting and just as real as the life and bliss of the righteous in heaven.

Jesus did not say the unrighteous will go into eternal sleep, or into a temporary punishment. He did not say He will annihilate the unrighteous and they will cease to exist. These are false teachings which are not biblical truth. Rather, they have been added to scripture, or taken scripture out of context by the enemy (Satan) to trick people into believing that hell is not real.

There are many other scriptures which also describe the horrible reality of hell. Hell is described as an "unquenchable fire" (Matthew 3:12), "shame and everlasting contempt" (Daniel 12:2), a place where "the fire is not quenched" (Mark 9:44-49), a place of "torment" and "fire" (Luke 16:23-24), "everlasting destruction" (2 Thessalonians 1:9), a place where "the smoke of torment rises forever and ever" (Revelation 14:10-11).

Perhaps the most sobering and literal description is found in the book of Revelation. Similar to parables, this book is filled with symbolic imagery meant to teach ACTUAL TRUTH about ACTUAL EVENTS which have occurred or will occur in the future. Therefore, do not brush aside its contents as fictional or merely symbolic. Revelation 20 describes the judgment of Satan, an actual event which will take place after the millennium (1000 year) reign of Jesus Christ on earth.

Revelation 20:7-10 says, "When the thousand years are over, Satan will be released from his prison and will go out to deceive the nations in the four corners of the earth—Gog and Magog—and to gather them for battle. In number they are like the sand on the seashore. They marched across the breadth of the earth and surrounded the camp of God's people, the city He loves. But fire came down from heaven and devoured them. And the devil, who deceived them, was thrown into the lake of burning sulfur, where the beast and the false prophet had been thrown. They will be tormented day and night for ever and ever."

Satan knows his fate. He hates God and he hates people who are made in God's image. His only avenue of revenge against God is to destroy the only hope people have of being saved from the torment which awaits himself and his fallen angels. Satan knows the ultimate destiny of all unbelievers will be to join him in the lake of fire. (Revelation 20:15) Therefore, he tries to alter the message of the bible to diminish the reality of the coming judgment. He uses truth, such as God is love, to spin the lie that "a loving God would never send a person to hell."

He distorts the character of God just like he did in the garden when he deceived Eve. "Did God really say you must not eat from any tree in the garden?" Later he says, "You will not certainly die". On the issue of hell Satan says, "Did Jesus really teach there is a hell?" And he adds, "You will not go to hell. Hell is not real." Do not be deceived! HELL IS REAL! To say it is not diminishes the sacrifice Jesus endured to save us and makes Him out to be a liar. It also distorts the holy, righteous character of God who has promised to bring wrath and punishment against all unrighteousness.

Fellow Christian, we cannot comprehend the magnitude of God's grace, mercy, and love for us without recognizing the magnitude of His holiness, righteousness, and perfection. We cannot begin to understand the incredible sacrifice made by Jesus on the cross until we begin to understand the incredible weight of our sins which God placed upon His beloved Son! May God richly bless you all and fill you with the hope we have in Christ!

FOCUS QUESTIONS

How can having fear be a good thing?

What is the purpose of parables and symbolic imagery in the bible?

Who or what is the source of lies and deception, and for what purpose?

The Four Horsemen of the Apocalypse

The Tribulation refers to a seven-year period when the righteous judgments of God will be poured out on an unbelieving world. This is set to occur during the last days of Satan's reign as the god of this world. 2 Corinthians 4:4 says, "The god of this age (Satan) has blinded the minds of unbelievers, so that they cannot see the light of the gospel that displays the glory of Christ, who is the image of God."

The phrase "god of this age" (or "god of this world") indicates that Satan is the major influence on the ideals, opinions, goals, hopes and views of the majority of people. His influence also encompasses the world's philosophies, education, and commerce. The thoughts, ideas, speculations and false religions of the world are under his control and have their origin in his lies and deceptions. Thus, the Tribulation will come during the end times of history as we now know it.

The second half of this seven-year period is a time of particularly terrible suffering and is referred to as the Great Tribulation (Revelation 7:14). These judgments will be climaxed by the second coming of Jesus Christ in glory to the earth. Based upon world events and fulfillment of prophecies concerning the nation of Israel, it is the opinion of many Christians that we are very near this point in history. It is also the opinion of many Bible scholars that all Christians who are alive during these last days will be raptured (caught up with the LORD) from the earth just before the beginning of this Tribulation period.

The Four Horsemen of the Apocalypse are described in the book of Revelation, the last book of the New Testament. Chapter 6 tells of a "'book', or 'scroll', in God's right hand that is sealed with seven seals". The Lamb of God, or Lion of Judah, (Jesus Christ) opens the first four of the seven seals, which summons forth four beings that ride out on white, red, black, and pale horses. This is the beginning of the Tribulation. Although some interpretations differ, in most accounts, the four riders are seen as symbolizing Conquest, War, Famine, and Death, respectively. Let us examine each one.

The White Horse
"I watched as the Lamb opened the first of the seven seals. Then I heard one of the four living creatures say in a voice like thunder, "Come and see!" I looked, and there before me was a white horse! Its rider held a bow, and he was given a crown, and he rode out as a conqueror bent on conquest. (Revelation 6:1-2) The animal represents an unparalleled time of peace—a false peace that is short-lived. This first horseman likely refers to the Antichrist, a world leader who will deceive the nations into following him. (See Matthew 24:3-5) He will be given authority

over the entire world and will conquer all who oppose him. This antichrist is the false imitator of the true Christ, who will also return on a white horse. (Revelation 19:11-16)

The Red Horse
"When the Lamb opened the second seal, I heard the second living creature say, "Come and see!" Then another horse came out, a fiery red one. Its rider was given power to take peace from the earth and to make men slay each other. To him was given a large sword. (Revelation 6:3-4) The second horseman refers to terrible warfare that will break out in the end times. As horrible as this judgment is, it will be only the beginning pains of God's wrath! (Matthew 24:7-8)

The Black Horse
"When the Lamb opened the third seal, I heard the third living creature say, "Come and see!" I looked, and there before me was a black horse! Its rider was holding a pair of scales in his hand. Then I heard what sounded like a voice among the four living creatures, saying, "A quart of wheat for a day's wages, and three quarts of barley for a day's wages, and do not damage the oil and the wine!" (Revelation 6:5-6) The third horseman of the Apocalypse refers to a great famine that will take place, likely as a result of the wars from the second horseman. A day's wage will be barely enough to sustain one person. Many people in the world live in hunger right now, although we in America have been spared this type of suffering. But a time is coming when even the richest countries on earth are going to experience famine and scarcity.

The Pale Horse
"When the Lamb opened the fourth seal, I heard the voice of the fourth living creature say, "Come and see!" I looked and there before me was a pale horse! Its rider was named Death, and Hades was following close behind him. They were given power over a fourth of the earth to kill by sword, famine, and plague, and by the wild beasts of the earth." (Revelation 6:7-8) The fourth horseman of the Apocalypse is symbolic of death and devastation. It seems to be a combination of the previous horsemen. The fourth horseman of the Apocalypse will bring further warfare and terrible famines along with awful plagues and diseases. What is most amazing, or perhaps terrifying, is that the four horsemen of the Apocalypse are just "precursors" of even worse judgments that come later in the tribulation!

Fellow Christian, these prophecies of the coming Tribulation do not need to be a source of distress for us. We belong to the Lord Jesus Christ and nothing can change that! Jesus said, *"I give them eternal life, and they shall never perish; no one will snatch them out of my hand."* When we see and hear about the terrible events that take place each and every day, it serves to remind us of what is really important. Our Lord told us about the signs of the end times

(Matthew 24) so that we would be diligent in following the truth of His word and in living each day for Him. Let us all be bold in sharing the gospel and showing the love of Jesus to people around us. By doing so we may draw people to the hope found in Jesus that saves them from a world that is heading for death and destruction! May God bless you all!

FOCUS QUESTIONS

What is the Tribulation?

What does each horse represent?

The Rapture

"...For I am going away to prepare a place for you. And when I have gone and have prepared a place for you, I will come again and take you to Myself so that where I am, you also will be." (John 14:2-3) These words from our Lord Jesus were spoken shortly before His death on the cross. His disciples were troubled and fearful about the disturbing news that Jesus was soon going to leave them. But our Lord gave them comfort with the promise that one day they would be reunited with Him. These words also give you and I comfort knowing that our Lord is preparing a place for us to be with Him for all eternity and that one day He will return for us. Hallelujah!

It is true the word rapture is not found in the bible. Nevertheless, the bible teaches about an "end times" (eschatological) event where Jesus Christ will return to earth to gather His Church. Believers who have died and those who are "alive and remain shall be caught up together...in the clouds to meet the Lord in the air." (1 Thessalonians 4:16-17) The Greek word used in this passage for "caught up" is "harpadzo" meaning to remove, seize, or take away. The English word used to describe this biblical event is "rapture", which means "to be transported by a lofty emotion or ecstasy". Semantics aside, the bible clearly teaches us that Christ will return for His church and this is a blessed hope all Christians can look forward to!

1 Corinthians 15:51-52 says, *"Take notice, I am telling you a secret. We shall not all die but we shall all be changed, in a moment, in the twinkling of an eye, at the last trumpet call. For the trumpet will sound and the dead will be raised imperishable, and we shall all be changed"*. The Rapture is the time of the resurrection, when each Christian will receive his or her newly resurrected body. The first to receive their new bodies are those Christians who have already died. Immediately afterwards the Christians who are still alive will also receive their new bodies and all Christians will be joined together with our Lord!

Christians do not need to grieve like unbelievers over the death of fellow believers. Of course we grieve over the loss of loved ones, even Jesus did, but our grief differs because we have the hope of eternal life. Philippians 1:21-23 says, *"For me, to live is Christ and to die is gain. If I am to go on living in the body, this will mean fruitful labor for me. Yet what shall I choose? I do not know! I am torn between the two: I desire to depart and be with Christ, which is better by far"*. And 2 Corinthians 5:8 says, *"We are confident, I say, and would prefer to be away from the body and at home with the Lord."*

Christians have the blessed hope that when we die, our dead bodies go into the ground like all other people, but our souls leave to go be with the Lord. Once there we consciously await the day when our souls will be reunited with our newly resurrected bodies. This will occur at the time of the Rapture. 1 Thessalonians 4:13-14 "Brothers and sisters, we do not want you to be uninformed about those who sleep in death, so that you do not grieve like the rest of mankind, who have no hope. For we believe that Jesus died and rose again, and so we believe that <u>God will bring with Jesus those who have fallen asleep in Him</u>."

Continuing in this passage, 1 Thessalonians 4:15-18 says, "According to the Lord's word, we tell you that we who are still alive, who are left until the coming of the Lord, will certainly not precede those who have fallen asleep. For the Lord himself will come down from heaven, with a loud command, with the voice of the archangel and with the trumpet call of God, and the dead in Christ will rise first. After that, we who are still alive and are left will be caught up together with them in the clouds to meet the Lord in the air. And so we will be with the Lord forever. Therefore encourage one another with these words."

Some fear to think of the Christians who have been dead for centuries, buried at sea, or burned up and had their ashes scattered. But the God who created the heavens and the earth from nothing certainly has the power to resurrect these bodies in a moment of time. Thus the resurrected and translated bodies of all Christians will be reunited with our Lord Jesus from that moment and for all eternity to follow. The death and resurrection of Jesus Christ are among the best attested facts in history. Since Christians know these events took place, they can be equally certain that the souls of believers who have died will return with Christ when He comes for His living saints. These certainly are encouraging words!

When will the rapture happen? Scripture does not encourage us to try to determine the date of Jesus' return. Rather, we are to "keep watch, because we do not know on which day our Lord will come." (Matthew 24:42) And we are to "be ready, because the Son of Man will come at an hour when we do not expect Him." (Matthew 24:44) Therefore, we do not know when it will occur, but we do know that it will be instantaneous, in "the twinkling of an eye". We also know that it will happen at the time of the tribulation.

The tribulation is a seven-year period that immediately precedes the return of Christ and the establishment of His millennial kingdom, which will last for 1,000 years. The first 3 ½ years of the tribulation will be a time of peace and cooperation and the second 3 ½ years of the tribulation will be a time of war and catastrophe. At the midpoint of the tribulation, the Antichrist will proclaim himself to be god and require worship from all people of the world.

Many will bow down and worship the Antichrist, including taking his mark of worldwide registration. Some will refuse to worship the Antichrist and receive his mark, and many will be killed for this act of disobedience. The second half of the tribulation is referred to as the "Great Tribulation." There will be extraordinary catastrophes all over the world during this period.

There are three views among Christians as to when the rapture will occur in relation to the tribulation. The **pre-tribulation** view is that the rapture will happen immediately before the tribulation period begins; the **mid-tribulation** view is that the rapture will occur half-way through the tribulation period; and the **post-tribulation** view is that the rapture will occur at the end of the tribulation period.

The pre-tribulation rapture is a wonderful hope for believers in Jesus Christ. Revelation 3:10 says, "Since you have kept my command to endure patiently, I will also keep you from the hour of trial that is going to come on the whole world to test the inhabitants of the earth." This verse is viewed by many to support a pre-tribulation rapture of the church. However, whether we live to see a pre-tribulation, mid-tribulation or post-tribulation rapture, or whether we die prior to any type of rapture at all, the key to eternal salvation is, in all cases, our belief and faith in Jesus Christ alone. Be secure in your relationship with Christ and nothing else really matters.

Consider this, God created the heavens and the earth in six days. Jesus has been gone for 2,000 years. Can you imagine how magnificent a place that awaits us? No you can't! No person can. "What no eye has seen, what no ear has heard, and what no human mind has conceived--the things God has prepared for those who love Him." (1 Corinthians 2:9) May this blessed hope fill your hearts with peace and joy! May God bless you all!

FOCUS QUESTIONS

When a Christian dies, what happens to the body and the soul?

Who will be "caught up" to be with the Lord?

What are the three views as to when the rapture will occur?

Lasting Treasure Part 1

The Word of God is very clear about this point: A person cannot work their way to heaven! Ephesians 2:8-9 says, "For it is by grace you have been saved, through faith-- and this is not from yourselves, it is the gift of God—not by works, so that no one can boast."

This verse reminds us of the amazing grace our God has lavished upon us through the finished work our Lord Jesus Christ on the cross. He did for us what we could not do for ourselves, and it is only by His shed blood that we may be washed clean of our sins and be set free from the power of sin and death! This is the power of the gospel unto salvation and praise be to God for it!

However, God's grace does not give us license to live as we please. Paul addressed this many times in his letters to the churches and so did James, the leader of the early church in Jerusalem. James wrote, "You foolish person, do you want evidence that faith without deeds is useless? Was not our father Abraham considered righteous for what he did when he offered his son Isaac on the altar? You see that his faith and his actions were working together, and <u>his faith was made complete by what he did</u>." (James 2:20-22) James reminds us as believers that our faith without deeds is useless, and that faith is made complete by our deeds. The point is that even though our deeds do not save us, they are an integral part of living our lives for God.

Let us refer back to the passage in Ephesians 2. We just read in verses 8-9 that we are saved by grace, but now let us read verse 10. It says, "For we are God's handiwork, created in Christ Jesus to do good works, which God prepared in advance for us to do." So you see, God has prepared good works for us to do while we are here on earth.

These works are to bring Him glory and to be a blessing to others and our Lord has promised to reward His followers for their efforts on His behalf. 2 Corinthians 5:10 says, "For we must all appear before the judgment seat of Christ, so that each one may receive what is due for what he has done in the body, whether good or evil." As believers we must give an accounting for what we have done with our lives as Christians.

1 Corinthians 3:11-15 says, "For no one can lay any foundation other than the one already laid, which is Jesus Christ. If anyone builds on this foundation using gold, silver, costly stones, wood, hay or straw, their work will be shown for what it is, because the Day will bring it to light. It will be revealed with fire, and the fire will test the quality of each person's work. If what has been built survives, the builder will receive a reward. If it is burned up, the builder will suffer loss but yet will be saved—even though only as one escaping through the flames."

Gold, silver, and precious stones represent durable work that stands the test of divine judgment; symbolic of pure Christian doctrine and living. Our Lord will reward us for this type of work. Wood, hay, and straw represent worthless work that will not stand the test; symbolic of someone's teaching and life that merely confuses or actually misleads believers. We will suffer loss of reward for this type of work, yet we will not lose our salvation. The emphasis is on teaching the pure word of God.

Don't we all get the same rewards in Heaven?

The rewards that saints receive in Heaven will vary greatly. Some people think the term "eternal reward" just means that all saved people will be given the reward of eternal life, but the Word of God promises five different crowns for the people who qualify for them. Let's look at one of them.

The Imperishable Crown –

"Do you not know that those who run in a race all run, but one receives the prize? Run in such a way that you may obtain it. And everyone who competes for the prize is temperate [disciplined] in all things. Now they do it to obtain a perishable crown, but we for an imperishable crown" (1 Corinthians 9:24-25)

This crown is given to believers who faithfully run the race, who crucify selfish desires in the flesh and point men to Jesus. God calls some people to do things that will require sacrifice in the way they will live and conduct their lives. Some may be called to be a missionary in a far off and poor country where they will literally be working for almost nothing in earthly terms. They will have to sacrifice the money, possessions and life style they could have had if they stayed home in their own country. Believers will also receive this crown for the sacrifices they were willing to make for God in order to successfully complete the call and mission God has for them.

In Paul's time athletes competed for a laurel wreath, a crown that could only be worn for one day before it withered. He urges the believers in Corinth to strive for an imperishable crown, one that won't wear out and will be waiting for us when we meet our Lord Jesus Christ. Likewise in Matthew 6:19-21, Jesus urges us to not store our treasures on earth "where moth and rust destroy, and where thieves break in and steal", but instead to store up our "treasures in heaven". We must remember that all things on this earth are subject to decay and will perish.

Therefore, earnestly run whatever race God has set for you and be the best you can be for Him. Be willing to make whatever sacrifices there may be to successfully complete the mission God has set out for you knowing that He will gladly reward your efforts! That is all for now, please return next time as we look at more crowns our Lord has promised to those who love Him. May God bless you all!

FOCUS QUESTIONS

Do believers work their way to heaven? Explain.

What kind of work will survive God's testing?

Lasting Treasure Part 2

In part one we learned that we are saved by God's grace through faith in Jesus Christ, and that salvation is a gift of God. However, we also learned that Christians are God's handiwork, created in Christ Jesus to do good works (Ephesians 2:10). Thus, our works do not save us but they are expected by our Lord, and He has promised to reward us in heaven for them. So far we have read about the Imperishable Crown. Today we will examine two more crowns of reward that we as believers and servants of Christ can look forward to.

The Crown of Rejoicing –

1 Thessalonians 2:19 says, "For what is our hope, or joy, or crown of rejoicing? Is it not even you in the presence of our Lord Jesus Christ at His coming?" And Luke 15:7 says, "I tell you that in the same way there will be more rejoicing in heaven over one sinner who repents than over ninety-nine righteous persons who do not need to repent." This crown has also been named the **soul winner's crown**. It is given to those who faithfully witness to the saving grace of God and lead souls to Jesus.

Telling others about the grace of God given through His Son Jesus Christ is the greatest thing you can do for someone here on this earth. When you help to lead someone to the Lord, you have been used as a vessel of God and that person will inherit eternal life. They are rescued from an eternal separation from God for all eternity in hell, a place created to receive sin and death. It is an awful place and should motivate us to share the gospel to those who don't know the way to heaven.

American culture is becoming increasingly secular and more openly hostile to Christian theology. How often have we seen Christians labeled as being close-minded and intellectually stunted in their thinking by the media and by educators in our schools and universities? If you dare take a stand for the gospel you take the risk of being called a sexist, homophobe, flat-earther, intolerant, or many other derogatory names. There is even a movement by those opposed to Christianity and the bible to have pastors prosecuted for hate speech if they dare to teach in their churches that homosexuality is a sin!

Despite this disturbing trend, sharing our faith is a fear we must overcome. Many Christians are not willing to be used by God, or are too busy to help lead others to the Lord. God will judge us by our willingness and desire to be used by Him to witness to others. Remember, God is the one who actually does the saving through the working of the Holy Spirit, we are simply His messengers. God will bring opportunities for us to witness for Him if we allow Him, and some of those He brings could be our unsaved friends, co-workers, or even our own family members. The next crown awarded to believers is the Crown of Glory.

The Crown of Glory –

"To the elders among you, I appeal as a fellow elder and a witness of Christ's sufferings who also will share in the glory to be revealed: Be shepherds of God's flock that is under your care, watching over them—not because you must, but because you are willing, as God wants you to be; not pursuing dishonest gain, but eager to serve; not lording it over those entrusted to you, but being examples to the flock. And when the Chief Shepherd appears, you will receive the crown of glory that will never fade away."(1 Peter 5:1-4)

Though Peter is addressing the elders, we must also remember that the crown will be awarded to all those who long for or love His appearing. This is the pastor's crown and will be given to the ministers who faithfully feed the flock of God. This probably could also include preachers, teachers, Sunday school teachers, missionaries and all those who teach the Word of God in their respective ministries.

This crown may signify the importance and sacrifices of bringing up others into the ways of God. God wants those who are saved to grow and learn as much as they can about Him, His Son and His Holy Spirit and to do that He uses mature believers who are willing to teach others. God can use you to teach and shepherd others. God shows you the extreme importance that He is placing on those who teach and preach the word. Being willing to teach and educate others after they are saved is one of the greatest things you can do for them this side of heaven. That is all for now. Thank you for reading and God bless you all!

FOCUS QUESTIONS

Why is the Crown of Rejoicing known as the soul-winners crown?

Is the Crown of Glory only for pastors? Explain.

Lasting Treasure Part 3

In parts one and two we learned about three crowns our Lord has promised as rewards for us in heaven. Today we will examine the last two crowns of reward that we as believers and servants of Christ can look forward to.

The first is **the Crown of Righteousness** –

2 Timothy 4:8 says, "Finally, there is laid up for me the crown of righteousness, which the Lord, the righteous Judge, will give to me on that Day, and not to me only but also to all who have loved His appearing." And Philippians 3:20 says, "But our citizenship is in heaven. And we eagerly await a Savior from there, the Lord Jesus Christ "

This crown is awarded to us for living a good and righteous life for God the Father with what time we have left on earth. If you are a believer you have been made righteous before God the Father as a result of Jesus dying on the cross for all of your sins. This means that the righteousness of Jesus has now been imputed to you. This is known as Justification. You are sealed by the Holy Spirit of God and you become an heir with Christ to receive an eternal citizenship in heaven. You did not earn this because it is impossible for you as a mere mortal sinner to live a perfectly righteous life. When God looks at you He sees the righteousness of Jesus and He accepts you as His child. Praise God for this!

Even though you and I as Christians cannot live a perfectly sinless life, our Lord calls us to grow in our faith and knowledge of His word so that we may increasingly live better lives on earth. Our good works should be a proof and reflection that our faith is real, and sinful habits and actions should be decreasing. As we allow the Holy Spirit to reign in our hearts and thoughts, we begin to produce fruit of the Spirit, and we become more like Christ our Lord. This is known as Sanctification.

There are some people who are saved in God's eyes, but at times do evil works that the unsaved do. We all have our weaknesses and certain temptations that we struggle with. God is not looking for absolute perfection but He is looking for us to head in the right direction, towards lives characterized by love, joy, peace, patience, kindness, gentleness, goodness, and self-control. (See Galatians 5:22-23)

This crown is not for those who depend upon their own sense of righteousness or of their own works. Such an attitude breeds only arrogance and pride, not a longing, a fervent desire to be with the Lord. This crown is for those who love the appearing of Christ, who anxiously wait and look forward to the day when He will return for His saints. This crown is given to those who have lived a good and righteous life for God while living down here on earth.

The Bible says that, we all have sinned and have fallen way short of the glory of our God. We all know right from wrong! God just wants each one of us to choose to do the right thing when faced with temptations or choices to do something bad. To live a righteous life for God will really be worth your while as you look forward to receiving this crown from God Himself once you enter into heaven.

The last crown we will learn about is the Crown of Life –

Revelation 2:10 says, "Do not fear any of those things which you are about to suffer. Indeed, the devil is about to throw some of you into prison, that you may be tested, and you will have tribulation ten days. Be faithful until death, and I will give you the crown of life." And James 1:12 says, "Blessed is the one who perseveres under trial because, having stood the test, that person will receive the crown of life that the Lord has promised to those who love Him."

This crown is for those believers who endure trials, tribulations, and severe suffering, even suffering unto death. This crown is also referred to as **the martyr's crown**. Being willing to die for your faith in God would be the ultimate sacrifice. It is the greatest act of courage and love that you can show God. Christians who have been martyred for their faith throughout history will not only be given this crown of life, but other rewards once they enter into heaven.

James tells us that this crown of life is also for all who love God. The question then is how do we demonstrate our love for God? The apostle John answers this for us: "For this is the love of God, that we keep His commandments. And His commandments are not burdensome" (1 John 5:3). As God's children we must do our best to keep His commandments, obeying Him, and always remaining faithful. Of course, this is impossible for us to do on our own strength. We must daily surrender our hearts and minds to Christ and constantly look to Him as our example. Hebrews 12:2-3 says "...fixing our eyes on Jesus, the pioneer and perfecter of faith. For the joy set before Him He endured the cross, scorning its shame, and sat down at the right hand of the throne of God. Consider Him who endured such opposition from sinners, so that you will not grow weary and lose heart." Dear brothers and sisters, we can endure the inevitable trials, pains, heartaches, and tribulations of being a Christian knowing that our Lord Jesus is with us and will reward us with the crown of life.

What is the purpose of us receiving crowns?

Consider this scene in heaven recorded by the apostle John. "The twenty–four elders fall down before Him who sits on the throne and worship Him who lives forever and ever, and cast their crowns before the throne, saying: You are worthy, O Lord, To receive glory and honour and power; For You created all things, And by Your will they exist and were created."(Revelation 4:10-11) These elders place their crowns at Jesus' feet.

When we finally meet our Lord face to face and the pain and suffering of this world are a distant memory, we will finally see clearly the magnitude of the sacrifice He made for us. We will be overwhelmed with thankfulness and full of love as we never have been before. We will long to give gifts to our Lord for what He has done, but what shall we have for Him? Let's revisit a passage we read in part one.

1 Corinthians 3:11-15 says, *"For no one can lay any foundation other than the one already laid, which is Jesus Christ. If anyone builds on this foundation using gold, silver, costly stones, wood, hay or straw, their work will be shown for what it is, because the Day will bring it to light. It will be revealed with fire, and the fire will test the quality of each person's work. If what has been built survives, the builder will receive a reward. If it is burned up, the builder will suffer loss but yet will be saved—even though only as one escaping through the flames."*

The gold, silver, and precious stones represent durable work that stands the test of divine judgment and our Lord will reward us for this. Wood, hay, and straw represent worthless work that will not stand the test and we will suffer loss of reward for this, yet we will not lose our salvation. When our Master says to us "Well done, good and faithful servant! You have been faithful with a few things; I will put you in charge of many things. Come and share your master's happiness!" (Matthew 25:21), we will want to place whatever crowns we may have at His feet. And we will "suffer loss" knowing that we did not do all we could for Him who did everything for us!

Keep the faith and do not grow weary of living each day for our Lord! Let us look forward to the Day when we meet Him and strive to please Him with all we do now! May God bless you all!

FOCUS QUESTIONS

What is justification?

What is sanctification?

What is the purpose for us to receive crowns?

Chapter 8

Do Miracles Exist?

"Always, everywhere God is present, and always He seeks to discover Himself to each one" — **A.W.Tozer**

Do Miracles Exist? Part 1

It is necessary to first establish a foundation before delving right in to the topic of miracles. So today, in part one, I will start by making the case for the existence of the supernatural. You see, in order for miracles to be possible, there must be a supernatural realm. After we establish that point, that opens the door for us to examine together the concept that our physical realm coexists with a supernatural, or spiritual realm. And we will look at what the Bible says about that subject and the implications for us as God's creation. Then we may proceed to examine the topic of miracles, including the reasons God performs them. But that is further down the road.

Let's begin with a definition for the word supernatural. It is as follows: **manifestations or events attributed to some force beyond scientific understanding or the laws of nature.**

If something occurs that can be documented as actually have taken place, and nothing within our human understanding and experience of how the universe works can rationally explain it, then it is by our definition a supernatural occurrence.

Now let us consider people's worldviews, which can be placed into one of four basic categories: Atheists or materialists believe matter and energy are the prime reality, the thing from which everything else comes from. Deists believe in a personal God who does not intervene with His creation. Pantheists believe in an impersonal god, or many gods, who is a part of everything (e.g. Hinduism, eastern religions). Finally, theists believe in a personal God who does interact with creation (e.g. Judaism, Islam, and Christianity).

So for the deists, theists and pantheists, their differences in beliefs are primarily a matter of who or what God is; is God active in the world today; is there one or many gods; or if we are all a part of god. But they all believe in the supernatural idea of god. But understand that no worldview has an absolute certainty! <u>They all require faith, including atheism!</u> It is the atheist, or materialist, who believes the laws of nature are everything and that's it! From that person's perspective, there is nothing supernatural that exists outside of space and time, like say the God of the Bible. Okay, so let's look at the subject of space and time logically to see if this materialist view about the supernatural holds up.

First let us define the words finite and infinite: If something is finite, then it has a beginning and end. If something is infinite, then it has no beginning and no end; it exists outside of space and time as we know it and it cannot be explained using the laws of nature.

Now let's ask the question; what if the universe is infinite? If the universe is indeed infinite, then it has no beginning and no end. This is actually the best argument against God's existence because if the universe had no beginning, then it doesn't need a creator. However, if the universe is indeed infinite, this is by our definition a supernatural phenomenon because it cannot be explained logically using science and the laws of nature!

The laws of nature state that something cannot create itself! Every event must have a cause. This is called the Law of Causality. Therefore, the concept of a universe that has always existed and was not created is beyond our scientific understanding. Just like the concept that there is an almighty powerful God who has always existed and was never created. The two ideas are one and the same. <u>The materialist has simply replaced the idea of a personal God with the idea of an impersonal god in the form of matter and energy.</u>

On the other hand, what if the universe is finite? If the universe is indeed finite, then it must have a cause for it to have a beginning. There must be something that exists outside of space and time, something supernatural, to cause it to come into existence. Refer to the post "The Bible: A True Story of Epic Proportion! Part 1". In it I present scientific evidences from Big Bang Cosmology which provides a very strong case that the universe is indeed finite and had a beginning.

However, regardless if the universe is infinite or finite, both answers point conclusively to the existence of something supernatural. For theists like you and me, a finite universe supports our belief in the existence of a creator. I believe the God of the Bible to be that creator. For the materialist, an infinite universe is a supernatural thing that no natural law can explain. So for them, the universe itself is their god, even though they won't call it that. Either way, something supernatural exists. We can't escape it. This brings us to **MAIN POINT #1: THE EXISTENCE OF THE SUPERNATURAL IS LOGICALLY UNAVOIDABLE!**

To this point we have approached the concept of the supernatural logically. But now that we have arrived at the conclusion that the supernatural exists, our logical reasoning cannot to take us any further. Why? Because by definition the supernatural is beyond our capability to explain using scientific understanding or the laws of nature. <u>Therefore, in order to for us to learn about and grow in our knowledge of the supernatural, it is completely legitimate for us to seek answers from a supernatural source.</u> Since natural law limits our ability to understand the existence of a supernatural being like God, we must rely on a source that claims to be of supernatural origin; a source like the Bible.

So if you are in a discussion about the existence of God and someone tries to argue believing in God is illogical, this infinite universe versus finite universe comparison is a strong argument. Because the evidence for God's possible existence starts with the basic question – does something supernatural exist? Using this argument the answer is 100% yes! This doesn't prove God's existence, but it makes His existence a viable option that directly silences the claims that the idea of God is "pie in the sky thinking" or a "fairy tale." That is all for now. I hope you will return for part 2. May God bless you all!

FOCUS QUESTIONS

How is the word "supernatural" defined?

A person's worldview can be placed into which four categories?

How does an infinite universe point to something supernatural?

How does a finite universe point to something supernatural?

Do Miracles Exist? Part 2

In part one we learned the existence of the supernatural is logically unavoidable. Our reasoning showed that God's existence is a viable option and it is legitimate for us to seek answers from a supernatural source like the bible. The next question we can ask is which worldview about God makes the most sense and offers the best explanation? That is another series of sermons altogether, but I believe Christianity offers the best explanation of who God is. Therefore, I am going to approach our explanation of the supernatural from the Christian point of view.

Refer to my recent posts in which I provide an argument supporting the authenticity and reliability of the Bible. This book is unlike any other and I believe it is what it claims to be. God's communication to mankind answering all of the essential questions concerning our existence: Where we came from? Where we've been? Where we are headed? Having taken a look at the preponderance of the evidence, the Bible by far offers the best explanation; the bible makes the most sense. Now let's look at the contents of the Bible concerning the supernatural.

Ecclesiastes 3:11 says, "He has made everything beautiful in its time. He has also set eternity in the human heart; yet no one can fathom what God has done from beginning to end."

This passage sums up what we covered in part one. In it we read that God has placed within each one of us the idea of eternity, or the infinite. It is not an idea we would logically arrive at on our own. Everything we know about our universe and how it works and the laws of nature would not lead us to conclude the infinite to be possible. Yet, we have an inner longing for more than what is temporal, but we cannot comprehend or understand it. We have a notion that there is more to our existence than what we can see, feel, and touch; yet, it is literally beyond our physical grasp.

As Christians, you and I can look to the God of the Bible as the supernatural source to explain our existence, and we can read His words to help us comprehend that although we live in a physical realm, a realm we can see, feel, and touch, a realm that can be observed and quantified; we also live in a spiritual realm, a realm that is unseen, that exists outside of the laws of nature, that can't be observed and quantified. This leads to **MAIN POINT #2: OUR SENSE OF THE INFINITE COMES FROM GOD**

Why would God plant within us the idea of eternity? Let's look at more scripture to find out. In this passage Jesus is having a discussion with His disciples and He began by asking them "Who do people say 'the Son of man' is? Their response was some say you are John the Baptist, others say Elijah, others Jeremiah or one of the prophets. Then Jesus continued…"But what about you?" He asked, "Who do you say I am?" Simon Peter answered, "You are the Messiah, the Son of the living God." Jesus replied, "Blessed are you, Simon son of Jonah, for this was not revealed to you by flesh and blood, but by my Father in heaven." (Matthew 16:15-17) One of the truths we can learn from this passage is that God the Father is not flesh and blood. He does not have a physical body like we do.

John 4:24 says, "God is spirit, and His worshipers must worship in the Spirit and in truth." Here we learn God is spirit, confirming He does not have a physical body. And notice that His worshipers must worship in the Spirit. This is referring to the Holy Spirit of God. This and many other passages confirm that people must have the Holy Spirit within them in order to worship God in truth, in order to be "Born Again", in order to have salvation.

Salvation occurs when a person believes Jesus Christ to be the Son of God and that He died for our sins and that He has risen from the dead, and accepts this by faith, with the understanding it has not been earned. It is by God's grace which He imparts to us when we ask Him in faith to be Lord of our lives. The implications of receiving the Holy Spirit means for you, me, or any person to worship God, there must exist within each of us the spiritual capacity to do so. Now let's look at a familiar passage in the book of Genesis.

"Then God said, "Let us make mankind in our image, in our likeness, so that they may rule over the fish in the sea and the birds in the sky, over the livestock and all the wild animals, and over all the creatures that move along the ground." So God created mankind in His own image, in the image of God He created them; male and female He created them." (Genesis 1:26-27)

God created mankind in His own image. But people have physical bodies of flesh and blood. And God is not flesh and blood, He is spirit. So what is it about a person that makes us created in God's image? Let's look for clues from one more passage to drive home the point I'm making.

Psalm 139:13 says, "For You created my inmost being; You knit me together in my mother's womb." Here the psalmist is praising God's creative power in making Him. We read God created our "inmost being". What does that mean? Think about it. It is who you really are. You are more than flesh and blood; you have a soul, or a spirit. God created that spirit. Why? Because He created us in His own image with the capacity to reason, to imagine, and to create. We also possess the ability to demonstrate compassion, mercy, forgiveness, and love. These are abilities that are not necessarily measureable in a science lab, but they exist, just like He exists. And God gave them to us so that we can come to know about Him and that we can have fellowship with Him.

God also created us physically. It says "You knit me together in my mother's womb". I believe that is referring to Him putting our physical parts together. Modern science has discovered the existence of a very complicated process involving the exchange of incredible amounts of information, which takes place at the genetic level of all living cells. Biologists have learned that the DNA molecule contains sequencing which is essentially coded information. <u>All of our scientific experience teaches us that you cannot have information without an intelligent source.</u> The laws of probability are staggeringly against the idea that the coded information in DNA could be the product of random chance, despite the so-called billions of years of evolutionary history! Microsoft has yet to develop anything remotely sophisticated as the storing, retrieving, and distribution of information that takes place at the genetic level of living cells. DNA screams of intelligent design! That designer is the God who has revealed Himself to us in the Bible.

Here is one more scripture. "The Spirit himself testifies with our spirit that we are God's children."(Romans 8:16) This passage affirms that God has given each person a spirit and placed the idea of the infinite within each one of us so we would seek Him and desire to have fellowship with Him. And when we become a child of God, the Holy Spirit comes to dwell within us and has fellowship with our spirit, and we become a child of God with a hope and a future that is secure! This leads us to **MAIN POINT #3: PEOPLE ARE BOTH PHYSICAL AND SPIRITUAL BEINGS.** I hope you will return for part 3. Thank you and God bless you all!

FOCUS QUESTIONS

Why did God plant within us the idea of eternity?

Why did God give each person a spirit?

Do Miracles Exist? Part 3

To this point, we have learned that the existence of the supernatural is unavoidable, no matter what worldview you may have. We've learned God is not flesh and blood, but is spirit. We also learned that God created people in His image, with a spirit as well as a physical body. Now let's look at scripture for the next main point of our lesson.

1 Timothy 1:17 says, "Now to the King eternal, immortal, invisible, the only God, be honor and glory forever and ever. Amen." And Colossians 1:15 says, "The Son is the image of the invisible God, the firstborn over all creation." Because God is not a physical being He is invisible to us. It is not possible for people to see God in strictly a physical sense. And even if He chose to show Himself to us, it is an experience we could not survive.

1 Timothy 6:15-16 says, "God, the blessed and only Ruler, the King of kings and Lord of lords, who alone is immortal and who lives in unapproachable light, whom no one has seen or can see." And Exodus 33:20 says, "…you cannot see my face, for no one may see me and live." It is true that Moses saw a glimpse of God's back, but He could not look at God's face and live. No one can. God lives in "unapproachable light" and His glory and majesty are too intense for mere mortals to confront.

Since we can't see God physically, then how are we to know of Him? It is possible to see him with other forms of sight. The first is rational sight; sight in the sense of intellectual perception. The bible clearly states that truth about God can be inferred from the natural order of creation. Romans 1:20 says, "For since the creation of the world God's invisible qualities—his eternal power and divine nature—have been clearly seen, being understood from what has been made, so that people are without excuse." And Psalm 19:1-4 says, "The heavens declare the glory of God; the skies proclaim the work of his hands. Day after day they pour forth speech; night after night they reveal knowledge. They have no speech, they use no words; no sound is heard from them. Yet their voice goes out into all the earth, their words to the ends of the world."

In these passages we have a clear statement that God's character and power can be seen through the measureable, observable, physical creation He has made. Again, this called rational sight. Some of the early scientists who were pioneers in their respective fields approached their work with this very mindset. Many of the great scientists in history were Christians. Men like Sir Isaac Newton, James Clerk Maxwell, and Sir Robert Boyle thought they were discovering design in nature that came from an intelligent God. And their theistic worldview in no way prohibited them from doing great science. Newton and Maxwell are considered among the top three physicists of all-time, the third being Alfred Einstein. Boyle is considered the father of modern chemistry.

But the culture among scientists has changed drastically the past 150 years. Today science and Christianity always seem to be at odds with each other. There exists a cultural bias among modern day scientists that is opposed to anyone with a theistic worldview. The prevailing idea among the scientific community is that a serious scientist cannot be a Christian, or that a Christian cannot be a serious scientist. This should not surprise us. The Bible speaks of such prejudice. Let's again read the passage in Romans 1, including the verses before and after verse 20.

Romans 1:18-21 says, "The wrath of God is being revealed from heaven against all the godlessness and wickedness of people, <u>who suppress the truth</u> by their wickedness, since what may be known about God is plain to them, because God has made it plain to them. For since the creation of the world God's invisible qualities—his eternal power and divine nature—have been clearly seen, being understood from what has been made, so that people are without excuse. For although they knew God, they neither glorified him as God nor gave thanks to Him, but <u>their thinking became futile</u> and their foolish hearts were darkened." This pretty much sums up the humanistic thought process of our modern secular world.

Not only can we can see God through what He has made, but since we have a spirit, we can also see God using spiritual sight. Spiritual sight uses the "eyes of the heart", that is, perception of the soul that comes through faith and through communion with the Living God by the power of the Holy Spirit. Ephesians 1:18 says, "I pray that the eyes of your heart may be enlightened in order that you may know the hope to which He has called you, the riches of His glorious inheritance in His holy people…"

When Christians look at God through the "eyes of our heart" we are opening ourselves to allow Him to work in us. Through the working of the Holy Spirit we begin to see Him for who He is and we begin to change. These changes are not physical changes, they are spiritual changes. They are fruits of the Holy Spirit and they become more and more evident in our daily lives. The spiritual fruits of joy, peace, patience, kindness, goodness, faithfulness, gentleness, self-control, and most importantly love. These qualities are manifested by the Holy Spirit in those who willingly submit themselves to the living God. This brings us to the next main point, which is **MAIN POINT #4: GOD REVEALS HIMSELF IN BOTH THE PHYSICAL AND SPIRITUAL REALMS.**

In closing, the God of the Bible also intervenes in human history; He is active in this world. One way He intervenes is when He allows or causes the spiritual realm to intersect with the physical realm in a manifestation that can't be explained by natural law, in a supernatural event that we would call a miracle. He does so in order reveal Himself to mankind and also to achieve His glorious purposes. But that is really for next time. I hope you will return to read it. May God bless you all!

FOCUS QUESTIONS

What is intellectual sight?

What is spiritual sight?

Do Miracles Exist? Part 4

In parts 1-3 we established key ideas which provide a foundation for us to build upon today. First, we learned that no matter what worldview a person may have, the existence of the supernatural is logically unavoidable. Even the atheist, if they are honest, must grapple with the notion that the supernatural exists. This brought us to the understanding that not only do we live in a physical realm, one that we can see, feel, and touch, a realm that can be observed and quantified; we also live in a spiritual realm, a realm that is unseen, that exists outside of the laws of nature, that cannot be observed and quantified.

Next we established that the God of the Bible is spirit and His followers must worship Him in Spirit and in truth. The Bible makes it very clear that in order to receive salvation, a person must accept by faith the forgiveness for sin offered through God's Son Jesus Christ. When they do the Holy Spirit of God comes to dwell within that person and they become of child of God, with a hope and a future that is secure.

We also learned God created people in His own image, with a spirit as well as a physical body. He did this so people can have the capacity to know about Him and to have fellowship with Him once they receive the Holy Spirit. Today, we will build on this foundation, first learning the importance of understanding about miracles. Then we will define what a miracle is and is not, and we will see the existence of miracles is logically possible.

Why is understanding miracles important?

In modern secular society, miracles are often challenged as being nonsensical fantasy and therefore a legitimate reason to dismiss the Christian faith as a viable worldview. This is especially true in our universities and institutions of higher learning, where our young Christian men and women are constantly confronted with a secular worldview, and many have had their faith weakened or lost it altogether. Therefore, as Christians, the existence of miracles is a topic that you and I need to think about very carefully. Why?

Because as Christians, we must say we believe in miracles, otherwise how could we say we believe in an Almighty God who exists outside of space and time and who created all things and holds all things together? How can we say we believe Jesus to be the Son of God who was born of a virgin, who was crucified to death, who rose from the dead and is alive today? We could not say we believe these things to be true if we do not believe in miracles.

Let's define what we mean by the word miracle: **A miracle is a supernatural event that can't be explained by science or natural laws and is considered to be of divine origin.**

Miracles are supernatural events and because they can't be explained, they either violate or suspend natural law. Examples from the Bible are God stopping the sun in the sky for about a day to allow Joshua more time to defeat the Amorites (Joshua 10:12-14), the parting of the Red Sea by Moses so that the Israelites could cross on dry ground to escape Pharaoh's army (Exodus 14), or Jesus raising Lazarus back to life after he was dead four days (John 11:38-44). These events fit our definition of a miracle, a word that we have a tendency to misuse. Here's what I mean.

When a mother suddenly gets a worried feeling and runs to the bedroom just in time to prevent her toddler from sticking a paper clip into a wall socket, or when you get a much needed check in the mail for the exact amount you had prayed for, or when a friend calls at precisely the right moment and gives you much needed encouragement when your faith is reeling; these are not miracles. God is certainly at work in these events and they are just as real as miracles. But they are not events which violate or suspend natural law. They are acts of divine providence, whereby God is orchestrating natural events so that they do what He wants them to do. I believe this is the primary way God chooses to work His will on earth.

God communicates to us with unspoken words in our spirit, like the mother worried about her toddler. God uses people of faith, people who are willing to serve Him to bring blessings and help to others; the person who mailed that check, or the person who made that phone call. We might call this being the "hands and feet of Jesus". God also uses His people to bring the hope of the Gospel message to a lost world, rather than miracles, signs, and wonders. We will see why in a later post.

Some will argue that miracles cannot occur because it is impossible to violate the laws of nature. That is true for those whose existence is confined within the laws of nature, but it assumes that nothing exists outside of the laws of nature, something supernatural.

In our first lesson we learned that the existence of the supernatural realm is logically unavoidable. We pointed out that there is strong scientific evidence which shows our universe is finite, in other words, it had a beginning. And the Law of Causality states there must be a cause for it to have had a beginning because nothing can create itself. Therefore, there must be something that exists outside of the laws of nature, something supernatural like the God of the Bible, to have caused our universe to come into existence. Because of these reasons, it is logically possible for events to occur that cannot be explained by science.

This leads to MAIN POINT #5: SINCE THE EXISTENCE OF THE SUPERNATURAL IS UNVOIDABLE, THE EXISTENCE OF MIRACLES IS ALSO UNAVOIDABLE.

Since a miracle is a supernatural event, it is beyond our ability to explain using scientific understanding or the laws of nature. Therefore, in order to explain miracles, we must rely on a source that claims to be of supernatural origin; a source like the Bible. Please return next time when we will begin to explore the bible to learn more about miracles. God bless you all!

FOCUS QUESTIONS

How is a miracle defined?

Explain the difference between "miracles" and "acts of divine providence".

Do Miracles Exist? Part 5

In our last lesson, we learned that a miracle is a supernatural event that can't be explained by science or natural laws and is considered to be of divine origin. Since there are over 100 miracles recorded in the Bible, we have a tendency to think that miracles were a common occurrence during biblical times. But that really isn't true. We need to understand that the books of the Old Testament cover about 4000 years of history. If we chart the history of God intervening in human history through miracles, we see that there are long stretches of time when He is silent.

The first recorded miracle in the bible is when God took Enoch away to heaven (Genesis 5:24), 987 years after the creation of Adam. The next recorded miracle is the flood which took place around 2400 B.C., about 700 years after the taking of Enoch. Other noteworthy miracles and their approximate dates are: the confusing of the languages at Tower of Babel (2000 B.C.), the destruction of Sodom and Gomorrah (1892 B.C.), the many miracles during the Exodus of Israel from Egypt (1445 B.C.), Elijah calling down fire on Mount Carmel (875 B.C.), the rescue of Shadrach, Meshach, and Abednego from the fiery furnace (600 B.C.), the many miracles performed by Jesus during His ministry, and those performed by the apostles during the establishment of the early church. Therefore, our next point is **MAIN POINT #6: MIRACLES ARE RARE IN HISTORY.**

Now that we've seen miracles are rare, let's explore why God performs them. To help us answer this question we will look at two of the early miracles. First, why the Flood?

Genesis 6:5-6 says, "The LORD saw how great the wickedness of the human race had become on the earth, and that every inclination of the thoughts of the human heart was only evil all the time. The LORD regretted that He had made human beings on the earth, and His heart was deeply troubled." And Genesis 6:11 says, "Now the earth was corrupt in God's sight and full of violence."

Recall that God's creation was initially very good. But the rebellion of Adam and Eve had now progressed to the point where evil completely dominated the human race and God's creation. God was deeply grieved by the immorality practiced by those He had created in His own image. And it was apparent that left unchecked, mankind would be lost to Him forever and would destroy itself completely. But there remained a shred of hope for the human race. Genesis 6:8-9 says, "But Noah found favor in the eyes of the Lord…Noah was a righteous man, blameless among the people of his time, and he walked faithfully with God."

Understand this; Noah was born just 126 years after the death of Adam and Noah's father Lamech was born during Adam's lifetime. Adam's grandchildren were still living when Noah was born! Think about that. The very first man created, who knew God intimately and who walked with God in the garden was still alive when Noah's father was alive. It is evident that God's existence was known by virtually everyone during this point in human history! Yet, mankind still lived in active defiance against God! Noah's faith was not just the belief in God because that was surely common knowledge at that time. Noah's faith was in his obedience to God, in giving God His rightful place in his life. Therefore, God determined to intervene in human history through the hope found in the one man who still had faith in Him.

Why the Tower of Babel? Let's read the account in Genesis to find out.

"Now the whole world had one language and a common speech. As people moved eastward, they found a plain in Shinar and settled there. They said to each other, "Come, let's make bricks and bake them thoroughly." They used brick instead of stone, and tar for mortar. Then they said, "Come, let us build ourselves a city, with a tower that reaches to the heavens, so that we may make a name for ourselves; otherwise we will be scattered over the face of the whole earth." But the LORD came down to see the city and the tower the people were building. The LORD said, "If as one people speaking the same language they have begun to do this, then nothing they plan to do will be impossible for them." Genesis 11:1-6

As the world repopulated after the flood, people again rebelled against God! This time they united together in a proud attempt to seize control of their own destiny, removing God from their plans and from His rightful place in their lives. Without intervention, there would be no limit to their unrestrained rebellion against God. If allowed to carry out their plan the result would be the establishment of a godless human kingdom, replacing God's plan for His future kingdom; a kingdom of righteousness and perfection that could only be realized by the coming of Jesus Christ, the Savior of the world. Without God's intervention, people would again be lost to Him and again be destined to self-destruction as before the flood.

The remainder of the Old Testament books all point to the day when God will rescue His creation through the coming Messiah and we see that His actions in these two accounts and all accounts have the purpose of ensuring that this happens.

When God allowed Joseph to be sold into slavery in Egypt it was to preserve Israel from the coming famine (Genesis 45:7). He allowed the Israelites to be enslaved by the Egyptians so that they would grow to be a large nation, instead of being destroyed by the more powerful nations living in the land of Canaan. And when they were numerous enough, He sent Moses to free them from captivity and lead them to the land promised to Abraham, Isaac, and Jacob (Exodus 1-12). God protected and preserved them in the desert and He fought for them during the conquest of Canaan under Joshua. Despite repeated rebellion and disobedience by the nation of Israel, God continued to preserve them and eventually the promised Messiah, Jesus Christ, was born.

So our next point is **MAIN POINT #7: GOD USES MIRACLES TO SHAPE HISTORY.** Please return next time to find out more reasons God performs miracles. God bless you all!

FOCUS QUESTIONS

What was the culture of mankind during Noah's time?

Why did people band together to build the Tower of Babel?

Why did God intervene with miracles during the historical times of the Old Testament?

Do Miracles Exist? Part 6

In part 5 we learned that God used miracles to shape history in order to ensure the Messiah Jesus Christ would be born. This fulfilled God's plan for the redemption of mankind and paved the way for the establishment of God's kingdom on earth, instead of an ungodly human kingdom. We also noted that Jesus performed miracles during His earthly ministry, including many miracles of healing. But the Gospels rarely refer to them as such. Instead, Jesus' miracles are almost always referred to as "signs". Why would the Bible use the word "signs" instead of "miracles"?

John 14:11 says, "Believe Me when I say that I am in the Father and the Father is in Me; or at least believe on the evidence of the miracles themselves." And John 2:23 says, "Now while He was in Jerusalem at the Passover Festival, many people saw the signs He was performing and believed in His name." You see, the primary purpose of the miracles Jesus performed was not just to provide people with physical healing. He did them to serve as a witness to the truth of His ministry. The signs attested to the fact that He was the promised Messiah and that the Kingdom of God was near.

Let's look at one of Jesus' miracles of healing to emphasize this point. Mark 2:3-12 says, "Then men came to Him, bringing a paralytic who was carried by four men. And when they could not come near Him because of the crowd, they uncovered the roof where He was. So when they had broken through, they let down the bed on which the paralytic was lying. When Jesus saw their faith, He said to the paralytic, "Son, your sins are forgiven you." And some of the scribes were sitting there and reasoning in their hearts, "Why does this Man speak blasphemies like this? Who can forgive sins but God alone?" But immediately, when Jesus perceived in His spirit that they reasoned thus within themselves, He said to them, "Why do you reason about these things in your hearts? "Which is easier, to say to the paralytic, 'Your sins are forgiven you,' or to say, 'Arise, take up your bed and walk'?

"But that you may know that the Son of Man has power on earth to forgive sins"-- He said to the paralytic, "I say to you, arise, take up your bed, and go to your house." Immediately he arose, took up the bed, and went out in the presence of them all, so that all were amazed and glorified God, saying, "We never saw anything like this!"

The Pharisees were right to object by saying "only God can forgive sins". To dispense a legal pardon for sins could only be done through a sacrifice and from God. Jesus healed the man of his palsy in order to show that He, as the Son of Man, had the authority to forgive sins and that He was in fact God! Jesus healed what the people could see to prove He was able to forgive the sins that they could not see. So our next point is **MAIN POINT#8: JESUS' MIRACLES PROVED HIS DEITY AND LEGITIMIZED HIS MINISTRY.**

After Jesus ascended back to heaven, miracles, signs and wonders continued to occur with His apostles and followers, which at that time numbered about 120. The first significant miracle is the Day of Pentecost recorded in Acts chapter two. It says, "When the day of Pentecost came, they were all together in one place. Suddenly a sound like the blowing of a violent wind came from heaven and filled the whole house where they were sitting. They saw what seemed to be tongues of fire that separated and came to rest on each of them. All of them were filled with the Holy Spirit and began to speak in other tongues as the Spirit enabled them." (Acts 2:1-4)

"Now there were staying in Jerusalem God-fearing Jews from every nation under heaven. When they heard this sound, a crowd came together in bewilderment, because each one heard their own language being spoken. Utterly amazed, they asked: "Aren't all these who are speaking Galileans? Then how is it that each of us hears them in our native language? Parthians, Medes and Elamites; residents of Mesopotamia, Judea and Cappadocia, Pontus and Asia, Phrygia and Pamphylia, Egypt and the parts of Libya near Cyrene; visitors from Rome (both Jews and converts to Judaism); Cretans and Arabs—we hear them declaring the wonders of God in our own tongues!" Amazed and perplexed, they asked one another, "What does this mean?" (Acts 2:5-12)

With the power of the Holy Spirit Peter addressed the crowd and gave a rousing sermon. He said, "Fellow Israelites, listen to this: Jesus of Nazareth was a man accredited by God to you by miracles, wonders and signs, which God did among you through Him, as you yourselves know. This man was handed over to you by God's deliberate plan and foreknowledge; and you, with the help of wicked men, put Him to death by nailing Him to the cross. But God raised Him from the dead, freeing Him from the agony of death, because it was impossible for death to keep its hold on Him." (Acts 2:22-24) "God has raised this Jesus to life, and we are all witnesses of it. Exalted to the right hand of God, He has received from the Father the promised Holy Spirit and has poured out what you now see and hear." (Acts 2:32-33)

Notice that Peter reminded them of the miracles, signs, and wonders that God did through Jesus and their failure to accept Him as the Son of God. Instead, with the help of wicked men they had Jesus executed. Peter also points out that Jesus rose from the dead and explains the miracle they now are witnessing is from God. Then Peter really nails them.

"Therefore let all Israel be assured of this: God has made this Jesus, whom you crucified, both Lord and Messiah." When the people heard this, they were cut to the heart and said to Peter and the other apostles, "Brothers, what shall we do?" Peter replied, "Repent and be baptized, every one of you, in the name of Jesus Christ for the forgiveness of your sins. And you will receive the gift of the Holy Spirit. The promise is for you and your children and for all who are far off—for all whom the Lord our God will call." With many other words he warned them; and he pleaded with them, "Save yourselves from this corrupt generation." Those who accepted his message were baptized, and about three thousand were added to their number that day!" (Acts 2:36-41)

The book of Acts continues to describe miracles, signs, and wonders, all of which served to help the church grow. In chapter three Peter heals a man who was lame from birth, then he gives a sermon to the crowd of onlookers and the result was 2000 more believers were added that day!

The early church grew and was scattered as a result of persecution by the Jews, among whom Saul of Tarsus was most prominent. But Saul was confronted by Jesus on the road to Damascus (Acts 9), a miraculous event which completely changed his belief about Christianity. Saul changed his name to Paul and became a missionary to the gentiles, planting churches all over the Mediterranean and writing most of the New Testament. This leads us to our next point which is **MAIN POINT #9: MIRACLES WERE NEEDED TO BUILD THE EARLY CHURCH.** Please return next time to read the conclusion of this series. Thank you for reading this and may God richly bless you all!

FOCUS QUESTIONS

Why does the bible refer to Jesus' miracles as signs?

What was the result of the miracles performed by the early Christians?

Do Miracles Exist? Part 7

Now that we've seen God's purposes for miracles, let's examine their spiritual value. In other words, what value do miracles have in terms of conversion and salvation for those who witness them? Especially the public miracles that draw attention to God's work. John 12:37 says, "Even after Jesus had performed so many signs in their presence, they still would not believe in Him." This verse depicts the final days of Jesus' earthly ministry during the passion week in Jerusalem, just days before His crucifixion. Three years of miracles, signs, and wonders performed in their sight and yet, the Jewish leaders were plotting to kill Jesus, rather than accept Him as the Messiah.

One of the soberest warnings of how ineffective a miracle can be in getting people to change is seen by considering the people who are living during the end times before Christ's second coming, who witness endless miracles as described throughout the book of Revelation. What will be the ultimate reaction of such a godless generation to the divine intervention of God?

Revelation 9:20-21 says, "The rest of mankind who were not killed by these plagues still did not repent of the work of their hands; they did not stop worshiping demons, and idols of gold, silver, bronze, stone and wood—idols that cannot see or hear or walk. Nor did they repent of their murders, their magic arts, their sexual immorality or their thefts." This passage shows us that miracles, of and by themselves, don't necessarily cause people to repent of their sin and convince them to obey God.

Remember, Noah's generation had full knowledge of God, as did the generations that followed the flood. Yet, they still lived in active rebellion against God, choosing to follow their own self-destructive tendencies. The generation of Israelites who witnessed God's power in Egypt and in the desert continually rebelled against Him. The generation that witnessed Jesus Christ's miracles chose to have Him crucified rather than repent and be saved. And we just read that the last generation of people living just before Christ returns will also witness miraculous signs and wonders, yet they will refuse to change and give God His rightful place in their lives. Do you see the pattern? Has it changed at all over the course of history? No it hasn't.

It is also important that we Christians don't get caught up in wanting miracles and signs to confirm our faith, to prove that God is real. That can be spiritually dangerous! Speaking about the end times, Jesus warned His disciples that miracles can also be used to deceive. Matthew 24:4-5 says, "Jesus answered: "Watch out that no one deceives you. For many will come in my name, claiming, 'I am the Messiah,' and will deceive many." And verse 11 says, "...many false prophets will appear and deceive many people." People must not look for signs and wonders as proof as to where God and Christ are working today, if they do, then they run the risk of being deceived. So our next point is **MAIN POINT #10: MIRACLES DON'T SAVE US, FAITH IN JESUS CHRIST SAVES US!**

We have already seen that Jesus confirmed the truth of His message by the signs and wonders He performed. So the question arises, if people were healed by Jesus and the apostles, should we expect to see miracles of healing today?

Understand this, Jesus and the apostles instantly and completely healed people who were born blind, lame, mute, paralyzed, with a withered arm, and even raised people from the dead. All obvious and indisputable miracles, which even Jesus' enemies didn't challenge because of the overwhelming eyewitness testimonies of those who were there. Jesus and His apostles never did a miracle that was slow and they never did a miracle that was less than permanent.

The types of miracles that are being claimed by faith healers today are nothing like New Testament miracles. Today we have claimed miracles that are partial, gradual, temporary, sometimes reversed, and almost impossible to verify. Unfortunately, these faith healing ministries are simply money-making enterprises which prey on the desperate hopes of people. They are an obvious exploitation and misappropriation of a biblical truth that miracles exist. We can and should recognize that.

But what about the legitimate appeals to our heavenly Father to heal us, or heal a sick child, a loved one, or a friend? How often is the answer we receive to those prayers an immediate yes answer? I'm talking about the person is made well at that very instant, just like in the Gospels and the book of Acts. My personal experience is 0%. That is not to say God is incapable of answering those prayers or that He is indifferent to them. Nor am I saying that it has not happened to you or someone you know. God may choose to heal someone as an act of mercy, but it is not something that we should expect and demand from Him, nor is it dependent upon the strength of our faith. The reality is we do not see these kinds of miracles in our modern time. Why is that?

Well, let's look at our main points so far to help us find the answer. First of all, MIRACLES ARE RARE. We really should not expect them! We've seen that GOD USES MIRACLES TO SHAPE HISTORY to ensure the establishment of His kingdom on earth. MIRACLES CONFIRMED JESUS' DEITY AND LEGITIMIZED HIS MINISTRY; and we've seen MIRACLES WERE NEEDED TO BUILD THE EARLY CHURCH. But we've also seen miracles are not a source of salvation. We've noted that God works primarily through divine providence, within the natural laws He has created. He accomplishes His purposes mostly through ordinary people like you and me, who are willing to be the hands and feet of Jesus.

It is also noteworthy that the early Christians did not have the Bible as we do. Today, we have the complete Word of God and the Holy Spirit dwells within every believer. Therefore, miracles are not needed to point people to God; they can pick up His word and find Him. They can hear the gospel message shared by a person, they can see the testimony of a co-worker who lives their faith, and they can see that God is real through what He has created.

Our last point I hope will provide us what I consider to be the proper perspective on the subject of miracles, including miracles of healing.

Consider the following:

God spoke the universe into existence from nothing, and He created you and me in His image, with a spirit that allows us to know Him and have fellowship with Him. But we have a huge problem that keeps us from realizing our true purpose. It is our sin. Sin keeps us from having fellowship with the God who made us, not only here on earth, but also for all eternity. To remedy this problem, God took the form of a man, the man Jesus Christ, whose sole purpose was to come and be an atoning sacrifice for our sins. He paid the penalty of sin which is death, for you, for me, and for everyone who chooses to accept it. He suffered for us, more than we can ever know, in order to bring us back to God; so that we may enjoy for all eternity the miracle of life.

"He himself bore our sins" in His body on the cross, so that we might die to sins and live for righteousness; "by His wounds you have been healed." 1 Peter 2:24

When we accept Jesus as our Savior He sends us the Holy Spirit as a down payment, a guarantee that we belong to God, with a hope and a future that cannot be lost or stolen. In other words, **He heals us spiritually.** That is why He came. The reason He had to die on the cross was to bring spiritual restoration to mankind. The physical healings He performed were acts of mercy for sure, but the main reason He did them was to demonstrate the truth of His identity and ministry. Some have misinterpreted His purpose for the physical healings to mean that people can and should be healed if they only have enough faith. Again, Christ died so we may be healed spiritually, not physically.

Not only does the Holy Spirit bring spiritual healing, it also gives us supernatural power to change. Power to experience joy, peace, forgiveness, self-control, and love, which are fruits of the Spirit, and grow in the lives of those who are walking in obedience to God's Word. The person who was once full of anger and rage becomes gentle and kind; the person who was enslaved to drugs or alcohol is set free and finds joy in life; the person who never felt worthy of being loved finds peace in the love of God that fills their very soul. And there are many more examples which are too numerous to name, because each person who comes to Christ can name their own.

I once knew a kid who grew up in the suburbs. Like many kids today he was raised by a single mother. Luckily, she loved the Lord and encouraged him to do the same. He loved playing sports and was a decent basketball player. But like many of us he was selfish. He loved himself more than anyone else and he didn't care much for living his life for God, even though he believed God existed and had even accepted Christ as his Savior when he was five. God allowed this young man to experience the pain and consequences of living a life of sin, until that young man realized true happiness is only found in living for God through His Son Jesus Christ.

Slowly but surely this young man grew in his faith by doing those things all Christians need to do; praying, reading the bible, attending church and serving others; and by sharing his faith. Although he is not young any more, God was able to start using him to build up His kingdom and make a difference in the lives of young people for all eternity. This man is far from perfect and has a long way to go in his spiritual growth. Yet, I think his life is a miracle. I'm talking about myself. I would have never dreamed that I would be here today doing what I am doing now. There is a retired coach from my old high school that could not believe that the knucklehead kid he knew back then is now active in serving God by teaching His word. We have now arrived at our final point, **MAIN POINT #11: YOUR LIFE IS A MIRACLE!**

What's your story? What miracle has God done in you? What miracle has He worked in the lives of those close to you? God is real! God loves you! God can change you! God can use you to make a difference for all eternity! You just need to be willing. So let me ask you, are you willing?

FOCUS QUESTIONS

Does witnessing miracles always bring people to faith in God? Explain.

According to 1 Peter 2:24, why did Jesus die on the cross?

How has God supernaturally worked in your life, or the lives of those you know?